Tanabe Hajime and the Kyoto School

Bloomsbury Introductions to World Philosophies

Series Editor:
Monika Kirloskar-Steinbach

Assistant Series Editor:
Leah Kalmanson

Regional Editors:
Nader El-Bizri, James Madaio, Sarah A. Mattice, Takeshi Morisato,
Pascah Mungwini, Omar Rivera, and Georgina Stewart

Bloomsbury Introductions to World Philosophies delivers primers reflecting
exciting new developments in the trajectory of world philosophies.
Instead of privileging a single philosophical approach as the basis of
comparison, the series provides a platform for diverse philosophical
perspectives to accommodate the different dimensions of cross-cultural
philosophizing. While introducing thinkers, texts and themes emanating
from different world philosophies, each book, in an imaginative and
pathbreaking way, makes clear how it departs from a conventional
treatment of the subject matter.

Titles in the Series:

A Practical Guide to World Philosophies, by Monika Kirloskar-Steinbach and
Leah Kalmanson

Daya Krishna and Twentieth-Century Indian Philosophy, by Daniel Raveh

Māori Philosophy, by Georgina Tuari Stewart

Philosophy of Science and the Kyoto School, by Dean Anthony Brink

Tanabe Hajime and the Kyoto School, by Takeshi Morisato

Tanabe Hajime and the Kyoto School

Self, World, and Knowledge

Takeshi Morisato

BLOOMSBURY ACADEMIC
LONDON • NEW YORK • OXFORD • NEW DELHI • SYDNEY

BLOOMSBURY ACADEMIC
Bloomsbury Publishing Plc
50 Bedford Square, London, WC1B 3DP, UK
1385 Broadway, New York, NY 10018, USA
29 Earlsfort Terrace, Dublin 2, Ireland

BLOOMSBURY, BLOOMSBURY ACADEMIC and the Diana logo are
trademarks of Bloomsbury Publishing Plc

First published in Great Britain 2022

For legal purposes the Acknowledgments on pp. vii–viii constitute an
extension of this copyright page.

Series design by Louise Dugdale
Cover image © shuoshu / Getty Images

A catalogue record for this book is available from the British Library.

Library of Congress Cataloging-in-Publication Data
Names: Morisato, Takeshi, author.
Title: Tanabe Hajime and the Kyoto School : self, world,
and knowledge / Takeshi Morisato.
Description: London ; New York : Bloomsbury Academic, 2021. |
Series: Bloomsbury introductions to world philosophies |
Includes bibliographical references and index. |
Identifiers: LCCN 2021023356 (print) | LCCN 2021023357 (ebook) |
ISBN 9781350101715 (HB) | ISBN 9781350101708 (PB) |
ISBN 9781350101722 (ePDF) | ISBN 9781350101739 (eBook)
Subjects: LCSH: Kyoto school. | Tanabe, Hajime, 1885-1962.
Classification: LCC B5244.T34 M675 2021 (print) |
LCC B5244.T34 (ebook) | DDC 181/.12–dc23
LC record available at https://lccn.loc.gov/2021023356
LC ebook record available at https://lccn.loc.gov/2021023357

ISBN: HB: 978-1-3501-0171-5
         PB: 978-1-3501-0170-8
       ePDF: 978-1-3501-0172-2
      eBook: 978-1-3501-0173-9

Series: Bloomsbury Introductions to World Philosophies

Typeset by Integra Software Services Pvt. Ltd.

To find out more about our authors and books visit www.bloomsbury.com
and sign up for our newsletters.

Contents

Series Editor's Preface

Bloomsbury Introductions to World Philosophies will offer plural, hitherto unexplored pathways into the study of world philosophies. Instead of privileging a single philosophical approach as the basis of comparison, the series will provide a platform for diverse philosophical perspectives to accommodate the many different dimensions of cross-cultural philosophizing. While the choice of terms used by the individual volumes may indeed carry a local inflection, they will not foreclose critical thinking about philosophical plurality. The individual volumes will strike a balance between locality and globality.

Tanabe Hajime and the Kyoto School: Self, World and Knowledge is dedicated to the work of Tanabe Hajime (1885–1962), a co-founder of the Japanese Kyoto School. In Part One, the book weaves together Tanabe's concepts, ideas, and distinct argumentation to create a Tanabean understanding of the self, the world, and knowledge. Part Two supplements this reading through a translation of relevant excerpts from Tanabe's proliferous writings. The result is a fascinating account of Tanabe's meta-noesis, a knowing that includes both transcendent and immanent aspects. To know fully, is, as Morisato's Tanabe says, to accept the limits of philosophical knowing, while simultaneously becoming aware of, and accepting, the discontinuity in multiple forms of human knowing.

Monika Kirloskar-Steinbach

Acknowledgments

My Italian friends once told me that there is a delightful expression in their beautiful language, "Del maiale non si butta via niente" (You don't throw away anything of a pig).[1] As academics, we hope to materialize this wisdom: we read books and articles to prepare for a conference presentation, which serves as a recipe for a scientific article later on, and then after collecting a few of these dishes, we compile them into a book as a great course meal. There is one academic practice, however, that is extremely difficult to incorporate into this Italian ideal, namely, job interviews. We have to spend hours preparing for a life-changing event with such short notice and are often asked to give the best of what we do in less than an hour for the search committee, most of whom we have never met. When we are notified with the automated rejection message or never hear from them again, the world is just insipid like the salt without its savor. No matter what your families, friends, and close colleagues say, the future looks as gloomy and hopeless as it could be. What is worse, none of this will register as an academic achievement on your C.V.

At one of these interviews, a critic said, "Perhaps, Tanabe is too difficult to teach to undergraduates." I politely disagreed with the interjection, but had no way to sufficiently prove my point in a couple of minutes. Somehow the aftertaste of this passing question-and-answer stuck in the back of my mind and pushed me to write this introductory text on Tanabean philosophy. I am confident as a scholar of Japanese philosophy that this book would satisfy the acclaimed critics or the authority of the Kyoto school. But most importantly as a philosopher, I hope it speaks to many of my fellow academics as a silver lining, proof that my Italian friends were right: we can always make so much out of nothing!

The substantive explanations of the key terms regarding the "logic of species" in Chapter 1 is previously published as an article, entitled "Tanabe Hajime and the Concept of Species: Approaching Nature as a Missing Shade in the *Logic of Species*," in *Natural Born Monads: On the Metaphysics of Organisms and Human Individuals* (Berlin: De Gruyter, 2020). I would like to thank the editors, Andrea Altobrando and Pierfrancesco Biasetti, for their permission to use the substantive part of the chapter for this book. Chapter 2 is a revised and abridged version of a chapter on Tanabe in my first comparative monograph, *Faith and Reason in Continental and Japanese Philosophy: Reading Tanabe Hajime and William Desmond* (London: Bloomsbury, 2019).

The second half of Chapter 3 was initially presented as a lecture on the interdisciplinarity of Eurasian Studies at the workshop, *International Eurasia Humanism Research Group Research and Training Workshop: Transversal Anthropology of Knowledge*, at the University of Salamanca, Spain, on April 3–15, 2020. The presentation manuscript was published in the conference proceedings entitled "Japanese Philosophy and the Idea of Eurasia: Tanabe Hajime and Two Aspects of Scientific Knowing," and the lecture is available online at https://youtu.be/d0csjNfBjrU. Some parts of Chapter 3 in this book correspond to the essential part of this lecture. I would like to thank Alfonso Falero for providing me with a place to both express and develop this idea and also for the editorial permission.

Chapter 5 is an abridged version of James W. Heisig's complete and acclaimed translation of Tanabe's *Philosophy as Metanoetics* (University of California Press, 1991; Chisokudō Publications, 2016). Most specialists of Japanese philosophy owe much to his life's work in this field and as such it has become customary to thank him in our acknowledgments. I would like to renew my gratitude for sharing his excellent translation of Tanabe's work in this volume and to thank Chisokudō Publications for permission.

Lastly, I would like to thank all the members of "European Network of Japanese Philosophy" (ENOJP), who have been in one way or another a great inspiration for my scholarly work. Their constructive feedback and overdeterminate encouragement have never failed to help me improve my philosophical thinking and being. Special thanks to Cody Staton. His editorial suggestions and scholarly input have always provided me with the moral incentives to continuously improve my philosophical thinking and writing. What is not lucid in this text is probably due to the last-minute changes that I made on my own. I hope the readers may hear the ensemble of selfless voices, and their dedications to the field of Japanese philosophy, supporting the composition of my text.

Abbreviations

Preamble

Tanabe Hajime 田辺元 (1885–1962) is a co-founding member of the Kyoto School philosophy (*Kyōto gakuha*, 京都学派). This school is known as a group of thinkers from twentieth-century Kyoto in Japan who had successfully integrated various concepts available in the East Asian and Japanese intellectual traditions in the process of their critical engagements with European and North American intellectual traditions. Their various frameworks of thinking have arguably succeeded in both responding to and generating a set of philosophical questions that are pertinent to these various traditions. In doing so, Tanabe and those that followed in his path ignited interest in cross-cultural philosophical discussions unlike any hitherto in the history of philosophy. Just like his predecessor at the Imperial University of Kyoto (later Kyoto University), Nishida Kitarō 西田幾多郎 (1870–1945), who is considered the illustrious father of modern Japanese philosophy, Tanabe produced a number of significant philosophical works in the comparative tradition that indicate original contributions to the history of word philosophies. This book will lay out his major concepts, principal ideas, and characteristic arguments that will help us formulate a Tanabean rendering of the philosophical notions that this series interrogates—that is, "self," "world," and "knowledge."

The fifteen heavily bound volumes of *The Complete Works of Tanabe* (which is always referred to as *Tanabe Hajime Zenshū* 田辺元全集 and abbreviated by scholars as *THZ* in the field of Japanese philosophy) consist of sixteen monographs, numerous essays, and lecture notes that Tanabe has either published or delivered as public lectures between his philosophical debut in 1910 and his death in 1962. This massive oeuvre is generally divided into four parts and they represent methodical or thematic shifts in his philosophical thinking.

(1) Philosophy of math and science, and early essays on Neo-Kantian and Nishidian philosophy (the 1910s)
(2) The works on Kant and Hegel (the 1920s)
(3) The *Logic of Species* (1932–1945)
(4) Later works on the philosophy of religion (1945–1962)

Because of these divisions, it is impossible to read the entire Tanabean corpus as a seamless whole or to group them all according to a single term. We must simply pay attention to the period in which each text is written in order to understand its significance. However, some of the early essays already invoke the questions that will play a central role in the later texts. Also, the ways in which Tanabe struggles with some questions in the early texts express the reasons why he had to make a significant shift in his methodology or intellectual foci. It is important, in this sense, to maintain our openness to various connections across these categories while keeping in mind the main concerns of each historical period.

Most scholars recognize the origin of "Tanabean philosophy" (*Tanabe tetsugaku*, 田辺哲学) in the third period. That is precisely because, in the *Logic of Species*, Tanabe sets forth his critique of Nishida and strives to show how his own philosophical standpoint is different from the original works of his senior colleague at the Kyoto University. Despite his intent, however, it is quite difficult at times for contemporary readers to decipher how the "logic of species" breaks decisively from the Hegelian dialectic that he abandons as an incomplete form of thinking at the end of (2). Subsequently, it remains questionable to emphasize his fundamental difference from Nishida's dialectical logic of *basho* (partly because Tanabe detects in this logic the same problems that he diagnoses in Hegel's metaphysics). The most obvious systematic transition from the Hegelian model of speculative metaphysics takes places in (4). And here, Tanabe provides a much more forceful and compelling critique of Nishida as well. Yet he argues that his later philosophy of religion in (4) does not only mark a transition or conversion (*tenkan* 転換) from the previous viewpoint available in (3), but also completes the picture of the "logic of species." In other words, according to Tanabe, his mature philosophy of religion can salvage the metaphysical notion of the *specific* that he could not complete when he was working on that very logic for nearly fifteen years right up till the end of the Second World War. Unlike the developmental genesis of Nishida's philosophy, where we can recognize the consistency of his thinking from the beginning to end, Tanabe's whole *zenshū* will plunge readers into a hermeneutic nightmare, especially if we become eager to trace the chronological development of his thinking.

The best way to introduce Tanabe's key ideas then is to read the second half of the complete works backward.[1] Instead of beginning with periods (3) and (4) and trying to figure out where and how Tanabe shifted his standpoint, what he preserves in the process of this transition, and whether or not he was successful in doing so, we can simply take a look at the original standpoint that Tanabe (allegedly) provides in (3) from the perspective of (4) and further delve into the concepts that he elaborates on in the latter period. This way of treating Tanabe's oeuvre would be doing some violence to the dynamic development of his philosophical concepts, but I find it necessary for the sake of clarity, especially when the aim of the text is to introduce readers unfamiliar with Tanabe or let alone with works by philosophers who take up Tanabe. I would like my readers to keep this pragmatic approach in mind when they decide to further examine the works of Tanabe in the future.

His notable philosophical ideas are "logic of species" (*shu-no ronri*, 種の論理), "absolute mediation" (*zettai baikai*, 絶対媒介), "metanoesis" (*zange*, 懺悔) or "metanoetics" (*zangedō*, 懺悔道), "absolute dialectic" (*zettai benshōhō*, 絶対弁証法), and "philosophy of death" (*shi-no tetsugaku*, 死の哲学). As we can anticipate from the peculiar approach of this text to the works of Tanabe, it is not possible to neatly separate them apart from each other, and also, we are sometimes required to use one major concept to explain another. So, for instance, without understanding "metanoetics," it is impossible to paint the complete picture of the "logic of species." This is quite common to dialectical thinkers like Nishida and Tanabe from the Kyoto school. But it can also make their works inaccessible to undergraduate students in their first or second year of studying philosophy. Hence, in a few places in the early phases of this book, I will have to make small leaps to other major concepts (without giving a full elaboration of them), and even though I give it my best effort to explain these concepts in the clearest of terms, it might not become immediately evident to some readers until later exegesis in the book ties all the concepts together. In this case, I would like to encourage my readers to read through this text and come back to the parts that, upon first reading, were not initially clear. Unfortunately, this method of reading back and forth is inevitable when we deal with dialectical metaphysicians.

This book consists of two parts and six chapters. The first part will give three essays that explain the Tanabean understanding of self, world, and knowledge; the second part will provide translations of the excerpts from the original text that are relevant to these themes. The first chapter will introduce the "logic of species" and further examine how its notion of "absolute mediation" (*zettai baikai*, 絶对媒介) leads to a complex theory of self. The second chapter will shed some light on a Tanabean worldview by analyzing the central arguments and key concepts raised in his magnum opus, *Philosophy as Metanoetics* (1946). A renewed sense of philosophy based on the notion of nothingness gives a dialectical worldview, which is consistent with what we have found as the notion of self in the "logic of species." The third chapter gives a twofold approach to the notion of knowledge in Tanabe's philosophy, and once again, this investigation will follow the insight provided in the previous chapters. First, we will think about the relation of human knowing (i.e., *noesis* or philosophy) to what lies in the midst of and beyond it (i.e., *meta*noesis or religion); second, we will think about how the "absolute dialectic" in Tanabe's account would frame the appropriate interrelation between philosophy and other modes of human knowing (e.g., politics, history, art, social sciences, natural sciences, mathematics, among others). By examining the vertical limit and the horizontal interrelation of human knowing, we will acquire the Tanabean understanding of knowledge.

The chapters containing translations in the second part are complementary to the thematically organized chapters of the first part. Chapter 4 will give a partial translation of an essay from *The Logic of Species*, entitled "The Social Ontological Structure of the Logic" (1936). This abridged translation is indeed a fraction in comparison with the massive compilation of the thirteen essays in volumes 6 and 7 of the *Tanabe Zenshū*. However, it should provide us with a microcosmic representation of the whole logic of species in relation to some of the key points introduced in Chapter 1. It should also demonstrate how the philosopher was critical of his previous standpoints and continuously made an improvement to his theory of social ontology. The fifth chapter will provide the translation of the opening sections of the *Philosophy as Metanoetics*. This is precisely where Tanabe lays out the theoretical foundation of metanoetics and articulates it as the overarching structure of his "absolute dialectic": hence, a careful reading of these sections should enable readers to recognize the validity of the major points introduced in Chapter 2. The sixth and final chapter of this book will provide the essential passages from the essay, "Two Aspects of Education in Natural Science." This article was originally delivered as a lecture for the general audience at the pedagogical workshop on natural sciences organized by the Japanese Ministry of Education in 1936. It is rather accessible to those who wish to begin exploring the field of Japanese philosophy. More importantly, it shows Tanabe's application of the absolute dialectic to the structure of human knowing, where he argues for the autonomy of natural science vis-à-vis other domains of our knowledge. The abridged translation of this article is not only supplementary for our understanding of Tanabe's take on knowledge, but also exemplifies how we can apply his complex theory of knowledge to our contemporary issues in education (especially in relation to our ongoing endorsement of interdisciplinary studies). These translations in the second part, along with the introductory essays in the first part, will showcase Tanabe's original contribution to the history of world philosophies as a Kyoto School thinker and help readers dive into the heart of his philosophical thinking.

Part One

Essays

Tanabe Hajime and the Philosophy of (No-)Self

Three Senses of the Self and the Logic of Species

Tanabe's notion of "self" can be articulated in relation to the "logic of species," which includes the principle of "absolute mediation" (*zettai baikai*, 絶対媒介) and anticipates his later formulation of the "metanoetic" (*zangedō-teki*, 懺悔道的) worldview. To avoid obvious confusion over the term "self," I would like to emphasize here at the outset that it could convey multiple senses throughout his work. First, it could refer to the concrete, single individual that each of us can recognize as the "I." The singularity of one's existence as a *this/once* is an indispensable factor in ascribing this meaning to the term. Second, it could also mean a group of individuals that holds a certain identity or a characteristic by which we can distinguish its specificity from other groups of individuals. This represents a communal self that we can recognize as the "we." Tanabe strives to show how we cannot talk about the social and individual self apart from each other: hence, we have to keep in mind that they are integral to our process of defining one's selfhood. Last, the term could also function as a metaphysical notion or principle that gives an ideality of selfhood. This concept is foundational for the ways in which the first two senses of self are articulated. It could be seen as a merely formal and empty concept in itself, but plays a significant role in determining the singular and the communal sense of the "self." In line with the Mahayana Buddhist tradition (especially the Zen and the Pure Land schools in Japan), this self is recognized as praxis of "no-self" or what Tanabe later calls an "act of nothingness." It is certainly not anything we can call "self" in an ordinary sense of the word in English (or in Japanese). But without it, Tanabe thinks, we cannot talk about the proper relation between the individual and the societal self. These three senses roughly correspond to the threefold "logic of species" and we will examine in the following how this logic unfolds Tanabe's polyvocal understanding of "self."

The *Logic of Species* and the Absolute Mediation
(絶対媒介)

The *Logic of Species* in *THZ* consists of thirteen essays that are somewhat awkwardly compiled into two bulky volumes. The whole text amounts to more than 900 pages and even though they were supposed to establish his own version of "social ontology," Tanabe was never satisfied with the end result of these articles. Naturally, neither his colleagues nor his students, nor even influential publishers could convince him to turn them into a monograph, regardless of the fact that they were celebrated as the origin of Tanabean philosophy. His dying wish was to have them compiled into the complete works simply as a historical record and never to be criticized unless the critic has read them in their entirety.

The difficulty of restructuring this massive work into a single volume lies not only in its overwhelming size, but also in the fact that the main concern of the logic shifts from the early engagement with the question concerning the state's obligatory power over individual(s)—which includes a series of questions regarding a constitution of state authority, the unity of an ethnic, racial, or particular society (*minzoku*, 民族), and the rational foundation of state, etc.—to the later methodological question concerning the foundation of philosophy, which is examined in terms of the problem of "mediation" (*baikai*, 媒介). In relation to the later concern, Tanabe argues that the history of philosophy, in its ongoing task of achieving a comprehensive understanding of reality (including human existence), exhibits a constant struggle between emphasizing the primacy of the universal and maintaining faithfulness to the irreducibility of the single individual. In order to understand reality, we would have to take into account their proper intermediation and to do that, he proposes "species" as the middle term that serves as the foundation for grounding his insight. The threefold distinction of "genus," "species," and "individual" thus provides us with the ontological framework in which we can articulate the threefold sense of self.

There are two interrelated concepts that Tanabe develops as the general "method of philosophy": (1) "absolute mediation" and (2) "history." The former focuses on the proper way in which we can conceive of the intermediation between any opposing metaphysical terms, while the latter sets forth the ultimate standpoint from which we can understand reality in concrete terms, which is supposedly comprehensive of both the human and the nonhuman standpoint (and in Tanabe's terms, "world-scheme" or "space-and-time"). In the "Logic of Species and World-Scheme" (hereafter, LSWS), Tanabe argues that absolute mediation is the core structure of the dialectical logic of species and further claims that we have to attend to the way in which it intermediates both positive and negative terms. First, he claims that the logic of species, as absolute mediation, cannot be a kind of thinking that "abstract[s] the non-rational and include[s] what is rational alone as its content."[1] Rather, as proper dialectical reasoning,

> the logic that denies immediacy must suspend it (i.e., the negation of self) as the mediatory moment of itself and deny [the immediacy] by affirming it under the condition of absolute negation (which is a negation of negation); otherwise, the logic cannot truly deny the immediacy. Thus, [the] non-rationality that immediacy possesses should not be thrown out but must be maintained as the mediator of the logic. If we say that the logic that denies this [immediacy] is rational, it should not be that which abandons the non-rational by merely opposing it. But rather, it should constitute non-rationality-qua-rationality that affirms it through negating it. With regard to this sense of absolute rationality, [the] non-rationality of immediacy must be an indispensable mediatory moment in the process of establishing itself. This standpoint is the absolute mediation that turns the non-rational into the medium of its own self through maintaining [the non-rational].[2]

This intermediation of opposing terms like affirmation–negation, rationality–non-rationality, and universal–individual, based on the notion of "absolute mediation," continuously surfaces in Tanabe's philosophical writings, especially when he expresses his critical stance toward other thinkers. What is important to note here is that he proposes the notion of "species" as the middle ground, where we can be truthful to the concrete manifestation of the irresolvable tension between two contradictory terms. Species as the medium of the contradiction, therefore, cannot be the positive term that assimilates the negative into the further determination of the positive (even though it is possible to be mistaken as such). In this sense, we have no choice but to recognize it as the negative. However, we cannot simply equate it with the determinate notion of the negative that is placed in its opposition to the affirmative. As we will see, species is the principle of self-negation that transcends the binary opposition of the affirmative and the negative. It should be seen as the locus in which we can tarry with the negative (without quickly subsuming it into the affirmative). It is perhaps useful to note that Tanabe is adding the third term "species" to the two opposing terms of the affirmative and the negative as the greater negative, namely, the *neither/nor* in which we can keep the contradiction of these terms as what it is. This is what he means by "absolute mediation" in his logic of species.

Defining Genus

It is quite challenging, therefore, to define one of three metaphysical terms in a determinate and coherent fashion, precisely because each definition presupposes its relation to others in this dynamic structure of dialectical reasoning. Simply put, we cannot define one term in the logic of species without defining the others insofar as they are to be articulated through the complex process of the absolute mediation. If one term could mean a number of different things depending on how we formulate its relation to other terms, moreover, it is a matter of course that some parts of the explanations of the single term will have to wait for further elucidation vis-à-vis other terms and vice versa. In what follows, therefore, I will provide a preliminary outline of what Tanabe means by each term, in the awareness that this does not exhaust Tanabe's understanding of absolute mediation. This exercise is necessary if we are to demonstrate how Tanabe sees their mediatory relations to each other and why he speaks of the "logic of species."

By *genus*, Tanabe indicates the notion of the universal. It is an abstract notion or mere ideality when it is understood apart from other terms. In other words, it is nonexistent in and of itself. In the context of social ontology, he refers to it as the totality of all human beings (i.e., humanity) and further attributes the notions of the "state" and the "(divine) absolute" to it. In the context of metaphysics and the philosophy of religion, he argues that it represents the notion of "nothingness" as a polyvocal, open unity of all that is, and describes it as a "will to salvation" or the "city of bodhisattva" (from which all sentient beings are derived and to which they all return).[3] It, therefore, represents a sort of principle of unity and rationality that is at work in other terms such as species and individual. However, if we interpret genus merely as the totality of all beings in immanent terms, Tanabe argues, we must be mistaking it for an unmediated sense of species or reducing genus to a bad (i.e., unmediated) sense of species. To understand genus properly, as what it is, we must first conceive of it as "absolute negation" or negative unity that constitutes the inseparable unity of all terms without reducing their differences to an unmediated sameness. In this sense, the concept of nothingness is indispensable for properly interpreting Tanabe's rendering of genus. (We will come back to this notion when we examine his formulation of metanoetics.)

Defining Species

By *species*, the Japanese philosopher indicates the notion of the particular, that is to say, that which is more universal than the singular and more specific than the universal. It is described as the substrate (*kitai*, 基体) of all living beings, and, unlike genus, it can be seen as being both immediate and irrational in itself. Species in its immediacy, in other words, constitutes a continuous and particular whole that compiles a multitude of individuals into a relatively determinate group, and this specific group can serve as the foundation of individual lives. The prime example of this relation between species and individual would be the relation of a nation state and its citizens. If I reflect on my existence as a singular person, I can easily think of my nationality, Japanese, as a specific characteristic of it. The socio-political identification of the nation state is usually more or less given immediately (which is to say, it is usually easy to identify the nationality of an individual) and my citizenship in this particular country has provided me with certain elements that have enabled me to live my life as a free individual in this world.[4]

What is interesting about Tanabe's argument is that rationality ultimately belongs to genus. In view of this fact, a species can provide no rational ground for legitimizing its identity over the others. Its specificity is simply beyond reason. As I will explain later, Tanabe comes to argue that species can serve as the ground for manifesting the ideality of genus in concrete reality, thereby highlighting the possibility that various forms of species can be placed in a hierarchical order. In other words, he does not deny the possibility that one species or a small group of them can come to play a leading role in manifesting the ideality and rationality of genus vis-à-vis other species. However, even in this process of relativizing species by means of genus, this realization of ideality is made through the free act of individuals (guaranteed by the general practice of "social justice"), and whether its formal specificity should be defined in one way or another in relation to the manifestation of the rational whole, remains completely contingent. Precisely in this sense, Tanabe argues that the "species is the grounding source of [the] individual's immediate life and what ultimately ought to be denied [since] it only gives the expedient being that exists as the negative mediator of absolute nothingness's manifestation in this world."[5]

If we revisit the example of my nationality, the specificity of being Japanese can manifest its rational ground only when its citizens live up to the ideality of humanity (which Tanabe explains as practicing the act of nothingness or carrying out the act of no-self) and transform their socio-political belonging in the nation state into an enabling ground for an open community of free individuals. But this concrete manifestation of the universal ideal of humanity (genus) can be made through any specific group of individuals, and there is no reason why it has to be done by means of one form more than by some other, as regards their specific way of living their lives. When a group of individuals identifies the source of its individual life in a specific socio-political milieu (species) as the ultimate ground of all things (genus) and fails to recognize the contingency and irrationality of the former in its negative relation to the latter, then we witness the totalitarian dictum of ultra-nationalism, where the participants erroneously reduce genus to a bad (i.e., unmediated) sense of species. Tanabe was clearly against this reduction of the notion of genus to the unmediated sense of species.

To ground the contingency and irrationality of the specific, Tanabe notices that the notion of species must represent something more than the given irrational that we can immediately talk about as something irreducible to our individual existence *in concreto* or to the ideality of human existence *in abstracto*. In response to a criticism that Tanabe's rendering of species seems to lack any mediation, regardless of the fact that it should demonstrate an axis of absolute mediation, he replies in "Social Ontological Structure of Logic" how species' in-between status in relation to genus and individual represents the principle of self-negation. More precisely, it refers to an endless movement of auto-generated oppositions that has its source in nothing other than itself:

> Species does not possess the negative outside itself but within itself carries that which denies itself. This self-negation has nothing beyond itself that grounds it and it is the self-negation that is entirely specific to species. The reason why species is not universal but particular is because it is simply self-negating and does not give any absolute negation [that pertains to genus]. When we say that the particularization of the universal is universal's self-alienation, what we mean is that absolute negation [of genus] is reduced to self-negation [of species]. But without this self-negation, we cannot talk about species as species. Nor can we know its existence. The fact that we have already known and been talking about it [as the immediately given] presupposes some negation of, and opposition to, immediacy. We just have to understand species as that kind of self-negation.[6]

This insight certainly allows Tanabe to emphasize the contingent characteristics of species. There is no external reason why the series of divisions between diverse groups of individuals or species is made in the way it is, nor can we reach any teleological viewpoint from which we can place a number of species in a hierarchical order based on their specificities. Species, as the principle of self-negation, is just that which divides itself: hence, it is simply marked with contingent finitude, whereby no rationality can be ascribed to the ways in which it divides itself.

However, this insight also leads Tanabe to revise the initial definition of species as having a primitive unity or a continuous whole in its immediacy.

[The reason why we have to make this modification] is because, so long as we think that the essence of species is to divide itself through the principle of self-negation, whichever part of species we look at, we will recognize a conflict between the positive and the negative power; and thereby, based on this conflict, the division towards the negative opposition and the unification towards the whole that opposes the very division accompany each other. Species represents this unceasing movement that contains the double negation that tries to divide itself through the struggle between opposing powers while, in turn, trying to preserve its unity by opposing this division. We cannot possibly think of it as a fixed unity at rest.[7]

It is undeniable that we can articulate species as something that is directly involved with the life of the individual. We can see, for instance, that a specific nation state, an ethnic group, or a particular society can serve as an enabling condition for the possibility of one's existence as a free individual. Tanabe's qualification of species as a principle of self-negation, here, does not contradict this point. However, he qualifies that the determinate phase of species as the immediately given is only half of the whole picture. The specific socio-political, linguistic, or cultural milieu is contingent and subject to change (and in some cases, subject to extinction) regardless of the fact that it constantly strives to preserve its unity. That is because it carries within itself the seed of self-negation as species. It divides itself as it strives to preserve its particular identity and as a contingent particular, it is always subject to endless change or complete cessation. Thus, the notion of species represents the principle of dynamic self-negation that constitutes two opposing phases of immediate positivity (i.e., unity) and mediated negativity (i.e., disunity).

Two Types of Species and the Significance of the Individual

Species, in Tanabe's account, therefore, manifests itself in two types: (1) the positive type, which opens itself to ideality and the rationality of genus while recognizing its relativity vis-à-vis other species, and (2) the negative and unmediated type, which strives to preserve its relatively unified identity in immediacy and tempts the individuals that belong to it to regard it as the absolute ground of all things (i.e., genus).[8] It is quite helpful to think of this positive-negative distinction of species as something similar to Henry Bergson's formulations of "open" and "closed" society.[9] The question, then, is as follows: where precisely is the basis on which genus is (1) manifested through species without compromising its specificity, or (2) reduced to the partial picture of species as the immediately given (thereby disregarding its essential relativity vis-à-vis other species)? How can a specific group of individuals or society constitute an (1) open or (2) closed society? Tanabe answers that it lies in free choice and the act of the individual.

If the notion of species is to serve as the foundation of the individual, it cannot be a simple amalgamation of individuals, but must represent that which is both irreducible to and constitutive of an individual's concrete existence. When it is conceived as the negative and unmediated whole, moreover, its immediate unity has a propensity to "swallow up the individual" (as every form of nationalism tends to do).[10] Species constitutes the continuous whole that denies the individual, but at the same time gives the societal substrate as the foundation through which the individual can come to enjoy its existence. In this sense, Tanabe argues, "in their negative relation, individual and species presuppose that … the individual can discard species through its own power while simultaneously species can bring the individual to extinction."[11] In short, "species gives birth to individual as it kills the individual."[12]

The flipside of this dialectical argument is that the individual must also stand in an oppositional relation to species and, in that sense, Tanabe defines the individual as having the "will to power." What he means by this is "freedom" or the "ability to deny the essence of determinate identity (species) in itself; and [to] take this freedom as its essence."[13] This sounds quite natural to our ears if we apply it once again to the relation between a nation state and its citizen. A single individual owes much to her country for enjoying her life, but what grants her the status of the singular is her ability to transcend her national identity and to make her own decisions, which may support or go against what is expected of her as her civic duty in that particular sociopolitical climate. The examples of this "will to power" could range from an extreme case of a high treason to a milder instance of naturalization in another state. A humanitarian aid to citizens of other countries would also qualify as the exercise of this freedom. The point is that the individual has the ability to suspend species when their interests are in conflict with each other.

In the "The Logic of Social Existence" (hereafter LSE), Tanabe examines the source of the individual's radical freedom. His argument is that the individual's differentiation from species through the will to power cannot be self-given but must come from somewhere else. In the process of responding to a critique of his earlier engagement with Durkeim's totemic principle and Tönnies's *Gemeinschaft–Gesellschaft* distinction, Tanabe traces the rise of individual freedom in the conflict between particular societies.

The differentiation (分立) of the individual [from species] finds an opportunity in the mutual conflict between various species. Species is the womb of the individual and simultaneously unifies them all [into itself] as a whole. Nevertheless, its conflict and struggle with other species serves as an opportunity for the individual to differentiate itself from its species. The demand of the individual for its autonomy is awakened by the existence of other species (that it does not belong to) and begins to put itself in motion through the struggle among them. The external conflict and the internal opposition, in this sense, are always relative to each other.[14]

What takes place in this moment of conflict between species is that the individual "usurps" the self-negating power of species. In the LSE, Tanabe defines the condition for the possibility of exercising freedom.

> Only an individual who usurps the power of species that both determines and unifies all individuals can obtain the will to power through the mediation of this governing force pertaining to species. Stated succinctly, the individual can be established through its oppositional unity vis-à-vis species; and because of that, its will to power represents that which is mediated through species as the will to life.[15]

The essential determination of the individual, therefore, is that it can stand in opposition to species as it exercises its "spontaneity that transforms the determination of species into a medium of its establishment."[16] This self-differentiation of individual from species as radical freedom maintains a paradoxical relation between the two terms. On the one hand, the individual is completely in opposition to species, thereby claiming its irreducible difference to, and independence from, species. Yet, on the other hand, since the source of its division from species comes from the self-negating principle of the latter, there is a significant degree of indebtedness to what the individual is departing from.

This leads us to an interesting outlook on the relation between individual and species in reference to the two types of the genus–species relation. The negative sense of species generates a reduction of genus to species, where the latter mistakes itself for the absolute, while disregarding its specificity.[17] In this case, this species loses sight of itself, since—on the basis of its finite specificity—it maintains its quality in its relativity to other species. Under the reign of this "closed" species, the individual will experience conflict with other species. Additionally, as the species aims to preserve its identity, it fails to exercise its full potential as the principle of self-negation and makes a self-contradictory demand of unwanted service to the specific whole on the individual. In this case, the individual will be awakened to its freedom and bring its "closed" species to a transformation (if not extinction).

This transformative change of the closed species (or a revolution) only leads us to the positive sense of it that gives an open relation between genus and species, where the irrational substrate of species can manifest rationality of genus without losing its specificity that keeps its relativity with other species. The principle of self-negation with regard to this species is fully realized in this "open" species: hence, the individual is fully exercising its freedom and making possible the manifestation of genus in species. This is what Tanabe means by the absolute mediation of genus, species, and individual, or the triadic "logic of species." What is important in relation to the nature of the individual is that it plays the crucial role of realizing the open mediation between genus and species, thereby fulfilling the promise of its freedom as derived from the self-negating principle of species.

Absolute Mediation as the Logic of Species

We have seen that the rationality of genus cannot exist in and of itself, but only manifests itself through the species that serves as the substrate of life. Species represents the contradictory principle of self-negation: hence, it has a double directionality in its way of (re- or mis-)presenting the genus. On the one hand, it strives to preserve its continuous unity by imposing its immediate and determinate identity on the individual as the absolute whole (i.e., a counterfeit genus). In this case, the species mistakes itself as genus while losing sight of its finite specificity and equality with other species. On the other hand, it also strives to deconstruct its determinate identity and constantly calls for a transformation that brings itself in its relativity to other species. This self-contradictory nature of species serves as the foundation of freedom in the individual, and only by exercising this freedom in a particular way, can the single individual concretize genus in and through species.

Tanabe describes this formal structure of the logic of species as absolute mediation and an examination of this notion can help us sketch out the content of the intermediation between the metaphysical terms in question. In the LSE, he argues,

> Absolute mediation means that in order to establish one, it is always mediated through another. Thus, since one and the other mutually negate each other, it means that absolute mediation cannot be carried out unless every affirmation is made through negation as a medium of

its establishment. As the so-called negation-qua-affirmation, absolute mediation requires that an affirmation is always an affirmation through negation. Hence, it excludes all immediacy. Even for what we call the absolute, we cannot allow it to be established directly unless it takes any relative that negates it as the medium of its establishment.[18]

The double directionality in mutual affirmation-through-negation among three terms in the logic of species is much easier to picture in reference to the relation of species and individual. Species is conflicted between its self-preservation and self-negation, and because of that, this inner split ultimately characterizes its nature as the self-negating principle. The individual, then, takes on this principle as the basis of its freedom and can choose to contribute to the preservation of the species or the transformation of it into a different kind. However, the similarity of self-negation between the individual and the species does not necessarily exhibit what kind of action from the side of the individual will contribute to the conservative or the innovative formation of its species. The question remains as to which kind of action constitutes the full realization of freedom by the individual and how it contributes to the intermediation of other terms.

In the LSWS, Tanabe describes how the intermediation of three terms would look like with an emphasis on genus as the unity of species and individual.[19] He argues that the individual does not stand in an oppositional relation to genus, but genus enables the individual to recognize itself in its negative relation to other individuals. Also, since it negates species through itself as absolute mediation (or what Tanabe calls affirmation-qua-negation),

> Species does not disappear simply as species but at the same time it is preserved in the unity of genus that transcends species. Accordingly, the special characteristics of species, which is to stand in an opposition to other species, is suspended and thereby comes to demonstrate the relation of difference-qua-sameness or otherness-qua-self. Genus accepts an infinite number of species and transcends them. Here, genus exhibits the meaning of the absolute whole. ... In this whole, not only the individuals in the same species, but also the individuals that belong to other species maintain the relationship of equality, as they constitute the unity of difference-qua-sameness in the same genus (while belonging to different species), and they stand in the relation of self-qua-other whether or not they belong to the same species. In short, the reason why genus realizes the whole of absolute mediation is because [in it] all conflicts between species and individual; between single individuals;

and between multiple species are negatively unified, whereby they enter into their mediatory relations to each other.[20]

Genus, as the principle of absolute mediation, therefore, embodies an open whole that both unifies all opposing terms and preserves their differences. Once again, it grants them their equality with each other without disregarding their specificities. The content of the absolute mediation, in this sense, is a kind of agapeic or selfless release that non-insistently disposes autonomous power to what is other to itself and enables them to be what they are in their oppositional relation to each other. For this reason, Tanabe comes to describe this "open unity of species and individual in genus" as the notion of nothingness, and declares that individual freedom must carry out the act of nothingness so that, through its intermediation with other individuals, it can manifest the ideality of such universal genus in the substrate of species.

It takes a while for Tanabe, in his essays on the logic of species, to clarify what exactly the act of nothingness should look like. Given that genus provides some space for both species and individual to determine themselves, and also that species represents the principle of self-negation at work in the heart of individual existence, Tanabe argues that the individual must practice a kind of self-sacrifice as a negative mediator of one's own self-realization in its relativity to the self-negating nature of genus and species.[21] "The act of [the] individual as the subject," he further elucidates, "represents the transformation of self-negation pertaining to species into the absolute negation of genus and thereby [the] individual is established through the transformation (*tenkan*, 転換) into genus via the mediation of self-negation in species instead of simply by standing in an opposition to species."[22]

What he means by the term, transformation or conversion (*tenkan*), becomes clear only when he ties the practical notion of "metanoesis" (*zange*, 懺悔) to it in his later works. The last essay in the seventh volume of the *THZ*, the "Dialectic of the Logic of Species," which is a revision of an essay published in 1946, after *Philosophy as Metanoetics*, clearly indicates that the act of nothingness must represent a kenotic movement of self-negation, an agapeic selflessness that brings itself to nothing so that what is other to itself becomes everything. To embody and signify the absolute nothingness of universal genus in the particular species, therefore, [the] individual must be actively engaged in the act of constituting the intersubjective (net)works of love with other individuals, and this community of selfless individuals gives a particular manifestation of genus in their species.[23] What makes this logic triadic is that this open species of free individuals, as the concrete manifestation of nothingness, consists of multiple communities of individuals that recognize the source of their freedom in other relevant metaphysical terms. With three terms giving space for each other through their self-negation, individual freedom can be seen to complete the triadic logic of species.

The Threefold Sense of Self in the *Logic of Species*

Tanabe's logic of species is essentially concerned with the structure of the ways in which a specific group of living beings organizes itself and manifests its ideality through its interrelation with other species. It is quite straightforward for us to see how it generates the threefold sense of self: namely, a single individual, a specific group of individuals, and the ideality of herself and their existence (or what we can tentatively define as the notion of "humanity" in the context of social ontology). It is possible to look at each sense of self (as we can define the terms in the logic), but as Tanabe's arguments demonstrate, each of them must be understood in its mediatory relation to the other. In this sense, we must take all of three senses and their interrelations into account if we want to articulate the fullest sense of one's selfhood in relation to Tanabe's logic of species.

For the sake of clarity, let us use an example of an individual, Pauline, and see what kind of self-understanding this logic can produce for her. Suppose Pauline is a Canadian national. We can easily imagine how her nationality is an instance of species and integral to her self-identity just as much as her citizenship in this particular country has enabled her to live her life as a free individual in this world. Now Tanabe's framework of thinking does not frame species as a simple amalgamation of individuals. Nor does it claim a constitutive form that gives any unifying intelligibility to the individual beings (whereby it serves as the ontological ground of its existence). So, we cannot argue that her being Canadian gives her an essential characteristic that is both necessary and indispensable for defining her unique existence as *this* Canadian person. Rather, the notion of species represents the irrational substrate of life that transmits its ontological energy to the individual, the power of existence that is torn between two contradictory movements toward its continuation and discontinuation. That is to say, every specific group of people has a natural propensity to encourage growth and to even preserve its continuous whole beyond the death of individual members. The Canadian society does aim to provide a sufficient level of social security for Pauline (among others) and hopes to guarantee the possibility of her pursuing prosperity and happiness with her family over generations. Yet what makes her nationality a specific whole is the principle of self-negation that limits itself in relation to other specific groups and ultimately negates its existence. It is ultimately finite and, as there is no species that can escape extinction, there cannot be an indefinite preservation of her society. This may sound shocking to many members of modern society (especially if they come from economically privileged countries that enjoy an arguably coherent narrative about their long national history). But Tanabe is saying that there is no rational ground for demonstrating or claiming that any specific group of people should last forever. Pauline should certainly enjoy Canada's prosperity and greatness and do everything in her power to pass that legacy to her descendants (if she wishes to have a family and/or continue to live in the lands that we currently call Canada), but Tanabe's argument claims that she could not expect Canada to exist indefinitely. To conceive of this possibility or hold it as the telos of social self would be to conflate the distinction of species and genus, thereby stepping into the problem of mistaking unmediated, closed species as the counterfeit double of genus.

Additionally, in reference to other species in the genus of humanity, there is no reason why the individual has to be a Canadian rather than a Korean or a Chinese. The notion of species in Tanabe's account identifies radical contingency with a specific way of being vis-à-vis all the other possible ways. Not only could a Japanese have been a Korean or any other specific nationalities in the world, we cannot give any rational ground or teleological reasons for prioritizing one specific group over the others. When they are properly understood as various manifestations of the same genus, we ought to see them as being equal to each other (without disregarding their differences). Certainly, this does not prevent Pauline from feeling proud of her own nation (and the logic of species does provide a ground in which she can praise a specific culture or society without discrediting its fundamental equality with others). But precisely because of the radical contingency of her social selfhood, her loyalty to her society cannot or should not be unconditional. If she regards her love of her country as the rational basis for disregarding other countries or recognizing them as being less valuable than her own, then she is once again stepping into the problem of constituting the closed species/society.

Tanabe further argues that the source of Pauline's ability to go beyond her national identity or to break away from her nation's continuous propensity to its self-preservation lies in the very specific group of people she belongs to. Because the ideality of human existence is present in her (or she is embodying it as an individual through her interaction with others in a specific community), she has the potentiality to recognize the equal value of other nations as different manifestations of human existence. However, what enables her to do this, Tanabe argues, is the contradictory nature of the specific group of people (species). As much as it is obsessed with its self-affirmation through closing its boundaries over against others, the Canadian society is capable of opening itself up to the others and allows its members to move beyond its borders. Because of the finitude of the social self, the individual self can move from one community to another as different self-expressions of human existence.

The notion of humanity as genus cannot refer to any concrete existence in the world, but demonstrates an idea that ought to be manifested through different groups of individuals. In this case, the idea of genus enjoys rationality and necessity, unlike species: hence, this seems to imply, at least in Tanabe's account, that its extinction should be avoided at all cost. However, note that there cannot be any direct preservation of genus and that there can only be proper or improper manifestations of it through various forms of species (or diverse human societies in this case). This implies a paradox: that is to say, a series of improper manifestations of genus through species that primarily focuses on its self-affirmation or self-preservation (at the cost of engendering other species) could lead to an extinction of itself and of the genus. In order for a specific group of people to enjoy a lasting prosperity and continuously express its richness as a unique expression of humanity, it must consist of individuals that can recognize its finite particularity and open themselves up to other groups as being equal to their own.

The triadic logic of species, moreover, indicates that genus represents the kenotic principle of absolute negation. Tanabe defines this notion of selfhood as "nothingness" and, as we will see later in his metanoetic worldview, it presents more of the act of "no-self" or the saturated *dunamis* of "selflessness" than any particular understanding of selfhood as a social or an individual self.[24] As the ground of determinate selfhood, however, the notion of humanity as genus has an inexhaustible wealth of potentiality and, through emptying itself, manifests its ontological richness through various forms of species in reality. What makes this kenotic movement of genus (or no-self) possible is also the intersubjective acts of individual humans that have a visible impact on the (trans)formation of their specific societies. A species, according to Tanabe, cannot continue its existence when each of its members puts itself above the other members, or when the species as a whole dominates other species with the same principle of self-determining self-affirmation. In both cases, the delicate balance of the human economy that aims to guarantee a sustainable supply to a specific society's demand for its survival is put under enormous pressure. For the specific society to fulfill its mediatory function as the place in which humanity can manifest its rich content through the interrelational acts of human individuals, each single individual must, then, carry out a kind of selfless actions and dedicate itself to the well-being of others. As a result of embodying the ideality of genus as self-negation, the interrelation of multiple societies must also exhibit the kind of behavior that mirrors the self-negating self-realization of genus and individual.

The logic of species, therefore, conceives of Pauline's self through the intermediation of the threefold sense of self. Her individual self is conceived as a manifestation of the universal self, the meontic notion of human existence that is irreducible to any specific determinations of human individual or societal selves. Partially because of this, she has the capacity to move between different groups of individuals and criticize any of them on the basis of their faithfulness to the ideality of humanity as intrinsically selfless and caring. The universal self is rational and necessary (and because of that it is inviolable), but it cannot be real in and of itself. Nor can it bear any ontological significance when we approach this concept in its immediacy. According to Tanabe, it can only be manifested through determinate expressions of it as the individual and the communal self, but at the same time it remains irreducible to any of these finite determinates. The universal self is described as an open whole that represents the inexhaustibly potentiality of human existence.

Pauline's social self indicates any specific group of people that she can identify her individual self with, and the term "species" in this Tanabean sense could refer to any of her cultural, socioeconomic, political, ethnic, religious, or even family backgrounds. They could all constitute the complex face of her social self, but for the sake of clarity in this chapter, we have referred to her nationality as an example of species. We have seen that the social self is finite and contingent (regardless of the fact that it could last longer than an individual life in many cases). It is essentially characterized by its contradictory nature. It is torn between its propensity toward self-preservation and self-destruction. The social self that is integral in defining Pauline's selfhood, therefore, faces two possible ways of being: it could either (1) manifest the rich content of humanity by opening itself to the multitude of other communal selves while recognizing their equal value to itself or (2) mistake itself as the sole (re-)presentation of the universal self at the cost of subjugating or engendering other social selves. The former, on the one hand, represents the open society that lives up to the diverse potentiality of human existence by promoting open dialogue and mutual understanding. It is the proper manifestation of the universal (no-)self. The latter, on the other, represents the closed society. It brings about the dark night of ultra-essentialism, which ironically pushes this community, obsessed with its self-preservation and self-promotion, one step closer to its extinction.

The fate of the social self lies in the free choice of the individual. Whether Pauline's country becomes a great nation that opens itself to others and promotes open dialogue with each other or becomes the harbinger of ultra-nationalism, which is often nothing more than the nightmare for the rest of the world, depends on whether or not she is going to live her life in accordance with the principle of self-negating compassion. The social self, in other words, is incapable of making any decisions on its own, and when it is seen to make one, it is only reflecting the choices that the individual members are making. This is almost always intuitive for members of a modern democratic society and yet might sound a bit too harsh for those who have no choice but to live in countries that are under military dictatorship or communist regimes. But note here that Tanabe is talking about this during the 1930s and early 1940s in Japan. According to his theory, the Japanese people should be held accountable for what the Japanese government decided to do regardless of the fact that the political system that can recognize voices of the individual was not in place for making the decision that affected the whole community. Only the individual self has the choice to act under any circumstance either for or against the ideality of humanity, and that decision will show its effect in what kind of society she lives in.

Pauline fortunately enjoys her life in the great democratic nation of Canada (where we seem to be able to list a number of things that would fit with the notion of "open society"), but what makes it great is ultimately her act as the individual. She can choose to live her life in accordance with the ideality of humanity by opening her mind and heart to the other and to seek genuine understanding of them on their terms. Her care for the other through her great compassion will help her community to build an open society that recognizes the equal value of other nations and in this case her communal and individual self will be a faithful manifestation of the universal (no-)self. Of course, she can also choose to serve herself at the cost of others and let her social self (mis-)take itself as the most valuable existence, as if it were the one and only incarnation of the universal self. There are too many living examples of these closed societies today. But it is easy to imagine how we cannot hope for a genuine communication that would require us to remain attentive to different cultural contexts or a constructive self-criticism regarding social issues that we would be going through in this type of society. But even then, both types of society are integral to defining one's selfhood and they either reflect or disregard the ideality of the universal self.

Tanabe's logic of species, thus, provides a complex metaphysical theory of self that strives to conceive of human existence in and through the threefold system. It always conceives of the individual self in relation to the communal self, and the metaphysical notion of selfhood (that is abstract and empty in itself) is either properly manifested or distorted through the individual's interaction with others in their social selfhood. The specific group of people as the social self could represent a community of compassionate individuals that live up to the ideality of human selfhood as self-negating emptiness or the praxis of no-self. In this case, the group of such individuals constitutes an open society, where they dedicate themselves to the good of others both within and beyond the boundaries of this group. We can expect a genuine communication or mutual understanding among diverse groups of human individuals in this mode of (communal) living. The diversity of social identities is always celebrated therein as equal self-expressions of human existence.

The same group of individuals could mistake the unique identity of their community as the highest ideality of human existence while taking advantage of other groups as being inferior to their own. In this case, the group of such arrogant and selfish individuals constitutes a closed society, where they will either reject or assimilate what lies beyond the bounds of their social selfhood into their process of self-affirming self-preservation. This communal self may show itself to be open to others at times (insofar as they can be assimilated into its own framework of being), but there is no true sense of openness in its interaction with the others. We cannot expect any genuine communication or mutual understanding between this closed society and the rest of the world. Every individual is born into a variety of social selves that play a decisive role in defining her self-identity, and in a sense, she cannot always choose which type of social self she initially belongs. However, according to Tanabe, the social self cannot make any decisions unless the individual members exercise their freedom. It is up to her, therefore, either to (trans-)form her society into a unique expression of human existence in its harmonious relation to others or watch the world burn and her community in the midst of it.[25] The social self that defines the individual is defined by her action in relation to the ideality of human selfhood. This triadic intermediation of individual and social self in relation to the universal self frames the Tanabean understanding of "self" in the logic of species.

Questions for Class Discussions

Q1. Tanabe argues that species indicates a social self or corresponds to specific groups of individuals that gives immediate identity to the sense of who you are. This book provided nationality as an example. Raise as many examples of a social self that you can think of, discuss how important they are for your self-identity; consider how similar or different they are from each other; and keep the list of your social self when answering the following questions.

Q2. According to Tanabe, the social self is finite and contingent. Because of this, it bears a contradictory movement toward self-preservation and self-disruption. What does this mean for the senses of social selves that you raised in response to Q1?

Q3. Tanabe argues that the rational ideality of the human self (i.e., genus) manifests through the social self (species) when individuals regard each other with mutual respect and openness of generosity. What should your social self (or selves) look like? What is the reality of your social self in comparison to that ideal?

Metanoesis and the Tanabean View of the World

The "World" in the Tanabean Oeuvre

The term "world" plays a specific role in the *Logic of Species*. In relation to Heidegger's phenomenology (especially in *Being and Time*), the term is deployed as representing a dialectical unity of time and space. This allegedly allows Tanabe to argue that his philosophy transcends the limitation of Heidegger's ontology precisely because it fully takes into account both individual self-consciousness (time) and the intersubjective side of human existence qua species (space).[1] In his critical appraisal of Karl Jaspers's existentialism (which is evaluated as being superior to Heidegger's phenomenology), Tanabe argues that the limit of existentialism lies in its static (self-)awareness of the opposition between existence and transcendence, thereby failing to achieve the "active conversion of transcendence-qua-immanence, other-qua-self."[2] This transformative act that bridges the gap between existence and transcendence is only possible through the practical notion of nothingness in the Mahayana Buddhist tradition and, on the basis of this concept, Tanabe refers to his philosophy as containing "world dialectic"[3] and "world ontology."[4]

As the logic of species begins to spread its branches in multiple directions in the later 1930s and the early 1940s, the "world" begins to be inclusive of a plethora of other meanings (e.g., history, reality, historical reality, historical manifestation of reality, human state, absolute reality, humanity, and practice). However, it is not entirely clear how we can systematically frame these concepts in relation to the whole logic of species (and perhaps this is another reason why the collection of the dense papers was never treated as a finished work by the author). These terms seem to mean somewhat different things at the beginning and at the end of the thirteen essays. Certainly, I am not saying that Tanabe was carelessly throwing around these terms without thinking about their mutual implications and then just suddenly dropped them when he came up with a more comprehensive framework of metaphysical thinking in his later philosophy. Many historical accounts on his editorial process and textual evidence from manuscripts testify that he was too systematic and meticulous to do anything like that; and when he did recognize a problem from his previous writings, he acknowledged his carelessness and explained how it should be rephrased or understood differently if it was to signify anything meaningful in the ongoing process of perfecting his metaphysical thinking. In fact, I believe his later philosophy of religion, especially in the trilogy of *Philosophy as Metanoetics* (1946), *Existence, Love, and Practice* (1947), and *Dialectic of Christianity* (1948), exhibits a far more coherent outline of the "world" or "reality." In these works, Tanabe's rendering of the absolute (i.e., nothingness) more consistently and more visibly plays a decisive role in determining his understanding of historical reality. In this chapter, therefore, we will investigate the general outline of Tanabe's metaphysical view of the world in reference to his central notions such as absolute critique, *metanoesis*, absolute dialectic, nothingness, self-power and other-power, *ōsō ekō* (往相回向) and *gensō ekō* (還相回向), and the intermediation of these opposing terms in the (net-)works of love.

Self-Awareness as a Passage to Nothingness: Absolute Critique as the Theory of Metanoetics

The foundation of Tanabe's metaphysical understanding of the world/reality is the notion of nothingness. As we have seen in his description of the logic of species, we cannot determine any positive significance of the term (nothingness or genus) in and of itself (otherwise it would be something other than no-thing). It is always to be understood in its mediatory relation to other concrete terms like individual and species. In fact, it represents a kind of "dynamic (dis)unity" that enables the intermediation of the other terms as what they are in their mediatory relation to each other and to itself. Tanabe articulates that this nothingness as the absolute in the foundation of his metaphysical system cannot be the content of intellectual intuition. This is quite different from many classical formulations of the absolute in the European metaphysical tradition. There is no direct access to this foundational metaphysical concept, but we can always recognize its manifestation through a certain act of an individual as well as its intermediation with other individuals in their communal form of existence.

Tanabe sets out to give an account of nothingness through an account of theoretical self-reflection or according to the Kyoto School's technical term, "self-awareness" (*jikaku*, 自覚). This is what he calls "absolute critique" in *Philosophy as Metanoetics* and it begins with a critique of the Kantian critical project. The basic argument is that many forms of European philosophy (especially Kant and German Idealism) suffer from a propensity to fix the absolute in immanence seeking to mitigate the gap between the absolute and the relative from the side of the relative (namely, itself) such that the relative is treated as the absolute merely in immanent terms. This clearly leads to the loss of self-awareness as the finite relative and when we lose our sight of the basic condition of human existence in its fundamental opposition to the infinite absolute, we also lose the sight of the absolute as that which exceeds the confines of the relative. Much in consonance with Kierkegaard, Tanabe is disturbed by philosophers' general inability to be truthful to their existence as finite, contingent, and uncompromisingly relative humans. For instance, in relation to Kant, he argues:

> Though a critical philosopher, [Kant] did not venture into criticism of the very possibility of criticism. It would seem he was convinced that if criticism is the proper task of reason, as he believed it was, philosophy becomes possible only when we presuppose and admit criticism; and moreover, that the possibility of criticism itself cannot be called into question without negating reason and abandoning philosophy. In this, he was from first to last a philosopher of reason. Yet it takes no more than a moment's reflection to locate the problems with such an idea of criticism.[5]

If the subject of reason's critique is exempted from the critique itself, the critique of reason can never be fulfilled. That is to say, Kant never begins to question *self-critically* the possibility of the critique of reason itself, thereby failing to ask the crucial philosophical question as to how one can thoroughly practice the critique of reason without calling into question one's critical project as a whole. But the flip side of this negative assessment of Kant is that we ought to remain truthful to the spirit of criticism. To do so, we must turn the critiquing subject into the object of critique and further put our critical reason to the task of self-critical questioning. If, however, we take this path of radical self-criticism, Tanabe thinks,

> We end up in an infinite regress where each critique gives rise to a critique of itself. We would then be forced to conclude that the thoroughgoing critique of reason in its entirety is simply impossible, involving a contradiction beyond the means of analytical logic to resolve because of the antinomies into which the infinite process of self-awareness is doomed to fall. ... [T]he self-criticism of reason [must] run aground on the impassable antinomies of the one and the many, the whole and the

individual, infinity and finitude, determinacy and spontaneity, necessity and freedom. Criticism has no alternative but to surrender itself to this crisis of self-disruption, and to overcome it by allowing itself to be shattered to pieces.[6]

The absolute critique represents this intellectual passage of human self-awareness, where the thinking subject recognizes his unavoidable self-disruption in the end of the uncompromising self-critique. What this deconstruction or crisis of reason reveals is the fact that the self-critique of human reason cannot make itself complete through itself alone, and in order for it to be a thorough self-criticism, it requires something more than itself. This sign of finitude in the self-reflection of human existence indicates that philosophy (especially in terms of modern European rational universalism) has faced the deadlock in which it cannot sufficiently mitigate the discontinuity between reason and being; subject and object; universal and particular; absolute and relative; rational and irrational/natural; ideality and reality; and self and other in addition to the other relevant metaphysical terms that Tanabe just mentioned.

To arrive at the standpoint of nothingness through absolute critique, Tanabe argues that we must first submit to the destiny of the radical self-critique where the self comes to realize that it can neither intermediate the gap between itself and other only from its own side nor turn itself into the absolute as the comprehensive synthesis of relative self and other. We have to be truthful to the self-destruction of philosophy as the inevitable consequence of self-questioning from the point of view of the finite relative. Or to use the language in the logic of species, we cannot properly define the notion of self by only focusing on one term in the logic. Nor can we treat it as a necessary or eternal pole that we can call "absolute." Even the universal selfhood (genus) that holds the intermediation of individual and communal self (species) cannot be exhaustively explained in terms of a single individual or a specific group of individuals. The triadic logic always already requires *both* the relativity of one term to another *and* general openness to the whole structure (and because of that, we are even liberated to [mis]take one form as if it were the fixed, eternal self). This essentially means that philosophy as an autonomous project of attaining complete self-knowledge in and through itself is ultimately impossible. Tanabe indeed sounds like he is echoing the madman in Nietzsche's *Gay Science*. Except in this case, he is saying that the loss of the divine absolute in the European philosophical context should also lead to another realization that "philosophy is dead."

Nevertheless, there is more to the fundamental finitude, ultimate impossibility, or radical emptiness of philosophical thinking as the process of attaining our complete self-knowledge:

> If we submit obediently to this destiny, choose this death willingly, and throw ourselves into the very depths of these utterly unavoidable contradictions, reality renews itself from those depths, and opens up a new way, urging us to head in the direction in which actuality is moving and to collaborate with this movement. Accompanying reason's option for its own death, the gate of contradictions, which was barred as long as reason clung to self-reliance, is thrown open. Contradictions do not thereby cease to be contradictions, but restore reason to a transrational dimension, where it can serve as a mediator to, or collaborator in the transformative activity of the absolute.[7]

As Tanabe repeatedly argues, "reason must fully break down in the pursuit of full autonomy through its self-critique."[8] But the breakdown of reason does not conclude with the mere annihilation of philosophical thinking altogether or our total degeneration into complete irrationalism. Because reason's confidence in its self-identity is shattered into pieces, philosophy can for the first time find a "foothold from which to break out its crisis by breaking through itself and to be transfromatively resurrected into a new being."[9] This new kind of philosophy is transrational in the sense that it cannot be reduced into any rationalistic framework of thinking that is obsessed with the process of demonstrating the immutable self-identity of reason or self. This anticipation of a breakthrough to the new direction in which transrational philosophy can embrace the radical difference between itself and what is other to itself or any relevant metaphysical terms in the very process of its breakdown constitutes the essential function of absolute critique.

So long as the absolute–relative or infinite–finite relation is reduced to the immanent self-relation of the human relative(s) as the infinite absolute (namely, the "bad/closed species"), there is no way for the self-thinking thought of the finite relative(s) to think what is truly absolute and infinite beyond itself because it erroneously thinks itself to be the absolute infinite in immanence. Once again, however, the "final result of the demand for self-identical unity in reason is the self-consciousness that all things are in absolute disruption because of antinomies and self-contradictions."[10] When reason, or human self, forgets its original finitude and misconceives itself as the infinite absolute, it is destined to the end of absolute critique, namely, an absolute contradiction and disruption. When philosophy loses its confidence in reason's self-identity and its presupposition of reason's absolute autonomy is brought into serious question, then, it can wake up to a different kind of absolute that is other than itself. This is what Tanabe calls "absolute nothingness." In this awakening to the absolute as that which is other than what we can conceive of only in philosophical terms, we can, for the first time, begin to reconsider the intermediations of the irreducibly contradictory metaphysical terms, including the relation between the relative and the absolute. And precisely when we realize our inability to bridge the gap between these opposing terms within the conventional form of philosophy alone, we can be led to a kind of philosophy that is "reborn out of the denial of philosophy."[11]

Tanabe calls this "philosophy that is not a philosophy because, on the one hand, it has arisen from the vestiges of a philosophy I had cast away in despair, and on the other, it maintains the purpose of functioning as a reflection on what is ultimate as a radical self-awareness, which are the goals proper to philosophy."[12] The death-and-resurrection of philosophy does not mark only the inevitable consequence of absolute critique but also the proper reflection of the ultimate through the renewed sense of philosophy. In this case, humbled reason comes to hear the Buddhist notion of nothingness as the absolute beyond the immanent absolutization of human, relative existence. This awareness of ultimacy outside the conventional form of philosophy based solely on reason's autonomy now leads Tanabe to reconstruct a dialectical mode of thinking—a new form of dialectic that, in reference to the otherness of absolute nothingness—recalibrates the intermediation of the opposing metaphysical terms with full attentiveness to the result of absolute critique (namely, their irreducible difference). Tanabe calls this new form of dialectic "absolute dialectic" and holds it to be the consummate standpoint for delivering his own metaphysical worldview.

From Hegelian Dialectic to Absolute Dialectic: The Worldview Based on the Notion of Nothingness

Absolute critique aims to show the groundlessness or essential emptiness of human thinking/being, especially when it is set to achieve its self-knowledge through itself alone. Precisely because it is essentially empty in and of itself, a thorough self-examination leads to the experience of a breakdown, which could paradoxically lead its practitioner to a breakthrough to the sense of the absolute that is other to itself. This indicates a transformation of rational self to another kind of trans-rational self (or what Tanabe consistently calls "no-self"). The self was once fixated on the structure of being as all there is to be talked about. It was also obsessed with itself as the sole ground of comprehending the whole world (and itself therein). But now it becomes aware of the inexplicable ground of all things as that which is other to itself (namely, nothingness) and thereby exhibits its self-awareness as the finite self-aware self, which recognizes its limitation in its process of understanding the world (and even itself) as what it is. Hegel's absolute spirit is an exemplar of the former. It tries to mitigate the gap between opposing metaphysical terms in view of its self-completing self-determination, thus claiming the philosopher's mind and (his) state to be the sole determiner of the intelligibility of all things. Contrariwise, Tanabe's reason/self demonstrates its fundamental inability to bridge the same gap because a thorough self-examination reveals its fundamental inability to fully comprehend the foundation of all things. Like many postmodern thinkers, Tanabe sees the radical difference between opposing concepts in metaphysics, while exposing the modern project of philosophical reason for alleging to bridge them on the basis of itself—or what some contemporary philosophers recognize as the dream of "logocentrism"—as sheer madness.

Our awareness of the ineradicable equivocity between opposing meta-physical terms, however, does not lead to a sort of nihilism, where we consider the philosophical thinking of the human subject as having nothing to do with the structure of objective reality. The irreducible difference between them is not exclusive of their mutual implications but is, in fact, indispensable for thinking about their proper interrelations. In this sense, Tanabe argues that the notion of nothingness can fully allow us to constitute a dialectical mode of thinking that can save us from falling victim to the Hegelian formulation.

It is helpful, therefore, to think about the contrast between Hegel's and Tanabe's rendering of dialectic. As I briefly mentioned, Hegel's model pays attention to the initial opposition of two terms and tries to make sense of it as a self-determination of only one term. If we are talking about the "universal" and the "particular," they are initially conceived of in their opposition to each other, but if we stick with this simple binary opposition, we are making a categorical mistake. That is to say that the universal is reduced to the level of the particular (as another particular standing apart from it) and/or raising the particular to the level of the universal (as that which is equal to the universal). So, to understand their differences properly, Hegel proposes to see the particular as the self-particularizing moment of the universal in its process of determining itself as the more comprehensive universal that sublates the opposition between itself and the particular. In this dialectical self-determination, the universal moves from the abstract universal (in its initial opposition to the particular) to the concrete universal in and through the particular (as its particularized moment). One term moves out of it, reaches out to the other, and by recognizing this other as its self-othering moment, comes back to itself as the comprehensive unity of both.

There has been a number of forceful criticisms against this model, but here are two key counterpoints that Tanabe makes in consonance with those commentators: (1) the mediation between the two terms according to Hegel is one-sided and (2) there is the risk of instrumentalization that can cloud our genuine understanding of the negative term. These criticisms are mutually inclusive. The Hegelian dialectic focuses on the self-identity of one term, namely, the positive: consequently, it can recognize the otherness of the negative term only insofar as it serves as the means for the self-determination of the positive. In this case, there is no genuine otherness implied by the negative term in relation to the positive term (as that which is irreducible to the latter), for when its value is determined as a means for the self-affirmation of the positive as the absolute, there is no genuine intermediation of the two terms as they are so considered by Hegel. If the value of the negative has to be judged on the basis of its usefulness to the self-determining self-affirmation of the positive, it seems like the negative is semi-positive, at best, but never entirely negative. Many Kyoto school thinkers were often dissatisfied with this failure to properly understand the negative in Hegel's dialectic.

There has been some debate among Hegel scholars whether or not the concrete universal (or absolute spirit) as the end result of the Hegelian dialectic refers to a philosopher's mind or to a community of individuals (i.e., state) that embodies it. Either way, we should be able to see by now how Tanabe would regard both of them as the problematic absolutization of an individual or a communal self. This is unfaithful to the finite status of our existence either as individual or species. Tanabe's absolute critique shows that the Hegelian speculative model of self-thinking thought can also be confronted with its one-sidedness (just like Kant's critique of reason) and it should lead us to the same rude awakening before the radical otherness of the negative term. With a thorough cultivation of self-awareness, what we thought as the proper way of "tarrying with the negative" as a necessary means for our self-affirmation now enables us to see for the first time the true face of the negative. It contains a value that escapes the process of the positive's self-affirmation, the value of the negative irreducible to the dialectical circuit of self-determining reason.

When reason is equipped with its full self-awareness, Tanabe thinks that it should be attentive to its own finitude. In this case, it comes to open itself to what is other to itself and it is "restored to a transrational dimension,"[13] where it serves as the collaborative mediator of the absolute.

This transformative absolute that restores reason at a transrational level, Tanabe argues, corresponds to the Buddhist notion of nothingness, and this transformation of self/reason, through its submission to the notion of nothingness, constitutes what he calls "*zangedō*" (懺悔道) and "*zettai benshōhō*" (絶対弁証法) in Japanese. He translates *zangedō* into English in consonance with a biblical passage as "metanoetics" and clearly indicates that what he is getting at in this work is relevant to those who come from the Judeo-Christian tradition. However, the initial set-up of his argument depends much on his interpretation of the history of European philosophy in reference to East Asian and Japanese Buddhist traditions. To understand his metaphysical worldview, therefore, it is crucial to examine some of the philosophical notions pertaining to Mahāyāna Buddhism (especially of the Japanese Pure Land school) and further investigate how, through them, Tanabe comes to develop a renewed sense of philosophy as "metanoetics" or "absolute dialectic." In the following, I will introduce some key Buddhist notions that he deploys in his formulation of absolute dialectic and analyze how they set forth a unique metaphysical worldview in Tanabean philosophy.

Self-Power (*jiriki* 自力)

Tanabe describes a type of philosophy that is based solely on the self's autonomy (whether it is of will or reason) as the "philosophy of self-power" and his metanoetics as the renewed sense of philosophy that recognizes its ground in the "other-power." This distinction refers to the Buddhist notions of *jiriki-hongan* (自力本願) and *tariki-hongan* (他力本願). The concept of *jiriki-hongan* is often translated as "salvation through self-power." This means that a human being makes the original vow of Bodhisattva (Skt. *pūrva-pran-idhāna*, Jp. *Hongan*, 本願) and realizes this vow as Tathāgata (Jp. *Nyorai*, 如来) through her own effort toward perfection, or what is called the impermanent state of nirvana (Jp. *Nehan*, 涅槃). In the context of metaphysics, this is equivalent to saying that the movement from the finite to the infinite or the relative to the absolute is made only through the self's own effort to overcome its finitude and, therefore, the self becomes the infinite absolute through itself alone. The self-negating self-transcendence in the philosophy of self-power, in this sense, makes the one-way movement from the human relative to the divine absolute.

Under the label of "self-power philosophy" (*jiriki-tetsugaku*, 自力哲学), Tanabe includes not only the Kantian and the Hegelian philosophy that we have briefly examined above, but also what he calls "mysticism," Zen Buddhism, Heideggerian phenomenology, and Nishidian philosophy.

The ways in which Tanabe critically responds to these diverse systems of philosophy are quite complex and could significantly vary from each other (as we can easily imagine from reading their works). But there is a consistent thread by which he makes his argument. This is precisely his existential concern with the premise of the self-power philosophy. If the finite relative can overcome its own limitation and rise to the level of the infinite absolute, the consequence of following the logic of *jiriki-hongan* would amount to saying that only those who can autonomously realize the ideality of moral perfection (or successfully manifest their Buddha nature without relying on anything other than themselves) can access the path to the absolute. Tanabe gives a complex response to this logic of self-power. On the one hand, he praises this path as representing the "sacred way"[14] (i.e., *shōdōmon*, 聖道門) of the saints and sages who can realize their Buddha nature by fully exercising their self-power. There are many occasions in which Tanabe expresses his deep admiration for the Buddhists (especially in reference to the Zen tradition), who are known to have gone through a variety of spiritual exercises and managed to pass through this extraordinary passage to enlightenment. On the other hand, he also expresses his concern that, if he were to say that this sacred path to the realization of Buddha nature is accessible to him, he would end up being disingenuous with regard to the state of his own historical existence, which is quite ordinary and far from being morally perfect.

There is a mixture of existential and theoretical concern in his ambivalent stance toward the self-power philosophy. As the opening of *PM* testifies, Tanabe was greatly torn over his inability to reconcile his responsibilities, both as a philosopher and as a citizen of Japan, during and following the Second World War. What we see here is a confession of an intellectual who strongly felt the responsibility to speak against the evildoing of his nation and to express his strong disagreement with the military government. However, at the same time, as the citizen of a nation, Tanabe felt he was compelled to refrain from causing a split among his people at the time of war. In the face of the destruction that his nation had caused outside and inside the islands of Japan, Tanabe's health had also greatly degenerated at this time. In this state of intellectual and physical depression, Tanabe found it difficult to continue his life as a philosopher, while facing the self-destruction of his nation in the 1940s, let alone to believe in the sacred path of self-power (*jiriki-shōdōmon*) as his way to salvation. Tanabe repeatedly argues that he is hardly the wise and righteous man who is capable of ascending the sacred path of self-power to his perfection, but rather he is the "sinful, the ordinary, and the ignorant"[15] man that can do nothing but admit to his incapacity to rise to the level of the absolute through his own self-power.

This existential self-awareness also demonstrates the realization that the *shōdōmon* of self-power is not truthful to the reality of one's moral existence. Tanabe often refers to Kant's account of religion and the confession of St. Paul. Kantian moral religion suggests that a human being is equipped with the natural disposition toward the good and, thus, he is fully capable of autonomously bringing himself to moral perfection. However, even the best of humanity, such as St. Paul, suffer from the so-called propensity to evil (or more specifically the "frailty of heart"), as he confesses, "For the good that I would I do not: but the evil which I would not, that I do" (Romans 7:19).[16] Tanabe emphasizes that this confession of St. Paul demonstrates existential honesty, essentially testifying to one's inability to achieve moral perfection through oneself, and because of that, we must admit with St. Paul (and Kant) that we need grace for our salvation, which always provides something more than the mere autonomy of reason can conjure.

The self's incapacity to mediate the gap between the reality of his existence and the ideality of moral perfection is consistent with Tanabe's theoretical portrayal of reason's radical self-criticism. Absolute critique concludes that reason is incapable of accounting for its unity when it attempts to carry out a thorough examination of itself and also that such reason cannot fully account for the unity of the contradiction between itself and what is other to it by maintaining its alleged self-identity. Given the inherent finitude (i.e., antinomies, paralogisms, etc.) of reason, Tanabe argues that the idea of the "sacred way," where the rational self is supposed to be able to bring itself to self-identical unity, as well as to the unity of itself and other, leads to an absolute crisis:

The absolute self-disruption brought about in absolute critique is unavoidable for reason awakened to awareness of itself. The self-awareness that all things are in absolute disruption because of antinomies and self-contradictions is the final result of the demand for self-identical unity in reason. Pure self-identity is possible only for the absolute. Insofar as reason forgets its standpoint of finitude and relativity and erroneously presumes itself to be absolute, it is destined to fall into absolute contradiction and disruption.[17]

In the face of the unavoidable consequence of absolute critique, the self has the following choices: either submit itself to the death of its own reason and thereby humbly admit that its inherent finitude prevents itself from claiming its infinite status through itself or exploit its own relative independence over and against the absolute and commit the hubris of self-apotheosis. In this sense, Tanabe often argues that self-power philosophy, which tends to unite the absolute and the relative through the principle of self-identity, has the serious tendency to ignore the fact that "a human being as the finite relative cannot possibly have the power to break free from the sin through himself [and consequently,] the salvation or freedom (Skt. *mokṣa*, Jp. *gedatsu*, 解脱) from sufferings through self-power is impossible for humanity."[18]

The Other-Power (*tariki* 他力)

The notion of *tariki-hongan* (他力本願) is often (mis-)used in colloquial Japanese in reference to the heteronomy of faith, where one is seen to leave everything up to the heaven (or other people) and makes no effort whatsoever to match the ideality of moral perfection. However, in the original sense of the term in the Pure Land tradition (and especially in the works of Hōnen 法然 and Shinran 親鸞), this term actually means that Amida Buddha's original vow ultimately saves sentient beings—that is to say, the self-negating self-transcendence of the finite relative to the infinite absolute must be accompanied by the divine kenosis of the compassionate other. What clearly differentiates the common (mis-)understanding of the notion of *tariki* and its original configuration in the Pure Land school is the fact that the former maintains the rigid opposition between *jiriki* and *tariki*, while the latter construes a paradoxical relationship in which *tariki* denies the ultimacy of *jiriki* and yet, at the same time, sustains its possibility. For this reason, Tanabe maintains that, by means of one's total submission to the consequence of absolute critique, "what is impossible with *jiriki* becomes possible with *tariki*, though both *tariki* and *jiriki* remain complementary to one another."[19]

Naturally, the question is how the complementary relationship between self-power and other-power affects our understanding of human autonomy or self-power. Tanabe's answer (much in consonance with Shinran) describes other-power as the transformative power of the absolute (i.e., nothingness) that noninsistently enables the self-power of each human to move from the finite to the infinite. Tanabe further articulates this "correlativity" of the absolute and the relative by saying that

> As nothingness, the absolute is absolute mediation and, therefore, permanently correlative to being; it is a circularity of unceasing mediation. The absolute is not an ideal or goal that ultimately sublates the relative; it is, rather, a principle that supports us continually wherever we stand and makes it possible for us to engage in authentic action. It is not a point that lies forever beyond the reach of our advance, but the very force that moves us here and now. Wherever the relative exists, the

absolute is there as its correlative. In the realm of being, nothingness always mediates and is mediated. The absolute coexists with the relative and becomes manifest through its confrontation with the relative.[20]

The other-power of the absolute, in this sense, grants the relative selves (i.e., being) their self-power (i.e., freedom), and each of these selves, in turn, can play its mediatory role of manifesting the absolute other-power in concrete reality. This mediatory manifestation of the absolute is possible when the relative self transforms itself or more precisely allows itself to be transformed (through the transformative support of the other-power) into the natural embodiment of the other-power. To do this, once again, the self must cultivate its self-awareness. That is to say, it must recognize its inability to sustain its self-power through itself alone or that its self-power is minted with a contradiction of existence and oughtness, which it cannot bring to unity through itself alone. This is precisely what Tanabe means by the death-and-resurrection of the self or the self-negating process in which each self becomes the "empty being" (*kū-u* 空有) that embodies the ideality of the absolute in relative reality.

This transformation of self from its obsession with its own self-power into the self-power as the realization of the other-power requires that one should give up oneself for the sake of the other and engage in the act of charity with the heart-and-mind of great compassion. This point becomes much clearer as we continue our investigation into the nature of the absolute and its intermediatory relation with the relative in the following section. However, what is clear at this point is that Tanabe calls for the necessity of recalibrating our understanding of autonomy as something made possible through its relativity to the power that is irreducible to our own self-power. In this sense, the proper formulation for understanding our autonomy should not be the dualistic framework in which the self's autonomy (*jiriki*) opposes the other-power (*tariki*), but the dynamic interrelation in which *tariki* empowers *jiriki*, while *jiriki* is transformed to realize *tariki* in reality. Tanabe, in this manner, maintains that we should properly formulate the nature of human self-power as the *jiriki-soku-tariki* (自力即他力) or self-power-*qua*-other-power.

Absolute Nothingness: Self-Awareness of Tathāgata or Amida Buddha

The absolute-relative relation beyond the self-power of the relative self, according to Tanabe, does not compromise the autonomy of the human self because the nature of the absolute in Buddhism represents a transformative power of Tathāgata or Amida Buddha. The absolute, for Tanabe, is neither a rational postulate nor an ontic object of cognition, nor even a self-determining concept, but is inspired by the Buddhist self-awareness of nothingness, whose significance has a long lineage in various Asian intellectual traditions under the term *Śūnyatā*. Tathāgata or Amida Buddha is an exemplary manifestation (or more precisely, the perfect practitioner) of this nothingness. In Tanabe's account, this absolute represents an infinite activity of self-negating compassion or the divine kenosis of Amida Buddha that makes itself both transcendent to and immanent in the existence of the finite relatives.

It is very difficult to visualize this notion of the absolute, since it refuses to be intellectually grasped or intuited as a static concept, but represents the dynamic intermediation of itself as nothing and what is other to itself as all things. This means that this notion also has full existential significance for those who claim to understand its meaning as sentient beings (just like Socrates's knowledge of the good). To emphasize the practical implications of the notion, Tanabe often qualifies this term with other names—for example, absolute mediation, transformative power, the Great Compassionate Action (*taihigyō*, 大悲行), the act of love, self-negation, self-sacrifice, among others. These qualifications are also made against the standpoint of *jiriki* philosophy, which (Tanabe believes) wrongly claims to reach the standpoint of the infinite absolute merely through contemplative activities of self-thinking thought (*noesis noeseos*), the self-centered standpoint that fails to capture the dynamic nature and practical implication of the absolute as absolute nothingness.

Once again, the passage to our (self-)awareness of absolute nothingness in metanoetic philosophy lies in the end of the "absolute critique":

> Unlike the philosophies of sages and saints, which presuppose a standpoint of the infinite and the absolute, metanoetics is thoroughly conscious of its finite and relative limits. Since the critique of reason cannot avoid entangling itself in antinomies, and is finally brought by "absolute critique" to its complete undoing, reason has no choice but to let go of itself and acknowledge its own ineffectiveness. But once reason itself ... decides to die in the midst of contradiction, the gate to a "middle way" (*chūdō*, 中道) that is neither thesis nor antithesis opens up unexpectedly, and one is taken up into transcendent nothingness.[21]

Once the single individual realizes its finitude through its genuine self-criticism, it comes to realize its ground in what is other than itself. The otherness of this foundation as the absolute nothingness is recognized as being transcendent, because it is neither identical to nor exhaustibly explicable by any of the relevant metaphysical terms (i.e., the single individual, the particular/species, and the universal/genus). Rather, as another Kyoto School philosopher, Nishitani Keiji, succinctly comments, "it lies beyond the alternative of 'to be' and 'not to be'"[22] or the relative notions of being and nothing. The ultimate as nothingness, in this sense, gives the trans-ontic ground that exceeds any of the ontic terms.

Notice also how the realization of "death" is crucial for this awareness of transcendent nothingness in the interiority of one's existence as the finite individual. Tanabe emphasizes this point by describing the consequence of one's being "taken up into transcendent nothingness" in the following passage:

> Transformed into a mediator of an absolute transformation that supersedes the opposition between life and death, one is brought to faith-witness of the Great Compassionate Action (*taihigyō*, 大悲行). … This is why we may speak of self-consciousness of the Great-Nay-qua-Great Compassion (*daihi-soku-daihi*, 大非即大悲), or of Nothingness-*qua*-love (*mu-soku-ai*, 無即愛), as the core of metanoetics. Here the self is resurrected from the death it once died of its own decision and is raised up to a new life beyond life and death, or a "life-in-death." The self is restored to a state of "empty being" as a mediator of absolute nothingness. … It is here that the Great Compassion of the absolute, which revives the relative self by its transcendent power, realizes its quality of absolute mediation: it makes independent relative beings a skillful means (Skr. *upāya*, Jp. *hōben*, 方便) to serve the workings of its own Great Nay, and yet allows them their relative existence as an "other" to serve as mediators of absolute Other-power.[23]

The awakening to one's finitude, which is to submit oneself to the painful truth that one's existence (i.e., life) must come to an end (i.e., death), leads to one's consciousness of oneself as being given to be by absolute nothingness (i.e., life beyond life and death). In this state of being "made to live its own life" from the perspective of death or the actuality of "living, or being restored to life, as one who is dead,"[24] the self comes to experience the renewed sense of "dying life" or "living death" based on the fundamental principle of life beyond life and death. Tanabe argues that this self-consciousness of a finite being as being finite, that is, for each of us to properly recognize that we are mortal beings, constitutes a "self-consciousness based not on the continued existence of the self but on the passing away of the self"[25] and further elaborates the significance of this self-awareness by saying that

> It is a self-consciousness established in the witness of a self that lives as it dies. Even though the self has been restored to life, this does not mean

that life reappears after death to replace it. ... The dialectic of death and life consists rather in this, that just as death does not follow life but is already within life itself, so is life restored within death and mediated by it. The point at which the mutual transformation of life and death takes place is not a universal locus where death and life together are subsumed into a relationship of both/and. It is rather in the dynamic of the neither/nor itself, in the very transformation itself.[26]

Absolute nothingness is the dialectic of neither/nor (or the open dialectic that preserves the "middle way" between self and other), since it represents *neither* life *nor* death within the confines of life's becoming and yet enables them to be without subsuming them into itself in immanence of *both* life *and* death, as Hegel's absolute spirit would maintain. This means that the notion of absolute nothingness that appears in Tanabe's mindfulness of his own finitude through his self-reflection on death/finitude points him to the true meaning of life: that is to say, his life along with its self-power is ultimately given to him as his own by the other-power of absolute nothingness. This is precisely the sense in which he says that the relative self, when it submits itself to its finitude and recognizes itself as the dying life, experiences its resurrection through the self-negating fulfillment of absolute nothingness.

This existential awakening to the presence of infinite otherness within the self-consciousness of the finite life confronts the relative self with the truth that this absolute is also immanent in all sentient beings. Transcendent nothingness is immanent because, through its self-negating compassion (*daihi-soku-daihi*), it continuously empties itself to allow the finite self to be and let the relative self freely determine itself through its own self-power. That is to say, the divine act of great compassion as nothingness never lords over the sentient beings for its self-determining self-affirmation, but always already enables everything to be what it is and "makes room" for the relative self to freely determine itself.

Notice how Tanabe continues to dismiss the dualistic framework for understanding the proper relationship between *jiriki* and *tariki*, self and other, and finite and infinite. It is not that self-power is standing over here and the other-power is threatening from above to compromise it. The absolute in Tanabe's formulation does not impede an autonomy of the relative self. In other words, absolute nothingness, by definition, refuses to be conceived of as any ontic term such that:

Nothingness is always nothing and cannot be that which directly works [on beings] as a being. It always mediates being for its work. Being as a mediator of nothingness takes nothingness as its principle and acts as it is acted on [by absolute nothingness]. Also, since what makes this [being] act is not a being but nothingness, to be made to act [by the absolute] is [for the relative being] to act for itself. This precisely gives the other-power-*qua*-self-power (*tariki-soku-jiriki*). To be made to work by the other-power of nothingness means freedom in the sense that self is not restricted by any other existence than itself and acts in accordance with its own decisions.[27]

As Tanabe repeatedly argues, a proper understanding of the intermediation of two things cannot give "a relationship in which one party is subordinated to the other, but one in which both enjoy and maintain an independence made possible by the other; and there is no question here of a causal connection that would make one party subordinate to the other as its effect."[28] So, the proper intermediation of absolute nothingness and self-power of the relative self cannot diminish the integrity of the latter in the same sense. Since the other-power as the foundation of self-power refuses to be identified with anything that we can grasp as "being," the self-power of the relative self must be fully granted for itself. This means that absolute nothingness can empower the self-power of sentient beings without becoming trapped in dualism, precisely because it provides the transcendent ground as transformative power that is inexplicable in any of the determinate/finite terms.

In this manner, metanoetic philosophy based on the other-power of nothingness as Tathāgata or Amida Buddha, in consonance with the Pure Land/Shin Buddhist teachings, preserves a peculiar sense of the transcendence that exceeds the realm of sentient beings, and yet, precisely because it exceeds the ontic domain of sentient beings as the trans-ontological absolute, it remains forever at work in the self-power of all beings and the free processes of their continuous efforts toward the unconditioned state of perfection, that is, nirvana or reaching the Pure Land. Thus, the picture of the absolute in the works of Tanabe demonstrates the "infinite reserve" of nothingness as the transcendent ground of all things, while avoiding the problem of conceiving divine transcendence in its dualistic opposition to the immanence of sentient beings.

The Intermediations of the Absolute and the Relative as the Open Species or the Networks of Love

The self-mediating self-power of the relative self is impossible without the "mysterious" support from the compassion of absolute nothingness. However, since the absolute claims itself to be nothing and takes nothing away from the freedom of the relative self, the relative self can easily think that it enjoys its integrity of being and self-power without recognizing the presence of the divine mediator in the way of its being. In other words, the autonomy of self-power is empowered to be for itself by the other-power; hence, it can mistake itself to be the absolute. This is what we saw in relation to the logic of species as an unmediated/bad/closed species, where the communal self mistakes itself as the sole embodiment of universal selfhood. Tanabe repeatedly reminds us that this way of self-centered thinking is guilty of "radical evil" against the other-power of nothingness and criticizes various forms of self-power philosophy as committing this crime. For the process of becoming itself, therefore, the relative self must see that the absolute selflessly grants it to be and to become conscious of itself as an empowered self-powering being, that is, to become the "empty being" or "being there as the relative emptiness" (*kū-u*). In order to achieve this true self-awareness of the finite individual as the mediator of absolute nothingness, then, the self must dwell in its inability to fulfill its own desire to determine itself only through its own power and let go of the very self-centered desire to ground its own existence only through itself. This achievement of true self-understanding—or the Buddhist praxis of no-self—requires the transformation of the self from the self that is incapable of coming to know (and determine) itself through itself alone to the self that opens itself to the other and comes to know (and fully become) itself through its intermediation with the other.

Tanabe argues in many occasions that this transformation from the self-determining self to the self-negating self requires an act of metanoesis—that is, a penitent confession of one's selfish tendency to think about oneself through oneself and also an earnest praxis of following the self-negating logic of nothingness. To know the presence of great nothingness in the foundation of one's self-awareness means that one must existentially engage in the act of true generosity and dedicate oneself to the other by learning to let go of its self-determining desire. To do this, we must go through the conversion from the standpoint of *eros* to that of *agape* (to use Plato's distinction). This means that I must dedicate myself to you not for the sake of myself, but for you, and when I succeed in doing so, I will be filled with the overflowing spirit of great-negation-qua-great-compassion (*daihi-soku-daihi*). Only then, I will truly come to realize that I am enabled both to be and to know my autonomous existence through the generosity of what is other to myself. In order to see the essential logic of this self-negating self-transcendence toward the absolute, one must "sacrifice one's own self compassionately for the sake of others"[29] and continuously engage in the act of love, "for the self-negation of absolute nothingness stands for nothing but love."[30] This practice of "dying" to oneself through the self-negating act of love, therefore, is indispensable for achieving one's self-awareness of absolute nothingness.

Ōsō-ekō 往相回向 and *Gensō-ekō* 還相回向: Manifestation of Absolute Nothingness through Networks of Love

There are at least two important points that we can draw from this existential/ practical implication of the metanoetic philosophy for the ongoing discussion of Tanabe's metaphysical worldview. The first can be found in the following passage summarizing his take on the absolute-relative relation:

> Metanoesis seeks throughout to maintain a standpoint of action-faith through Other-power, and thereby to insist on a relationship of reciprocal mediatory transformation between the absolute and the self. The redeeming truth that the absolute can function only as the power of absolute mediation can reach self-consciousness by way of reciprocal mediatory activity between relative selves. In this sense, the transformation through vertical mediation between the absolute and the self must also be realized in horizontal social relationships between my self and other selves.[31]

Tanabe clearly points out in this passage that there has to be a two-way intermediation between the relative self and absolute nothingness. In various places in his later works, he describes this absolute-relative intermediation in terms of the Buddhist notions of *ōsō-ekō* (往相回向) and *gensō-ekō* (還相回向). The *ōsō-ekō* literally means the "going toward the Pure Land from this world" while *gensō-ekō* refers to the "returning of Amida Buddha from the Pure Land to this world."[32] To make these terms relevant to the general context of philosophy, however, Tanabe slightly modifies the notion of the *ōsō-ekō* to represent the upward movement of the self to the absolute or the self's ascent from the inferior to the superior, while the *gensō-ekō* indicates the downward movement of the absolute to the relative or the self's descent from the superior to the inferior. What Tanabe is trying to say in this quoted passage is that one's vertical movement from the relative to the absolute (i.e., *ōsō-ekō*) must be accompanied by the *gensō-ekō* of the absolute to the relative, and at the same time, this vertical transformative intermediation(s) of the absolute and the relative is inaccessible unless the relative is practicing the act of generosity and compassion to other relative selves by transforming herself within the realm of sentient beings.

Tanabe incorporates these notions of *ōsō-ekō* and *gensō-ekō* into the mediatory relation of the absolute and relative by referring to the *Larger Sutra* and the *Meditation Sutra*.

> The mediatory significance of relative being may be understood in the two senses. First, the relative has being and significance only as a mediator of the absolute as an *ōsō*. But second, this function is fulfilled in a higher stage of self-consciousness: the vertical relation of *ōsō* must also be mediated by the horizontal relation between relative beings, which is the true import of the *gensō*. In other words, the absolute-relative relationship has also to be mediated by a relative-relative relationship wherein each relative being fulfills a mediating role in the salvation of other relative beings. This is the concrete form of "returning to" mediated by the activity of the relative. Hence the absolute itself is able to perform its *gensō* function only when it is mediated by the relative.[33]

This *ōsō-gensō* relation shows that the transformation of self-centered self-power to the selfless use of the self-power for the sake of the other (which is precisely to become an instance of other-power and to function as the mediator of absolute nothingness) in the communal networks of love is always made effective through the *gensō* movement of the other-power to the relative self; the intermediations of the self-negating relatives are the concrete manifestation of the transformative power of absolute nothingness. The relative *gensō* movements among the finite selves are a kind of *imitatio Dei*, an imitation of the absolute *gensō* movement of Tathāgata as nothingness toward the communities of the finite selves themselves. Thus, Tanabe's metanoetic philosophy understands the two-way mediations of the divine absolute and the human relative selves as the "two-fold dynamic of Amida Buddha," namely, the *ōsō*-qua-*gensō* (*ōsō-soku-gensō*, 往相即還相) or the self-power-as-other-power.

The Primacy of *Gensō* and Other-Power

With respect to the absolute-relative intermediations as the *ōsō-qua-gensō*, Tanabe emphasizes that there is an essential asymmetry between the *ōsō* movement of the relative to the absolute and the *gensō* movement of the absolute to the relative despite their inseparability from each other. This would be the second point that we can draw from the practical implication of the other-power philosophy as *gensō* metanoetics. Besides the transcendent status of absolute nothingness in relation to the realm of sentient beings,

Tanabe emphasizes the asymmetry between the *ōsō* and the *gensō* relationship between the absolute and the relative by saying that (1) the "bridge from the relative to the absolute" (i.e., *ōsō-ekō*) cannot be made from the side of the relative, and also that (2) the essential nature of humanity as the finite relative prevents us from either engaging in the *gensō* movements or initiating our act of metanoesis through our self-power alone.

To elucidate the priority of the absolute as the foundation of the two-way mediations between the absolute and the relative, Tanabe points to the "greatest contradiction" lurking in the foundation of religion, namely, the fact that the "self must free itself from the heart-and-mind of seeking freedom of the very self and desiring its own salvation [through itself alone] because the heart-and-mind that seeks the faith in itself could be the biggest obstacle for the same faith."[34] What is emphasized here is that only when the self can let go of itself, empty itself before the absolute, and dedicate itself for the other through the act of love—that is, to engage in the act of nothingness—there is the conversion (metanoesis) of the self from the self-centered use of its self-power to the selfless transformation of it as the mediator of absolute other-power. This *gensō*-mediation of human *ōsō*, Tanabe argues, is "not something that we can achieve only through *jiriki* but only originates from the grace of the absolute."[35]

The contradiction in one's effort to make oneself absolute or to attempt to travel the *ōsō* passage only through self-power is for the self to think that her act of nothingness (i.e., to love the other for the sake of the other) is her own. This contradiction is often condemned as the temptation of the "making of the Buddha" (*sabutsu*, 作仏) by problematically "desiring to become the Buddha who desires nothing." To force one's salvation through the other-power by means of one's own self-power is to commit this self-contradiction of *sabutsu*, which amounts to the radical evil of absolutizing the relative self. Tanabe clearly criticizes this attitude of egoity: "The salvation through *sabutsu* is impossible for human beings; for the bridge to absolute cannot be built from the side of the relative."[36] This asymmetry between *gensō* of the infinite absolute and *ōsō-ekō* of the finite relative also implies that the act of metanoesis—the very transformation of our self-power into the other-power as the manifestation of absolute nothingness—is also impossible unless the other-power of the absolute is operative in our self-powering existence as the relative self and our interactions with each other:

> Metanoesis does not come about merely as a result of self-reflection carried out under self-power. It suffices to ensure conversion and salvation only when the Other-power of the absolute is performing the work of transformation. Metanoesis is not simply a process of human

consciousness, not merely an intellectual dynamic within consciousness brought about through the self-power agency of the soul. It is not through a mere idea but through a real power that the soul is converted and turned in a new direction. Accordingly, metanoesis may be termed an inner action determined by Other-power.[37]

The transformation of ourselves through the inner act of metanoesis and the external act of love has to originate from the *gensō-tariki* of absolute nothingness. This is because we are finite individuals. Finite individuals are incapable of engaging in the infinite act of *gensō* to the same degree as the infinite absolute. Nor can we love each other at all times without failing to empty our egoity and dedicate ourselves entirely for the other. Nor can we initiate any of these activities through our own self-power alone. The very self-power that enables us to intermediate with the absolute as the means for its temporary manifestation in immanence (*upāya*) and/or tempts us to mistake ourselves for the absolute is ultimately the gift of the great compassion. Thus, the intermediating relation of the absolute and the relative, and the absolute *gensō* of nothingness as the foundation of our *ōsō(-qua-gensō)* movement point to the superiority of the absolute to the relative, thereby signaling the priority of the divine *gensō* in relation to the *ōsō* movement of the finite relatives toward the absolute.

The Metanoetic Worldview

Tanabe's metanoetic philosophy provides an "open dialectic" based on the notion of nothingness. It argues for the undeniable relativity of opposing metaphysical terms while refusing to prioritize one over the other, and because of that, their mutual implication always reserves the unsurpassable tension of their oppositions. This difference, in turn, makes room for their genuine intermediations rather than one-sided self-determination. If we think of it in terms of the universal and the particular or subject and object, the metanoetic worldview would hold that there are necessarily mutual implications between them, but also that we cannot collapse the distinction by thinking that the side of the universal/subject can somehow explain away everything about the side of the particular/object or vice versa. There is infinite reserve in the particular or object such that we cannot exhaustively make sense of them merely in terms of our universalizing articulation as the thinking subject (just as much as we cannot reduce our understanding of experience as the subject to the structure of objective reality). The basis for a human self to recognize this ineradicable difference between itself and what is other to itself, moreover, is its confrontation with the notion of absolute nothingness through a genuine practice of self-examination or a continuous cultivation of self-awareness. Tanabe thinks that by facing the groundlessness, mortality, or finite relativity of its own existence, a human self can come to recognize its undeniable dependence on the trans-ontological foundation that holds its irreducible otherness both to the self and to the totally of all beings. This trans-ontological source of being that is other to the self gives the inexhaustible otherness to all that is. Because of that, reason/self is marked with the givenness that it cannot fully account for itself through itself alone. There is much more to reason/self than it can understand on its own terms, and the same goes for being/other that stands in opposition to it with the same givenness.

This absolute, for Tanabe, once again, is emptiness or nothingness understood in accordance with the Mahayana Buddhist tradition. Hence, it involves a kind of dynamic self-withdrawing creativity, or active passivity, which, by always already making itself nothing, makes what is other to itself everything, thereby letting everything be and be free for itself.[38] The Tanabean absolute is, in this sense, both radically transcendent to, and immanent in, all that is. It is transcendent because, as nothing, it is not irreducible to anything in the realm of being, but also radically immanent to everything because, through its self-negating compassion (*daihi-soku-daihi*), it always remains at work in the free process of all sentient beings' striving toward the unconditioned state of nirvana or moral perfection.

The standpoint of *jiriki-hongan* maintains that the passage from the relative to the absolute or from sentient beings to the state of impermanence (i.e., nirvana) can be achieved through the self-power of the relative, sentient beings. Contrary to this notion of *jiriki-hongan* and *jiriki-shōdōmon*, Tanabe proposes the paradoxical path of Other-Power Pure Land (*tariki-jōdomon*). This configuration of the absolute-relative relation does not straightforwardly reject the standpoint of *jiriki-hongan*. The self-negating self-transcendence (i.e., *ōsō-ekō*) of the relative self in view of absolute nothingness is always accompanied by the self-negating self-transcendence of the absolute toward the relative (i.e., *gensō-ekō*). Tanabe expresses this two-way mediation of the absolute and the relative always as the *ōsō*-qua-*gensō* and *gensō*-qua-*ōsō*. This understanding of the absolute-relative intermediations, deriving from the notion of *tariki-hongan*, indicates that the autonomy of sentient existence is always already empowered to be for its own self-power by the other-power of absolute nothingness. Tanabe, in this sense, clearly argues that the movement from the relative to the absolute cannot be a one-way movement, whereby the relative self determines itself to be the absolute (which he sees as the central structure of various *jiriki* philosophies), but must adopt the standpoint of intermediation where it can pay proper attention to their mutual implications and compassionate asymmetry.

Tanabe often articulates the absolute as the transformative (other-)power of Tathāgata or Amida Buddha and continuously emphasizes its practical and existential implications as the act of love or of great compassion. This means that we cannot demonstrate the validity of his worldview based on the notion of nothingness without making any existential commitment to the notion. Or put more simply, there is nothing to be seen in the notion of nothingness if we approach it intellectually as a merely conceptual framework of thinking or if we continue to live the life of self-determining, self-obsessed self-power. Tanabe seems to suggest that we can only recognize its presence in our self-awareness once we self-consciously *embody* it. If we take this point seriously, then what we are asked here is a transformation of a relative self from its obsession with its own self-power to its selfless application of self-power for the sake of the other—thereby transforming itself into a mediator of absolute other-power as an "empty being" (*kū-u*).

This brings us back to the insight that Tanabe has provided in the logic of species. In view of nothingness as the foundation of our thinking/being, we come to recognize that what we thought as our own was *given* to be as ours. In the face of this paradoxical truth, we are freed to take our autonomy for granted as if it were merely our own and continue to live the path of self-centered self-power or to become aware of the powerlessness of self-power, when it decides to serve nothing but itself or to live up to its promise by transforming it into compassionate other-power. What is noninsistently called for is our self-sacrificial acts of love for the other relative selves and actively constituting open communities of compassionate selves. This, according to Tanabe, bears witness to a grace of great compassion that allows us to exercise our freedom. Once again, as it was the case for the logic of species, it is up to each individual to constitute a society (or more precisely her communal existence with others) that affirms the absolute value of itself at the cost of all the others (where many individuals seem to follow the same logic of self-apotheosis) or to dedicate herself to an intersubjective network of love as open communities of compassionate individuals. It is up to each of us to continue living in the shadows of our self-imposed delusion, where we believe to be the infinite absolute or turn around to live for each other in the light of truth that shines through us. Whichever path we take, it is a gift of freedom and both of them can prove Tanabe's point. Only one of them, however, can show the whole picture of his worldview based on nothingness and its logic of selfless love.

Questions for Class Discussions

Q1. Describe what Tanabe means by the "death of philosophy." How can submission to it lead us to the resurrection of philosophy? What counts as our obedience to the end of philosophy?

Q2. The philosophy that has died is not the same as the philosophy that is revived. How do we explain their differences or similarities? (Or can we do explain them?) What would be problematic if we tried to determine a set of criteria by which we could compare them?

Q3. Explain the relation of the "self-power" and the "other-power" as understood in relation to each of these perspectives by answering the following set of questions:

- How does the perspective of "self-power" understand this relation?
  - How problematic is this perspective?
- How does the perspective of other-power ask us to reformulate our understanding of self-power?
  - What are we asked to do to achieve this perspective of other-power?

The Boundless Bounds of (Meta-)Noesis: A Tanabean View of Philosophical Knowledge and Its Contemporary Implications

Trans- and Cross-Noetic Picture of Human Knowing

There are at least two ways in which we can outline Tanabe's understanding of knowledge. The first is to think about the relation of human knowing (i.e., *noesis*) to what lies in the midst of and beyond it (i.e., *meta*noesis). This requires us to think about how the metanoetic worldview that Tanabe has established with the notion of absolute nothingness portrays a proper relationship between philosophy as an epitome of human (self-)knowing and religion as its foundational other. The second is to think about the implications of absolute dialectic, which was initially formulated in the mediatory logic of species and further developed as metanoetics in the later works, with regard to the question of the appropriate interrelation between philosophy and other modes of human knowing (e.g., politics, history, art, social sciences, natural sciences, mathematics). The first roughly outlines the whole of human knowing to religion as that which both transcends and grounds human existence while the second asks the internal relation of various forms of human knowing in reference to the finite mode of our existence. Stated succinctly, the first asks a trans-noetic limit of human knowledge to what lies in and beyond it, while the second calls for our investigation into a cross-noetic picture of human knowing in relation to itself. Not surprisingly, Tanabean answers to these two questions are mutually inclusive as they both follow the insight that we have gained in the previous chapters on self and the world.[1]

To facilitate this process of demarcating the bounds of knowledge by responding to the two trans- and cross-noetic questions concerning human (self-)knowing, I would like to discuss the following two topics in reference to the works of Tanabe: (1) a common misinterpretation of his later philosophy of religion and (2) an understanding of interdisciplinary studies widely held among students and researchers in contemporary academia. By responding to these concrete questions, we should be able to see how Tanabe had envisioned the relation of philosophy to religion and how we would have to picture the proper intermediation of philosophy to other modes of human knowing in accordance with his framework of thinking.

Nothingness and Freedom: Is Metanoetics a Religious Philosophy?

The term "meta" implies a contradictory unity of transcendence and immanence in many of the works by the Kyoto School philosophers. Just as much as it means that which is excessive to the confines of what is modified by the prefix, it also implies its intimate presence in what is described in the root term. Meta-noesis in this sense means something that is both transcendent to and immanent in the process of knowing (noesis). However, this double directionality, especially in relation to the intimate aspect of the "meta," is often overlooked in contemporary philosophy. For instance, when we talk about "the death of *meta*physics," we are usually thinking about "meta" as insinuating some kind of transcendence or at least implying that the discipline of metaphysics generally ignores the dynamic presencing of the given reality in immanence. We should go back to the things themselves, examine how they appear to us, and let go of *meta*-physics that remains aloof to these concrete phenomena. These contemporary critiques of metaphysics (regardless of the fact that many of them are quite insightful in showing how some forms of metaphysics are indeed guilty of the charge) can solidify our impression of the term, "meta," as only referring to transcendence.

This one-sided conception of meta can also be conducive to a problematic interpretation of Tanabe's metanoetics. The common misunderstanding of his later philosophy, especially in relation to the trilogy of *PM*, *ELP*, and *DC*, is that they hold the position of "religious philosophy." What this phrase really means is that Tanabe's mature philosophy is understood to give up the autonomy of philosophical reason precisely by following the precepts of historical faith (whether they are derived from the Mahayana Buddhist or the Judeo-Christian tradition). Stated succinctly, the religious standpoint of transcendence (meta) dictates the terms of philosophical thinking (noesis) in immanence. In making this criticism, we are thinking that the religious aspect of the *meta* in metanoesis lacks any intimacy to the process of philosophical knowing, thereby turning a contemporary comparative philosophy of religion into another servile handmaiden to theology/religions.

The ways in which Tanabe introduces the *zangedō* also seems to fuel this misinterpretation. As we have seen in the second chapter, metanoetics is described as a "non-philosophical philosophy" (or a "philosophy that is not a philosophy") because it is no longer identical to the conventional framework of philosophical thinking that we can outline in the history of (European) philosophy (up until Tanabe's time in the early twentieth century); and also because, at the same time, "it maintains the purpose of functioning as a reflection on what is ultimate and as a radical self-awareness, which are the goals proper to philosophy."[2] This marks a resurrection of (new-)philosophy, and in pursuit of which, Tanabe argues, "it is no longer I who pursue [this] philosophy, but rather *zange* that thinks through me ... metanoesis itself that is seeking its own realization."[3] In the same vein of argument, he makes a striking reference to Augustine: "Metanoetics becomes philosophical self-consciousness when it is mediated by the performance of metanoesis through one's faith-witness. Hence the posture of *credo ut intelligam* is also applicable here."[4]

If the faith precedes reason, that is to say that we have to believe in the precepts of a certain historical religion before cultivating philosophical knowledge, and also if the former requires us to transcends the bounds of the latter, then their strong continuity only signifies the death of philosophy (which is precisely what Tanabe seems to be saying with the phrase "having no choice but to give up"). The philosophical process of acquiring knowledge of the "self" and the "world," in this case, ceases to be an autonomous practice. We can no longer ask questions about the world and ourselves for ourselves or search for their answers in and through ourselves.[5] Then we are left with a dogmatic discipline dictated by the religious teachings, some of which could certainly fail to be rational or sensible to any critical mind. The "resurrection" in this case is just paying lip service in the process of embellishing a zombified (non-)philosophy, a subservient state of mind that is surely more dead than alive.[6]

Freedom and Nothingness: Metanoesis as Trans-Philosophical Philosophy

This reduction of philosophy to religion, however, is very disingenuous to what Tanabe is actually trying to demonstrate through his notion of metanoetics. First, his criticisms toward other thinkers who tried to make sense of the notion of the absolute and its relation to human existence as the finite relative (which consequentially demarcates the boundary between philosophy and religion) is that they suffer from the problem of "either/or": *either* philosophy serves as a servant of religious faiths (thereby giving up the freedom of thought as a dogmatic philosophy) *or* sets itself up as a rational judge who makes a final verdict on the philosophical characteristics of religious teachings (thereby equivocating the significance of religion with that of philosophy). The former reduces reason to faith and the latter suffers from the opposite extreme. As one can easily imagine, these configurations of the religion–philosophy continuity both problematically end up cancelling one or the other.

What Tanabe is trying to show through metanoesis is the perspective of "neither/nor" that enables us to overcome the dualism of philosophy and religion. The standpoint of nothingness (which we can reach through a self-critique of philosophical reasoning), he argues, introduces the viewpoint of the religious that is excessive to the confines of the philosophical, thereby making room for the former; and yet, because the absolute does not refer to any of the philosophical terms that can be defined in immanence (i.e., individual, particular/species, or universal/genus), and also because it represents the trans-ontological principle of self-negation—or more precisely, it is that which empties itself to the point of nothing so that everything else in relation to it can be all that is—it can both ground and refrain from compromising the autonomy of all the relative beings. Tanabe's rendering of the absolute as absolute nothingness, in this manner, privileges *neither* philosophy *nor* religion while properly acknowledging their asymmetry as the basis for both of their undeniable intermediation and irreducible difference.

From this viewpoint of "neither/nor," Tanabe always qualifies his statement about the transcendence (i.e., meta) of the religious standpoint as regards the autonomy of philosophical knowing (i.e., noesis) with an emphasis on the former's radical immanence (i.e., meta) to the autonomous confines of the latter. This has something to do with the fact that he identifies the notion of the absolute not as any "self-identical substance," but as "negative mediation of nothingness" in accordance with the Mahayana Buddhist tradition.[7]

> Nothingness does not exist directly. Anything that affirms itself directly is not nothingness but being. It cannot … escape the relativity of mutual negation. Only nothingness, which manifests itself mediatively in this negation of being and affirms itself indirectly, is an absolute free of further negation. Still, absolute nothingness is realized in actuality only by affirming relative beings, negating the immediacy of its own absolute power vis-à-vis relative beings in order to give them life. This means, moreover, that absolute nothingness can actualize its function as

nothingness only through a self-negation of relative beings in the form of a reciprocal negation between beings.[8]

Absolute nothingness is abstract and empty in and of itself.[9] Furthermore, if we conceptualize its transcendence as something that is completely apart from the finite relative in immanence, we are problematically visualizing it as another relative that stands in its opposition to the finite. In this case, Tanabe argues, that what we are talking about is the relative that is not absolute and being that is not nothingness. At the same time, if we properly understand the notion of nothingness as that which is irreducible to any part or the whole of the finite relative as all that is, he continues to articulate, it cannot be seen as functioning apart from the free self- and inter-mediation of relative beings.[10] In fact, the mediatory nature of nothingness (i.e., absolute mediation) is such that it can only be manifested through the free self- and inter-mediation of the finite individual beings in concrete, historical reality.

This does not mean that the absolute somehow needs the relative to concretize itself in the manner of the Hegelian dialectic. It does not have this self-affirmative need to instrumentalize the relative finite for its self-determining self-realization as the concrete universal in immanence. The absolute mediation in Tanabe's nothingness is "not a relationship in which one party is subordinated to the other, but one in which both enjoy and maintain an independence made possible by the other."[11] The philosopher continues,

> there is no question here of a causal connection that would make one party subordinate to the other as its effect. Mediation is always and only a matter of a reciprocal relationship of independent participants, albeit one in which the independence of the one relies on the independence of the other. …
>
> … Far from functioning in an unrestricted manner, therefore, the absolute makes room for the independence of relative being, and to that extent imposes a restriction on its own determinative functioning, and through this self-negation functions affirmatively. … the absolute is truly absolute only when, through self-negation, it makes room for the independence of relative beings, permitting them to function as its mediators. This is why the absolute is nothingness. As the reality that realizes its own character of absolute nothingness in mediation with relative beings, it is a principle that, of its own accord, provides a basis for the independent existence of relative beings. And this is nothing other than love.[12]

The Tanabean absolute does not directly affect the movement of finite relatives in the immanent network of efficient causes. Nor does it need this finite other for its self-determining self-affirmation (as Hegel's absolute spirit needs the particular). As it represents a complete lack of egoity, it is termed as the "absolute other power" that, out of its great compassion, empowers the self-power of relative beings and grounds their autonomous existence for their individual and social existence in immanence. It represents a self-emptying other-power or self-kenotic "love" that gives itself to the relative other for the other, thereby affirming the self-powering existence of the finite relatives for these relative others.

The proper understanding of the relationship between the religious (i.e., meta) and the philosophical (i.e., noesis) in Tanabe's metanoetics, therefore, cannot give a dictatorial relationship in which the former controls the terms of noetic engagement in the latter. According to his description of the absolute as nothingness, religion can never directly intervene with the ways in which philosophers think about the world and themselves. In fact, religion must always "make room for the independence of" the philosophical knowing. This does not mean, however, that the standpoint of the religious transcendence has nothing to do with the dynamic process of the philosophical knowing in immanence (as Kantian formulation of their division, for instance, insinuates). Tanabe's insight is that the religious can be manifested through the free process of (self-)knowing in the realm of the philosophical, especially when philosophers take the task of noesis seriously and follow through with its demand to attain the complete knowledge of themselves and the world—that is, to attain "absolute knowledge." Far from compromising the free process of philosophical knowing, absolute nothingness calls for the free societal intermediation of the finite relative beings based on the principle of self-negating compassion, and through this free conversion of their self-obsessed self-power to self-emptying other-power (i.e., metanoesis), philosophers can both witness and embody the truth of religious transcendence in the free process of their philosophical (self-)knowing in immanence.

Thus, the intermediation of the religious and the philosophical does not rid philosophy of its freedom, but rather, through the autonomous process of philosophical knowing, we are confronted with the intimate presence of nothingness as the foundation of our finite existence. Our philosophical knowing seems to still be left with a choice in face of the otherness of religious transcendence. We can choose to believe that we can complete our philosophical (self-)knowledge through our autonomy and self-power alone, thereby retaining the duality of the philosophical and the religious (merely as the one-sided transcendence). Or with the (self-)awareness of the absolute nothingness as the foundation of our existence and freedom, we can convert our self-affirming self-power into other-power (that is to use our self-power for the sake of others), thereby constituting the community of selfless sentient beings as a finite manifestation of the truth of the absolute nothingness in immanence. The first passage will forever keep us in the dualism of transcendence and immanence (among other contradictory terms as the religious and the philosophical, meta and noesis, other-power and self-power, etc.); whereas the second "way of metanoia" (*zangedō*) can help us conceive their proper intermediation as "transcendence-qua-immanence,"[13] thus liberating us from the self-inflicted chain of dualism in the previous self-centered, one-sided way of thinking and being.

The Infinite Process of Absolute Critique and Its Inherent Diversity of Self-Knowledge

The process of coming to realize the foundation of our existence and freedom as the other-power of nothingness shows how philosophical knowing in metanoesis cannot be a passive reception of religious doctrines. As we have seen in Chapter 2, Tanabe has termed this procedure for coming to know the self, "absolute critique of reason," and argued that "reason [therein] is left exposed to antinomies that can only render it asunder and cast it into a state of absolute self-disruption."[14] The unresolvable antinomies of human existence are generated from reason's forgetfulness of its finite relativity, which often leads to its hubris of "erroneously presuming itself to be absolute." Only by recognizing its "absolute contradiction and disruption,"[15] can the self "awaken to its own finitude."[16] This is where it can reorient its standpoint from the self-powering egoity to a mediatory embodiment of other-power (namely, "empty being").[17] We have seen that only through thorough self-criticism, we can cultivate our attentiveness to the finitude of our own existence, and while giving up the impossible dream of achieving absolute knowledge through reason alone, the powerlessness of self in proper self-knowledge can be restored as the compassionate mediator of absolute other-power/nothingness.

Tanabe's choice of "giving up" philosophy sounds like something that many of us can easily accomplish simply by ignoring philosophy books or by thinking about complex problems that we can discover by ruminating on them. Tanabe does give an elaborate and systematic answer to this type of criticism against metanoetics as the "negative resignation" (in reference to the works of Goethe), but the simplest way to correct this confusion would be to take a look at the way in which he begins the *PM*.

The preface to this monumental text was written in the summer of 1945, a decisive turning point in the history of modern Japan. It simply gives a confession of an intellectual who strongly felt the responsibility to speak against the evildoing of his country and to express his strong disagreement with the military government. However, as the citizen of a nation, he was compelled to refrain from causing conflicts and confusions among his people at the time of war;[18] and in the face of destructions that his nation had caused outside and inside the islands of Japan, his health had also greatly degenerated. In this state of intellectual and physical depression, Tanabe found it extremely difficult to continue his life as a philosopher, while facing the self-destruction of his country in the 1940s. All of this happened toward the end of his most prolific and illustrious career as a philosophy professor for a quarter of the century at one of the leading national universities in Japan.

The historical context in which Tanabe pursued his philosophical investigation is far from giving an impression that we can enter the same path of *zange* by simply not reading philosophy books or disengaging ourselves from philosophical reasoning for the sake of pursuing blind faith. The circumstances in which we have no choice but to stop our philosophical knowing, too, would have to be as terrible as life in Japan at the end of the Second World War. Rather, this shows that only by employing reason to the fullest can we, for the first time, expect to make the limits of reason apparent. The process of absolute critique must take a life-time commitment to uncompromising self-criticism, and it seems that only at the limits reached by comprehensive self-examination will faith in nothingness arise.[19]

The structure of metanoesis also shows that it is not something that we can achieve at one point in history, and in accordance with this "paradigm shift" (as in Kuhn's *Scientific Revolution*) the rest of our philosophical knowing will automatically follow a different passage from its previous one. On the contrary, as Tanabe argues, the process of metanoesis must be both continuous and endless. That is simply because a human individual as a finite relative always faces the danger of falling victim to her own self-affirming egoity. She has been and will always be tempted to overcome her contradictory existence (that suffers from existential antinomies) through her self-power alone. The absolute critique of her reason that leads her to this insight, in turn, must be a continuous process that has no determinate completion at any point in the duration of her historical existence.

The best way to visualize this metanoetic relation of philosophical (self-) knowledge (i.e., noesis) and religious self-awareness (i.e., *meta*-noesis) is to think about the relation between ethics and religion. According to Tanabe, the most conscientious person would never say that she is perfectly ethical or absolutely content with who she is (including what she has done and how she goes about her life). In fact, if she were a type of person who would say after brief self-reflection, "I am totally an ethical person," it would be quite likely that she is highly an unethical person (probably in ways that she cannot even imagine). Tanabe's point is that the best person, who has cultivated an acute sense of justice and never fails to carry out a thorough self-examination, would say (once again in consonance with Paul and Kant) that she is far from being ethically perfect. This paradoxical truth about the ethical leads a single individual to witness the open unity of absolute nothingness as that which makes her contradictory existence possible. The religious standpoint of nothingness, therefore, is far from dismissing the standpoint of the ethical, but rather requires an infinite process of ethical self-reflection. In the same way, reaching the religious standpoint of nothingness cannot be seen to cancel the infinite process of philosophical knowing, but precisely because it requires an infinite praxis of self-awareness, philosophers must continuously be engaged in their endless acts of coming to know the world and themselves as what they are with the best of their abilities.

Additionally, Tanabe only gives a formal definition of absolute critique as the logic of metanoetics in the second chapter of the *PM*, and further continues to ground the validity of its insight by examining the works of major thinkers, which include Descartes, Spinoza, Pascal, Kant, Hegel, Schelling, Nietzsche, Kierkegaard, Shinran, Nishida, Heidegger, to name but a few. This implies two things: one, the act of *zange* must be practiced by each individual (and also especially in relativity to others in her communal existence); and two, the validity and soundness of the absolute critique can be tested in relation to a vast array of thinkers. In fact, Tanabe clearly states that he can only practice an absolute self-critique in relation to his existence as a single individual regardless of the fact that everyone should both individually and communally carry out the same transformative act of *zange*. The latter prohibits him to force others to tread the same passage of an examined life (otherwise it will not be a genuine, autonomous self-examination). Also, he argues, what he has shown as the validity of the absolute critique and the truth of metanoesis in this book is a particular passage: hence, he leaves open the possibility that philosophers after him would have to consult a greater number of thinkers from diverse intellectual traditions. Thus, we are given with a responsibility for making a greater effort to come up with our own formulations of metanoesis. In short, depending on when and where a reader of Tanabe's texts is coming from, her *zangedō* does not need to be limited to the history of the European intellectual tradition nor does one need to follow a specific formulation given by contemporary Japanese philosophy. She should be allowed to achieve a distinct form of philosophical knowing in relation to her historical context and to explore its specific openness to the sense of the religious absolute.

The trans-noetic relation of philosophical knowing (noesis) to religious self-awareness of the absolute (metanoesis), thus, shows an inter-mediatory relation in which the autonomy of the philosophical is never compromised by the standpoint of the religious. There is an open unity between the free process of human knowing and the religious self-awareness of the absolute as the notion of nothingness. Since metanoetics pays due attention to the double directionality of "meta," the standpoint of the absolute (nothingness) is both transcendent to and immanent in reason's endeavor to achieve complete knowledge of itself and the world. This metanoetic intermediation of the absolute and the relative, moreover, does not paint a subservient relation of the latter to the former: hence, no religious doctrine can dictate the terms of engagement in the domain of philosophy. Rather, when each thinker freely commits herself to genuine self-criticism in her own philosophical tradition and when such an examined life is lived to the fullest, she can come to achieve a self-awareness that this whole autonomous process of philosophical knowing is made possible (and even encouraged) by the compassionate other-power of absolute nothingness. Last, Tanabe only shows a particular metanoetic passage to the absolute in his critical engagement with European and the East Asian/Japanese intellectual traditions. As a contemporary reader of this passage, therefore, each of us is left with the task of "absolute critique" in our relativity to a specific intellectual and historical context of our own; and only when we fully commit ourselves to this continuous task of self-knowing, we can testify to the standpoint of the absolute (nothingness) as the intermediation of religious faith and philosophical knowing.

Cross-Noesis: Nature as the Other to Philosophy of Self

Tanabe's first monograph was on the philosophy of math and from his early writings on neo-Kantian epistemology to the later philosophy of religion, his *zenshū* is filled with references to mathematical concepts and arguments made by leading thinkers in the field of natural sciences (just as much as it cites numerous passages from poetry and premodern religious texts). The ways in which Tanabe wrote his philosophical texts demonstrate how vast and cross-disciplinary the range of his reading was, and how his openness to the other fields of study was indispensable for developing his original contribution in the field of philosophy.

What would strike contemporary readers as strange, then, is a lack of his reflections on "nature" in the logic of species. Despite the fact that terms like genus and species sound much more biological than ontological (even in his time) and also that there are some references to mathematical and natural scientific examples in his main arguments, what seems to be mainly at stake in these texts is not the natural scientific or biological notion of species, but only its significance for social ontology. When reading this text, it is not unreasonable to conclude that the *Logic of Species* is not concerned with setting forth a philosophical account of nature or other sentient beings in the world at all. The authoritative reference work, *Japanese Philosophy: A Sourcebook*, implicitly shares this view, since it translates the title of the work as the *Logic of the Specific*.[20] It succeeds in showing the Japanese term, *shu* (種), as having nothing to do with the biological concept of species in Tanabe's account and highlights the fact that it only denotes a metaphysical category. With this translation, we can defuse the tension between Tanabe's dialectical notion of species and the notion of species in natural science by showing that they are irrelevant to each other. That being said, I would like to point out in what follows that there are, however, some passages highlight the similarity between his account of social ontology and the domain of natural science.

On more than one occasion, Tanabe identifies the notion of species as the "will to life" (*seimei ishi* 生命意志), while contrasting it with the individual as the "will to power" (*kenryoku ishi* 権力意志) and genus as the "will to salvation" (*kyūsai ishi* 救済意志).[21] On the basis of these definitions, we can anticipate how the concept of species comes to signify a substratum of all living beings in Tanabe's mind. Moreover, in *LSE*, species is developed into that which is comparable to nature as genus is to the divine absolute, thereby signaling a strong connection between the notion of species and the realm of nature.[22] This is probably because Tanabe acknowledges that the concept of species, as the substrate of all living beings, originates from the Aristotelian understanding of the concept, which involves appropriate attentiveness to the characteristics of organic existence.[23] Tanabe remains critical of Aristotle's metaphysics on the basis of the fact that it emphasizes the ultimate primacy of form over matter, and construes an undifferentiated continuity between human/societal existence and nature. However, as far as the aforementioned passages are concerned, the notion of species has an indisputable connection with the notion of life: hence, Tanabe's social ontological account of self must address the notion of natural beings as the other, since it aims at a coherent grasp of human existence *in* nature.

The dialectical characteristics of the logic of species, moreover, guide Tanabe to recognize the significance of social ontology—or his conception of human existence (i.e., self) in society—as maintaining a comprehensive relation to its opposing term, "nature," regardless of the fact that his logic must maintain their mutually irreducible difference. In "Three Stages of

Ontology," for instance, the relation of nature and self becomes the standard model for outlining the structure of his dialectic, and it is laid out in relation to his critique of Hegel's philosophy of nature.[24] Additionally, in "Ethics and Logic," while explaining the mediatory relation of existence and ethical ideals, the philosopher weaves his understanding of absolute mediation into Schelling's view of nature. He argues,

> Nature that stands over against human action as an obstacle rather serves as the mediator that affirms the human action as the negative: so, to overcome nature through human action, in turn, must mean to follow nature. In this case, however, nature loses the meaning of "standing over against action." Rather it takes the human action as the mediator of its formation. In short, nature simultaneously comes to mean what human action produces. It is no longer nature that self must overcome as non-self but rather it turns itself into self as the mediator of self. Hence, it must be trans-natural, but at the same time trans-self because self follows the nature and so long as that takes place, nature turns self that is [initially] denied therein into an affirmation of it. The absolute mediation of self-qua-non-self or nature-qua-self makes self and nature as two moments of the absolute unity of subject-qua-object.[25]

In "Eternity, History, and Act" (hereafter EHA), Tanabe begins to label this transformative unification of nature and self as the work of "absolute nothingness," thereby adding a far more metaphysical (and even religious) tone to the notion of absolute mediation.[26] Once the notion of the transformative and metanoetic absolute is introduced to the logic of species, Tanabe's social ontology comes to mean something more than a metaphysical understanding of human existence because the concept of the absolute necessarily implies the transformed sense of the whole reality—including nature and all sentient beings—in relation to self's self-negating self-fulfillment in its communal existence.[27] Since, in this context, "self-awareness" based on absolute mediation comes to "represent reflections on the transformative unity of nature and self,"[28] the logic of species contains a line of thinking that extends far beyond the initial intention to examine the contradiction between the state's authority and individual freedom within human existence. This metaphysical development in Tanabe's writings can make us wonder what the renewed sense of nature under the dialectical logic of species would look like and invites us to apply this very logic to the study of reality and living beings in natural science.

There are some methodological suggestions that we can draw from Tanabe's passages. EHA states that "through the transformation of [absolute mediation or] absolute nothingness, both self and nature negatively become one; and this serves as the ground of comparative studies between nature and human action."[29] This statement alone proves that we may apply his logic to our study of nature or at least relate it to the biological concept of "species." In fact, as we will see later, the philosopher himself often applies his dialectical logic to the field of mathematics and theoretical physics. In this sense, our application of it to some branch of natural science (like physics or biology) should be a welcome addition to his philosophical findings.[30]

This interdisciplinary practice is further supported by Tanabe's metaphysical insight. He repeatedly emphasizes that his intention in making mathematical inferences or offering philosophical observations in matters of theoretical physics is not designed "to prove the structure of the historical world through the world understood in terms of physics as if it were the ground of existence."[31] However, he continues,

> Existence in physics is not anything that we can directly grasp through sense perceptions because it requires a negative mediation of the perceptual content and mathematical concepts. Hence, mathematics that belongs to a historical culture enters the world understood in terms of physics as mind's formal self-awareness; and thereby, the world picture that pertains to physics is not a mere reproduction of existence. Rather, it includes the historical fruit of mathematical thinking as its negative moment. In order for the historical world to reach the level of concrete self-awareness, therefore, it must include the structure of the world understood in terms of physics as a mediatory moment [for its establishment]; and if the logical structure of the latter is not understood as the abstract aspect of the logical structure in the former, then we would have to say that the understanding pertaining to the former is incomplete.[32]

This is to say that the logic of species, based on the notion of absolute mediation (i.e., nothingness), not only serves as the foundation for the comparative studies of philosophy and natural science among other academic disciplines, but also, without accounting for the significance of the worldview obtained through a certain structure of understanding in the specific field of science, the philosophical worldview (or what he calls "historical world") that we can access through the logic of absolute mediation remains an unfinished business. That is to say, philosophical insight can shed light on what is going on in the foundation of each of other scientific disciplines and at the same time, without them, philosophy can remain an empty theory or a contemplative practice that lacks any concrete content. To judge the validity and soundness of Tanabe's insight, therefore, it is crucial that it be compared with findings in other academic disciplines in order to discuss the structure of reality in the field of philosophy.

Thus, Tanabe's rendering of the relation between philosophical knowledge and other kinds of human knowing (like some branches of natural science that we have discussed so far) shows a reciprocal relationship. In one sense, philosophy seems to be able to provide a framework in which we can suggest some methodological implications in other disciplines (like physics or biology), but at the same time philosophy must wait for their findings to concretize its worldview derived from the very framework of self-critical thinking. Clearly, Tanabe welcomes interdisciplinarity in human knowing or at least implies the significance of the intermediation between various forms of knowledge in his analysis of *noesis*. We will further clarify in the following this cross-noetic constitution of human knowledge by paying attention to how Tanabe formulates it in terms of the dialectical relationship between philosophical and natural scientific knowledge.

Metanoetic Interdisciplinarity: A Common Viewpoint and a Tanabean Critique

Interdisciplinary studies has of late become a fashion in academia. It is often recommended to undergraduate and graduate students as the best path for education. More research funding seems to be available for projects that can belong to more than one academic discipline, while support for projects belonging to one particular field of study (especially in the humanities) seems downsized throughout most of the world. This is especially the case for philosophy programs. Many of our students struggle with a lack of apparent practical applications of their degrees, thus unable to earn money sufficient enough to shave off massive student loan debt or to have a healthy lifestyle with the rising costs of living expenses after graduation. Some suffer from their inability to justify their love of reading philosophy books to their worrying family members and, therefore, promise to go on with more respectable careers (like medicine or law) after giving up their dreams of becoming philosophers. Many philosophy professors and their program pamphlets are complicit, arguing that "philosophy is useful for cultivating critical/logical thinking, which is indispensable for scoring higher in the standardized exams for entrance to Medical or Law schools." This is not entirely surprising, given the constant threat of gutting philosophy programs to make room for other disciplines more suited to "train" students with so-called job skills. The lack of apparent economic and practical value in any academic discipline plays a significant role when recommending our students in philosophy to go beyond its boundary and to make sure that their study will provide them with certain tools necessary to survive the desolate job market around the world.

There is, of course, a much more positive motivation behind this push toward interdisciplinary study as well. In the course of my academic career, I have experienced different types of academic institutions in America, Europe, and East Asia. It is still shocking to see how many places structurally encourage specializations. For instance, at many universities in Europe, a student is admitted to a single program after an entrance exam. She then takes nothing but classes in the discipline of her major. Neither general studies nor elective courses are taken before choosing her major, as she is set to graduate with her mind cultivated in a single field of study. In some cases (especially in East Asia), students would have no choice but to major in one discipline (which is often not their first choice) and if they are to switch majors, they are subject to an amount of paperwork, time, and money disproportionate to the practical choice of switching, or so administrators argue. In this general context of specialization in higher education, college graduates gain a sophisticated and profound knowledge of one discipline; yet, their understanding of the world and of themselves (as far as what they have learned from universities) is often incredibly narrow and hopelessly uncritical.

Whether our thrust toward interdisciplinary study is motivated by the negative assessment of a single discipline or positive value of acquiring wider knowledge of the world and ourselves in higher education, the common understanding of it is very often to simply "cover the areas of topics that are pertinent to multiple disciplines." For example, if we are to examine a certain set of Buddhist artworks from medieval Japan, our investigation into these objects could belong to the disciplines of art history and religious studies. Some popular topics in philosophy nowadays deal with artificial intelligence (which asks the question of "at what point we can call a machine intelligent?") and the philosophy of technology, where we examine the immediate practical application of our findings (for instance, in relation to the question concerning the ethical responsibility of a car accident caused by an "automatic driving system"). World philosophies scholars too often take advantage of their proximity to anthropologists, historians, and cultural studies specialists, who can talk about the intellectual history of relevant geo-political areas, or articulate certain cultural traditions, or even translate world philosophical texts into European languages. Each discipline is like a dynamic circle (growing outwardly or declining inwardly at various rates in different historical periods) and a small set of questions shared between them (as in a Venn diagram) are qualified as the basis of generating an interdisciplinary research that is pertinent to both.

Tanabe's understanding of human knowledge, and of the constitution of academic disciplines, deems this widely shared conception of inter-disciplinarity problematic. Instead, he proposes a distinct way in which we should think about the complementary relations between different forms of human knowing. We can find this Tanabean outlook on the cross-noetic outline of interdisciplinary studies in a series of interesting essays published in the mid-1930s. In these texts, Tanabe discusses the boundaries of academic disciplines and further elucidates the importance of recognizing the double directionality in the education of a single discipline like natural science: namely, its strive toward the uncompromising preservation of its complete autonomy and, at the same time, remaining attentive to its restrictive relation to a certain set of value systems, which lie outside the bounds of natural scientific knowing (e.g., politics, culture, philosophy, history, etc.).

The Dual Nature of Natural Scientific Knowing

The most accessible and concise argument that Tanabe gives on the bounds of scientific knowing can be found in his essay, "Two Aspects of Education in Natural Science." This paper was originally delivered as a lecture at the "Workshop on the Study of Japanese Culture Instruction" hosted by the department of ideology at the ministry of Education in November 1936. It was later published as an article in *Japanese Culture Series* (by the same department) in the following year. The political and cultural climate at that time was defined by the nightmare of the totalitarian state: it was rather aggressively trying to justify the development of natural sciences in consonance with right-wing nationalism or what Japanese political historians would call the rise of "Japanism" or "*tennō*-centrism." Tanabe clearly indicates that the purpose of this workshop was to talk about how education in natural science should contribute to politics; namely, that the emperor should be the state sovereign rather than a branch of government requiring permission from the cabinet to make political decisions (including legislation and exercises of military power). There was a breach of political power and/or cultural judgment in the domain of natural science as much as the latter was attempting to emphasize (if not fabricate) its findings that seemingly justify the claims of the former.

To a contemporary reader, it seems obvious that Tanabe was invited as a prominent professor of philosophy from an *Imperial* University to both justify and praise this problematic continuity between science and politics. And as a servant of the state, he was expected to insert philosophy in the univocal mix. However, the philosopher's response to this request was quite cunning and, if we can read between the lines, it is not difficult to see how he was trying his best, both to criticize the government policy (and the very department of ideology), which was beginning to meddle with the domain of science, and to philosophically ground the independence of scientific investigations.

At the beginning of the lecture, Tanabe explicitly argues that the natural scientific way of thinking is to regard all phenomena as bound by necessary causal relations: hence, thinking from this standpoint cannot permit any (political or cultural) discourse that carries out a value judgment arguing that some things are to be accepted and others to be rejected. "What is normally thought as the natural scientific way of thinking is to regard that all existing phenomena in reality must be affirmed without any value discriminations and must be equally studied."[33] The language Tanabe uses here is in fact quite moderate; and immediately after this, he acknowledges that state politics needs science to complete its mission and also that science cannot hold its position without dealing with the limitation that comes from the outside. Nevertheless, he sets the tone at the outset that the autonomy of science should never be violated by any (political or cultural) value judgments. Nor should it be used to affirm these extra-scientific incentives regardless of the fact that it does face a limit when we pay attention to its proper constitution. He repeats this point again and again by making reference to both natural scientific and philosophical concepts.

Interestingly, Tanabe tends to swing his discussion of two (positive and negative) sides of scientific knowing by moving back and forth between two points: (1) the conflict of science and state politics and (2) the dual nature of scientific (and also philosophical) knowing in itself. I am quite certain that he was reading this paper at a podium for this event and that his posture hardly would have changed when he finished reading the introductory section that focuses on (1). Nevertheless, we can clearly see that he is now addressing his philosophical reflection on the nature of scientific thinking (2) to the fellow scientists, instructors of natural sciences, and other careful listeners at the workshop; all the while leaving behind the bureaucrats who wanted to hear his praise of the furtherance of natural sciences for the sake of affirming the ongoing political discourse. The basic gist of his argument is that the positive and negative sides of human knowing appear in various domains of human existence and this can be explained in reference to the sphere of natural science.

Tanabe explains this dual nature of human knowing with the concept of "mutual complementarity" (or Niels Bohr's *Komplementarität*) in quantum physics (which, according to Tanabe, was already applied to the field of biology by Pascual Jordan). He uses this concept to shed light on the two aspects of natural scientific knowing. He indicates that, in physics, the complementary relation of two terms means not only to compensate a lack in each other, but also refers to "complementary exclusiveness" (*komplementäre Außchliessung*), a relation in which one cannot appear in the standpoint where another appears and yet at the same time they mutually complement each other to constitute the whole. As an example, Tanabe highlights the dual nature of the universe perceived through quantum mechanics, where we have to combine mutually exclusive viewpoints of particle and wave theories to acquire a comprehensive understanding of a single object in nature (i.e., light or electrons).

To make this scientific and rather specialized insight palpable to the general audience, the philosopher further introduces two types of the "middle position" that is necessary for thinking about the interrelations of two different perspectives: namely, *secchū* (折中) and *shicchū* (執中). The term *secchū* literally means to "break in the middle." When two contradictory demands are made by two competing perspectives, and when taking one side means to reject the other, we can make a kind of "compromise" (*dakyō*, 妥協), where we suppress both of them to a certain degree to bring them to the point of agreement. Neither side is pursued to the fullest and, in exchange, we position them so as not to cancel either of them. There is a continuous relation between the two conflicting perspectives, and they are both present to us at the same time. This, however, also means that we will have to restrict them to the point of their mediocrity.[34] Tanabe argues that "[this middle position] is not the same as what he means by the unity or harmony based on the 'mutually exclusive complementarity.'"[35]

The term 執中 (*shicchū*) originates from classical Chinese philosophy. It indicates a performative wisdom where one is not obsessed with one perspective over the other, but by occupying the middle position, one can freely choose what is appropriate in a given circumstance regardless of the fact that this choice may look contradictory to another from a fixed position. This practice comes with a double posture of striving toward a complete dedication to each standpoint and of aiming at a full grasp of its limitation with attentiveness to what lies beyond it:

> Taking the middle is demarcating not *both* this *and* that but *neither* that *nor* this. When it problematizes this, we dedicate ourselves to it and when we problematize that, we completely dedicate ourselves in

the opposite direction. Unlike the method of natural science, or even in the very method, if we talk about the natural scientist or the subject that pursues natural science, one turns to this and that; and turns to that and this.[36]

When taking one perspective as a central problem of our critical discourse, we fully engage ourselves in the pursuit of our answer to it and when we deal with another competing perspective, we completely follow through with that process as well. A practitioner of natural science (among many other academic disciplines), according to Tanabe, must occupy this middle position in pursuit of complete scientific knowledge. What he is saying here is that this practice of "turning to this and that" is clearly what happened in the history of contemporary physics, which ended up unifying two contradictory perspectives of particle and wave theories as the nature of the universe.

What, then, enables the scientist to remain attentive to the dual nature of her own discipline (and further its complementary opposition to other kinds of human knowledge) lies in the fact that she is a human being:

> Taking the middle in the sense of *shicchū* means that when we take one standpoint, we only hold on to a single position: hence, it is not everything. It means to pursue one standpoint to the fullest while being (self-)aware that there is the opposite side to it. When we take the middle in this sense, we take one side as a problem and when it is necessary, we completely dedicate ourselves to it. When the other is necessary or it becomes a problem, we do the same for the other. This is a nature of human being that stands in between here and there and also when we go there, we have to be (self-)aware that there is here. When we go here, we have to be (self-)aware that there is there.[37]

Since the "mutually exclusive complementarity"[38] in the sense of *shicchū* indicates a radical discontinuity between two opposing views, Tanabe describes this transition between two sides of one academic discipline (in this case natural science) as a *tenkan* (転換).[39] He argues further that "there is no other word to describe the middle position of *shicchū*, which is neither this nor that, but the term 'nothingness.'"[40]

> If a being is the medium by which here is connected with there, this would give a negative compromise (*secchū*). However, if we talk about the transformation at the bounds of neither this nor that, there is nothing in the between. What lies between there and here is nothingness. By taking

nothingness as the medium, we can freely enter there and also freely enter here. I think something like this is necessary for the education of natural science.[41]

Now we can clearly see how Tanabe is talking about the metanoetic conversion and absolute mediation in relation to the comprehensive form of scientific knowing. He is saying that a natural scientist as a human being can hold the transformative standpoint of philosophical nothingness and, because of that, she can both recognize the mutually exclusive complementarity (or "contradictory unity") of two opposing perspectives in the natural scientific process of observing phenomena, and also, of the natural phenomena themselves.

Furthermore, this philosophical perspective allows the scientist to become aware of the limit of natural scientific knowing not only in relation to itself, but also to other forms of knowing without holding back her complete dedication to the study of nature. This insight is consistent with Tanabe's social-ontological explanations about the constitution of a specific group of individuals and its proper relation to other groups in the logic of species. We have seen that the ideality of selfhood (i.e., genus or nothingness) does not exist in and of itself; and since it is a mediatory point for other senses of self (i.e., individual and species) to be—and determine themselves to be— what they are, it can be manifested through a variety of individual and social selves. This diverse manifestation of the ideal selfhood, moreover, is nothing but what the individual human being constitutes by exercising freedom. Also, by remaining attentive to the radical contingency of species, free individuals must recognize the equal value of each social self to the others (regardless of the fact that some groups of individuals might be living up to the ideality of genus much better than others). The same logic applies to our understanding of a specific form of human knowing or a specific academic discipline, both in relation to itself and in relation to others.

If species is comparable to a specific kind of knowing, each academic discipline must be seen as being essentially finite and contingent. There is no rational explanation why one should look at what is given as reality in one way or another. Since no academic discipline can claim absolute knowledge of the world and of ourselves (i.e., the "historical world" in Tanabe's terms), it only gives one way in which we can look at them as what they are. In this sense, we have to treat all academic disciplines with equal respect while we refrain from (mis-)taking any of them as claiming absolute knowledge of reality (including human existence). This also means that insofar as we exercise our self-awareness in each of these disciplines, that is, to remain attentive to its limitation both in itself and in relation to other forms of knowing, it can equally manifest the absolute value of human knowledge in reference to the historical world in a distinct fashion.

Philosophy, according to Tanabe, seems to occupy a special position. In a certain sense, he places philosophical knowledge (*noesis*) of the absolute (i.e., nothingness) as the epitome of human knowing and also clearly defines its ultimate mission as to obtain knowledge of the historical world. Additionally, he seems to suggest that every academic discipline will face a great moment of antinomies (where they suffer from contradictory perspectives in relation to the object of their study) and at that moment of great crisis, the knower would have to step into the philosophical standpoint of nothingness, thus reaching the higher, more comprehensive standpoint, where she can arrive at the concrete unity of the contradictory perspectives in her own discipline. As we have seen in the case of "mutually exclusive complementarity" in science, philosophy (of *shicchū* or nothingness) seems to be able to serve as a foundation for the comprehensive unity of every other discipline.

However, I do not think that Tanabe's outlook on philosophy will give philosophers any privileged position in academia at all. Even if there is a philosophical transformation at a decisive moment in the development of another discipline, the field of philosophy as the study of theoretical and practical concepts cannot contribute to the development of particle and wave theories. Without them, we cannot even reach the moment of the crisis. Also, we can only observe how the scientists (like Einstein and Planck) are making a trans-scientific or philosophical move in their scientific endeavors to understand reality as what it is. Hence, both in theory and practice, the intellectual credit still goes to the scientists as the great thinkers rather than to the discipline of philosophy.

Moreover, there are two theoretical suggestions in Tanabe's works that would prevent us from privileging philosophical knowledge above all the others. First, the logic of species argues that so-called absolute knowledge— or more precisely, the comprehensive understanding of reality and human existence based on the notion of the absolute as nothingness—in philosophy is abstract and incomplete in itself: hence, it has to wait for the findings of other disciplines. Second, once again, the absolute critique in metanoetics demonstrates that philosophical reasoning cannot complete the task of achieving absolute knowledge, which it sets forth as the telos of that very philosophizing. *Noesis*, in other words, is minted with the destiny that it cannot be fulfilled through itself alone and cannot help but see this great contradiction. This grand antinomy of the human as a thinking being demands her to self-reflectively recognize the limit of her philosophical thinking. In both cases, philosophy is shown to depend on what is other to it just as much as the others would require a trans-disciplinary/philosophical transformation at the decisive moment in the history of their own development. The philosopher should be able to recognize the true ground of philosophical knowing by cultivating genuine self-awareness. In this case, she has to be aware that philosophical knowledge, too, must pay attention to its limitation and always make room for other disciplines to tell her about the truths of the world and her "self" in their own terms.

The cross-noetic constitution of knowledge requires us to pay special attention to the discontinuity of multiple forms of human knowing rather than to their unmediated continuity. The examples of interdisciplinary studies that we have mentioned earlier (such as an examination of Buddhist art works, contemporary questions of A.I. and the ethics of automated vehicles in the philosophy of science and technology, and world philosophers' collaborations with anthropologists, historians, and cultural studies specialists in discussions about the diverse histories of world intellectual traditions) are often structurally comparable to a Venn diagram. Multiple disciplines, in this case, are conceived as occupying different areas in the same dimension and the shared space represents an unmediated continuity between them. In this case, according to Tanabe, they are risking the danger of stepping into the problem of the negative compromise (*secchū*). The worst-case scenario with this kind of interdisciplinary studies is like dining at a terrible "fusion" restaurant. It claims to incorporate ingredients and techniques from multiple culinary traditions, but ends up creating a dish that is offensive to those who are familiar with any of them. Perhaps in the field of academia, the end result of interdisciplinary studies has not been as terrible as this culinary experience. In fact, there are some unmediated continuity between certain modes of knowing such that we do face questions that require this kind of continuous multidisciplinary examination (especially when the deployed disciplines do not necessarily suffer from any methodological conflicts against each other). However, when they make contradictory demands and their continuity is maintained through a compromise, it achieves nothing but mediocrity in each of them. This negative consequence of *secchū* could take place even when a philosopher collaborates with other specialists from humanities or social sciences.

In the context of world philosophies, this compromise can take place in the task of translating diverse intellectual texts into European languages. Suppose a philosopher, a philologist, and a historian look at the same Japanese text from the early twentieth century. When they agree on its significance (perhaps in relation to each of their disciplines) and set out to translate it into another language, a philosopher may be able to talk about the historical background and the literary style in which the text is written. However, she would engage in these discussions insofar as they are helpful for clarifying the significance of the concepts that it generates or for completing the task of translation that brought them together in the first place. Also, when she begins to talk about the philosophical significance of these ideas in reference to ongoing discussions in her own field, her research partners would quickly lose interest or find themselves lost in the cloud of her abstract arguments. To complete the collaborative work of examining and translating Japanese intellectual passages, the philosopher must refrain from philosophically engaging with the text before the others (just as much as the historian and the philologist would have to avoid asking too many questions that have no bearing on the task of translation or any relevance to the others' interests). As long as this interdisciplinary project is to be a joint investigation into a topic or a subject of study that is pertinent to the multiple disciplines, all participants would have to refrain from conducting a thorough examination of it in each of their own terms.

According to Tanabe, an interdisciplinary study that remains attentive to the cross-noetic constitution of human knowing cannot emerge from this "joint effort" of unmediated continuity, which avoids incurring any serious methodological conflicts or risking any communication breakdowns. In fact, if the historian looks at the intellectual text from the early twentieth-century Japan, she should examine it to the fullest as a historian, and she also has the obligation to talk about the historical significance of the text without suppressing any part of her analysis to be in line with the others' interests. Much of her historiographical explanation may be incomprehensive to those who are not familiar with her discipline, but that is perfectly acceptable in this metanoetic sense of interdisciplinarity. The philosopher and the philologist must make room for the historian to complete her investigation and the historian must also do the same for the others. That is to say, when the philosopher and the philologist approach the shared subject of their study (namely, the Japanese text), they should do so from each of their perspectives and strive to account for its significance in their own terms to the best of their abilities. Their explanations may turn out to be far from being useful for any part of the critical discussions taking place in other disciplines. However, according to Tanabe, it is imperative that each specialist is allowed to carry out a thorough and autonomous examination of the subject in her own way (where there might be no room for the other specialists to say anything about it) instead of making it accessible to all collaborators.

The Tanabean notion of interdisciplinarity, in this sense, demands an absolute mediation (or *shicchū*) of multiple disciplines. It calls for a metanoetic middle, where no discipline can claim itself to be superior to any others and yet simultaneously each is encouraged to pursue its interest without making any compromise vis-à-vis others. When a text is examined in the field of history, it should be seen as nothing but a historical document, and when it is taken up in the field of philosophy, it should be read as a philosophical text.[42] In this space of noetic freedom, moreover, a specialist in a specific form of knowing is further led to face some findings that she cannot fully make sense of within her discipline alone (just like the conflict of wave- and particle-theories in quantum physics or the case of "absolute antinomies" in philosophy). Only through her uncompromising commitment to a specific form of knowing can she awaken to this kind of fundamental problem that sheds light on the finitude/limitation of her *noesis*. Only then, Tanabe argues, can she come to recognize the complementary relation of her form of knowing to others while remaining attentive to their irreducible differences.

I do not think, however, that this cross-noetic "complementarity" needs to be always as dramatic or historically decisive as the antinomies in quantum physics or as self-disrupting as reason at the end of absolute critique in metanoetic philosophy. Sometimes philosophers are saved from grave confusion when they read an historian's analysis of the sociocultural and political contexts in which a text is written. Or an etymological account of a term (e.g., meta) could help us correct the widespread misconception associated with it. If philosophers give up the idea that we are the sole and final authority that can elucidate the meaning of a certain intellectual text and silence our egocentric propensity to claim absolute knowledge through our specific form knowing, we can begin to pay proper attention to what others say and sometimes reach a breakthrough leading to a series of solutions that we could not bring forth merely through philosophy. Thus, the "transformation [of noesis] at the bounds of neither/nor" (i.e., metanoesis) is necessary for placing philosophy in its equal status to other forms of knowing; for preserving each of their noetic freedom with an emphasis on its radical difference from the other; and last, for recognizing their inter-mediatory complementarity in their shared process of coming to know the world and the self as what they are.

Concluding Remark: Trans- and Cross-Noetic Constitution of Knowledge in Tanabean Philosophy

Thus far, we have examined the trans-noetic limit of human knowing in terms of the relationship between philosophy and religion; and the cross-noetic outline of human knowing in terms of interdisciplinary "complementarity." According to Tanabe, the vertical relation of philosophical knowing (noesis) to religious self-awareness of the absolute (metanoesis) gives an open unity. As the term "meta" in *meta*noetics indicates, both transcendence and immanence, the religious standpoint of absolute nothingness is constitutive of the self's philosophical endeavor to achieve complete knowledge of itself and the world: hence, the term "unity" or "harmony" refers to their binding relativity to each other. However, the absolute as nothingness is irreducible to any of the finite terms in ontic or ontological immanence (including the universal/genus, the particular/species, and the individual): hence, there is a radical difference between two terms of nothingness as the absolute and self as the relative. This trans-ontological asymmetry in metanoetics is described as their openness.

The intermediation of the absolute and the relative, however, is far from introducing a heteronomy of the religious over against the philosophical. Rather, since Tanabe's formulation of the notion of the absolute gives self-negating compassion to the overdeterminate other-power in accordance with the Mahayana Buddhist tradition, the standpoint of the religious is always understood as empowering the freedom (or self-power) of philosophical reasoning through its kenotic self-transcendence. This means that all religious doctrines must always make room for philosophy to speak the truth of its findings in its own terms and never dictate the terms of its engagement. Once again, each thinker is left with a free choice in the domain of philosophy. She can choose to continue chasing the impossible dream of completing her philosophical (self-)knowledge through her autonomy and self-power alone, thereby misconceiving the (counterfeit) duality of the philosophical and the (false) religious. Or she can bring herself to genuine self-criticism, where she can become aware of the limitation of her reason's autonomy.

When we choose to live such an examined life to the fullest, Tanabe argues, we can come to achieve the self-awareness that this whole autonomous process of philosophical knowing is made possible by absolute nothingness. This is not a passive resignation of philosophical thinking or a triumph of blind faith, but a profound self-transcending self-awareness that requires a life-long dedication to a complete self-examination in its relativity to a specific intellectual and historical context. Only when we fully commit ourselves to this continuous task of "absolute critique" can we testify to the religious standpoint of nothingness as the metanoetic foundation of our human knowing.

The interdisciplinary "complementarity" constitutes the horizontal inter-mediation between different forms of human knowing. This was understood when applying the (metanoetic) logic of species to our understanding of academic disciplines. If the notion of species represents a specific kind of knowledge, each discipline is essentially finite and contingent. This means that we cannot rationally argue for the superiority of one over the other, and also, none has the claim to absolute knowledge. Each gives only one specific manner in which we can observe them as what they are. The flipside of this argument in accordance with the logic of species is that, as long as we remain attentive to the limitation of each discipline, both in itself and in relation to other forms of knowing, it can be recognized as equally manifesting the absolute value of human self-knowledge and the knowledge of the world in its particular form.

We have seen that Tanabe argues for a kind of reciprocity between philosophical knowledge and other forms of human knowing. However, the Tanabean formulation of the dialectical relationship between philosophical and natural scientific knowledge leads us to a peculiar notion of inter-disciplinarity. What we ordinarily find in contemporary academia as interdisciplinary research often looks for a shared object of several studies and thereby focuses on making its findings as accessible as possible to all participating parties. The direct continuity between multiple disciplines, however, calls for some degree of negative compromise (*secchū*) and, as a result, we could end up with a mutually inclusive product of multidisciplinary mediocrities.

In accord with the logic of species, the Tanabean notion of the inter-mediation between multiple disciplines demands their absolute mediation of *shicchū* or "mutually exclusive complementarity." Each of them should be encouraged to pursue its interest without making any compromise over against others. This is to say, a philosopher should let the specialists of other disciplines speak the significance of their findings in their own terms regardless of the fact that there might be an epistemic rupture between their articulations and hers regarding the shared object of study. Only in this space of noetic freedom, Tanabe believes, can the philosopher be led to face some findings that she cannot fully account for within the bounds of her discipline alone. In facing the internal limit vis-à-vis her own discipline, she can bear witness to its genuine openness to other forms of knowing with an awareness that they constitute irreducibly different aspects of the same reality. Only then can she recognize the complementary relation of her specific form of philosophical knowledge to others while remaining attentive to their radical differences.

Questions for Class Discussions

Q1. What are the fundamental problems that Tanabe sees in the general practice of interdisciplinary studies? Is his alternative view of interdisciplinarity provided in accordance with his dialectical thinking conducive to the promotion of interdisciplinary studies? Or could it be detrimental to the purpose of pursuing interdisciplinary studies?

Q2. Tanabe provides an example of "exclusive complementarity" in relation to the example of electrons or the phenomena of rays of light in the discipline of physics. Are there any similar instances of the "limit case" in other disciplines of the natural sciences? Can we say the same thing about disciplines in the humanities?

Q3. Tanabe seems to say that this "limit case" or the "crisis" also takes place in the history of philosophy and further argues that metanoetics is a solution to this problem. How does metanoetics portray these two contradictory sides of philosophy and claim to overcome them?

Part Two

Translations

The Social Ontological Structure of the Logic

Notes on Translation

The original version of this article can be found in *Tanabe Hajime Zenshū* 6: 299–396. The collection of twelve essays, labeled under the "logic of species," is the largest body of work in the Tanabean oeuvre. It amounts to approximately a thousand pages, and each of these essays, by modern academic standards, would probably be read as a small booklet. The editors of the *Tanabe Zenshū*, therefore, had no choice but to awkwardly split them into two volumes of the complete works (namely, volumes six and seven). Tanabe also made a substantive revision, from one essay to another, regarding the mediatory nature of the key concept as he responded to various criticisms, which he received from other philosophers in the Kyoto School and beyond. He also claims that his overall thematic focus had shifted significantly in the process of writing these pages in the course of ten years (as we have seen in Chapter 1). Once again, Tanabe "discontinued" this project at the end of 1941 and remained unusually silent for one of the most prolific writers at that time in Japanese academia. Since he was thinking about giving up philosophy altogether, these essays were never complied into a monograph as a finished work. Even after his resurrection as a metanoetic philosopher in postwar Japan, they were left untouched. Thus, an attempt to present a comprehensive and coherent image of the "logic of species," with a single translation in the space of one chapter, requires some explanation.

A famous abridged version of the "logic of species," in Japanese, has been provided by Fujita Masakatsu through the Iwanami Bunko, a reputable pocketbook series and one of the first kind published by "Iwanami Shoten,"[1] the leading publisher in Japan. This version contains three essays:

(1) "Logic of Social Existence: An Essay on Philosophical Sociology" (1934–1935).
(2) "The Logic of Species and the World Scheme: A Way to the Philosophy of Absolute Mediation" (1935).
(3) "Clarifying the Logic of Species" (1937).

The first essay marks the advent of the term "species" in Tanabe's works, and the second tentatively lays the foundation of his unique social ontology. However, it received many criticisms over certain ambiguities that Tanabe himself recognized as serious problems. After giving his responses to these constructive counterpoints, he set the baseline of what would count as the logic of species in the third essay, which is the seventh of the twelve essays included at the end of volume six of the *THZ*. Tanabe certainly made more substantive modifications in the remaining five essays in volume seven. However, I must agree with Fujita that these three essays in the Bunko version are the best place to look for the emergence and the genealogy of the "logic of species."

There are several reasons why I did not translate these texts for this chapter. Neither the first nor the second essay provides a clear picture of the logic of species when each of these essays is presented alone. The third will assume the reader's knowledge of the criticisms that the second essay (and the subsequent ones) received. When we remove these critical comments, Tanabe's argument simply loses its force. The solution to this problem was to look at the essay that was published between the second and the third essay, especially the one that Tanabe wrote immediately before receiving the criticisms. "The Social Ontological Structure of the Logic" (1935) (hereafter SOSL) was precisely the article in which Tanabe polished the arguments he had provided in the second essay, and on the basis of which he later made his *respondeo*'s.

The SOSL is still over 100 pages. It refers to the history of European metaphysics, philosophy of science, mathematics, theoretical physics, social philosophy, and the Nishidian and Buddhist philosophy of nothingness. First, I translated the sections where Tanabe actually refers to the "logic of species." Then, I included the adjacent arguments that are integral to his claims in these sections. Where Tanabe refers to more than one subject for substantiating his insight, I selected only one, one which accounted for no more than a couple of pages in the original format. These should be accessible to the target audience of this book series. There are nine chapters in this essay. Chapters 4–6 provide theoretical examples in reference to the points which he made by the end of Chapter 3, and they range from Hegel's metaphysics, the philosophy of math (especially the number theories), the history of dialectic, an ambivalent critique of Nishida in reference to Plotinus, the philosophy of science, and to the dialectical notion of space and time. I removed these sections for two reasons: (i) much more concise versions of the points he makes in these sections are available in the earlier or the later chapters included in this translation and (ii) they are not necessarily helpful for readers even if they study these topics in other undergraduate philosophy or relevant courses. Chapter 8 contains a brief remark on the political implications of the logic, which are contained in Chapter 7, and Chapter 9 reiterates the point of the whole essay. However, unless one has read the entire text, this concluding section will make little sense. Most importantly, the main point that the article, as a whole, drives at is available in Chapter 7. This translation, I believe, covers the essential part of the essay which demonstrates Tanabe's understanding of the "logic of species."

The Social Ontological Structure of the Logic

1.

We have to think about the "logic of species." The most important reason for me to do this was the fact that a society cannot be understood solely on the basis of interrelations among individuals. Since the standpoint that conceives of the society in general as the interrelations of individuals is what we call "formal sociology," we can say that this reason lied in my recognition of the limit of formal sociology. Now I am not intending to criticize sociology, and also since formal sociology has lost its former position of authority and also since we are at the stage where almost everyone acknowledges the primitive form of community as the foundation of society, I do not think it is necessary to spend many words talking about the formal sociological understanding of society. However, if we pay attention to the fact that this standpoint itself is a product of liberalism (when it is seen in terms of its birth in society) and also that it precisely gives the nuclear view of society based on individualism, this is enough. Nevertheless, I do not think at all that this standpoint should be or can be rejected and excluded [from our understanding of human society]. Contrariwise, I think, once it has historically emerged, it must be something that should be forever preserved as a moment in the preceding views of society. Society cannot possibly lack the aspect that should be understood in terms of the individual interrelation in any case. It is a matter of course that sociology acknowledges this as an indispensable moment of society. In order for it to be established as a single empirical science, it necessarily uses an analytic methodology; and it is a matter of logical necessity that this standpoint [of individual interrelation] corresponds to this methodology. But what I cannot help but emphasize here is this: despite that this interrelation of individuals is an indispensable moment for [constituting] a society, we cannot describe it alone as the sole establishing principle of society; and that there has to be, in turn, the moment that negatively stands in opposition to it, the moment that is irreducible to the relation of individuals in every way, but rather seems like burying the individuals within [society] and annihilating them; and that this should be called "species" in opposition to the "individual." Society can be established as the medium of two moments that are in mutually negative opposition; the most primordial mode of it is the direct union of these two moments. Because of its immediacy, the species is necessarily superior [to the individual] therein: hence, the individual is fused with the species. ... [W]hat I call "species" is the grounding source of the individual that makes possible the denial of the individual. ... Hence, it cannot be reduced to the betweenness (*aidagara*, 間柄) of an individual and another. ... If the notion of species is to be understood as the between, it would have to be different from what I mean by "species." ...

I regard totemic society as a pattern of existing societies, where the moment of species is superior to the individual and the individual is directly fused with the species. However, I do not think that species in itself immediately constitutes the primitive society as a prototype of society. When we clarify the structure of society, we cannot constitute society based merely on the logical concept. ... I only raised the issue of totemic society as something that is closest to the society based on species (*shuteki shakai*, 種的社会) ... but I do not think that the totemic society indicates a prototypical society. I think that we can say that a clan society or a society that is based on blood relations generally belongs to the specific society (種的社会). Hence, it is not impossible to simply replace the *specific* society with the concept of the blood-relational society. Although we cannot deny that the "pure blood of all Japanese people" that is often discussed today is only a fiction, it does not prevent us from talking about the unity of blood as a specific society. Once I argued that species is that which stands over against species, but this was a result of my unrefined thinking. To clarify this point is one of the main purposes for writing this article and I would like to argue now that a species does not stand over against another species at all; but their relation must remain a matter of differences rather than one of opposition. Those that are different can continuously transition from one [species] to another and they can insert a composite layer without any limit in between them. This is the necessary consequence of species as a continuous whole. ... Accordingly, two species can be included together in a greater species, ... and they can coexist in a continuous whole. So, for instance, we can compare this to the coexisting relation of various and different colors in the continuum of color. In other words, we have to say that, every color as that which continuously transitions while being different from the other color in fact already more or less includes other species within it; and it is a matter of course that the absolute, pure species is merely a limit concept. ... Does this mean that there is no unity in species? No, this would be against the facts. For example, this can be seen in the case of color where it can be distinguished into seven colors as species. ... At any rate, in this manner, I emphasize the necessity of the fact that species as the continuous whole that negates the individual, and at the same time represents the fundamental medium that is born out of the individuals, is the substrate of society. Species gives birth to the individual as it kills the individual. ... [However,] what we call "species" is abstract and cannot signify the concrete substrate of life. This substrate is grasped only as the negative moment of logic and cannot appear in the standpoint of hermeneutics. … Rather, in expression, this type of species is negated and emptied as it is presupposed as the substrate: hence, it cannot enter into the hermeneutics of understanding. …

2.

The idea of mutual negation between species and individual that I mentioned in the previous section came from the demand to clarify the logic of social existence. However, at the same time, for someone like me who believes in the mediatory unity of being and logic in practice, it was clear that the category of social existence could make possible the concrete understanding of logic for the first time. …

However, this kind of philosophy had no choice but to result in my immature idea; and I have made this point clear to myself in the following manner. This problem is caused by the difficulty of thinking about the immediate negative opposition of the individual to the species. Indeed, the individual cannot be derived from the species at all (as I explained in the previous section), but in essence must constitute the negative opposition over against the species. However, as I just mentioned, the individual is sublated by and synthesized with the universal; and because of that, we can say that the "individual is the universal." Hence, in order for the individual to negatively stand over against the species, it would have to be mediated by the negative opposition of species and universal on the other side of the individual. Otherwise, if the individual tries to directly oppose species and, if the individual is itself immediate like the species, how could the individual also be this negative unity (as I have already argued)? The principle of individuation lies in the free, creative unity that denies the immediate essence of self and yet also makes the self what it is; an individual must clearly be the unity of contradiction; and the denied essence must be more than the fundamental medium of this self, and at the same time also the absolute negative that includes self-negation within itself and sublates this contradiction. In other words, it needs to be the universal that is already negatively mediated. That which is simply immediate cannot be the individual. In fact, the immediate, even if it is not aware of itself as the species that stands over against the individual, cannot help but be species in the sense that it is the immediate that stands in opposition to the individual as that which is negatively mediated. Since the individual is already that which is mediated, it is simultaneously that which realizes the universal and, in that sense, it is the universal. This is precisely the sense in which we say, "individual is universal." The individual cannot be thought as that which is simply immediate. … Thus, even if we try to think of the individual as the negation of species, so long as it cannot be directly determined as such, we cannot set it forth as that which directly denies species. That which is immediately set forth is precisely species. In this manner, the flipside of this argument is that it is necessary for the species to be negated. If the species is not negated, the universal that takes this as its medium is impossible; and at the same time, the individual that is established through the universal is also inevitably impossible. This is a negation of logic and an abandonment of thinking. ... Thus, since we must think of it as species and have it stand in its opposition to the individual and the universal, it would need to contain the principle that negates it. What then negates species?

As we have seen above, that which negates species cannot be the individual as the immediate. The immediate in general has no choice but to be species. In this sense, what is now required is precisely that which negates species. Then, the situation here is that we have no choice but to think that species negates species. In other words, we have to say that what negates species is also species itself and cannot be anything else but species. In short, it precisely provides the self-negation of species. The negation of species does not take place when the individual outside species immediately stands over against it, but the self-negation of species is the principle for the negation of species. Species does not have anything outside of itself that negates it, but contains within itself that which negates itself. This self-negation does not have anything more than itself that grounds it by means of a principle. This is to say that self-negation of species is utterly peculiar to species. The reason why species is particular and not universal is because it is simply self-negating and not the absolute negative. The particularization of the universal means that the self-alienation of the universal is at the same time the absolute negation degenerated to self-negation. However, without this self-negation, we cannot talk about species *as* species. Nor can we know its existence. That we have already known and been talking about it presupposes the negation or the opposite of the immediate. The self-negation of species must be acknowledged as such a thing. Instead of thinking about the individual as that which negates species, we have to think about the self-negation of species as that which is prior to it. The individual is mediated through such self-negation of species. I have argued that species serves as the foundation of the individual as it stands in opposition to the individual. If that is the case, then we must think about the individual as that which has emerged from inside the species. However, if species gives birth to the individual that denies it from within itself in this manner, we would have to say that species, in this sense, spontaneously denies its own self. Thus, even if the thesis that the individual negates species is correct, it does not change the fact that species negates itself. Only since I realized that the relation between the self-negation of species and the unmediated nature of the individual cannot be appropriately understood in this way of thinking, I must now terminate the proposition that the individual directly negates species and claim that what negates species is not the individual, but species itself and that species' self-negation in this manner rather mediates the individual. Thanks to this, the self-negativity of being that dialectic demands becomes complete and it is, therefore, reasonable to think that, when we presuppose the independent individual outside species and consider that it negates species, the structure of self-negation is incomplete. Neither can it escape the contradiction with the demand that the individual should have species as foundation of its generation. I must confess now that my previous framework of thinking included these inaccuracies and contradictions. ... This is the presupposition of logic and precondition for the logical nature of being and for the possibility of knowing it. ... The relation of one species to another is not an opposition but a difference. ... The negative opposition relies on the self-division of species itself. We have to think that species do not exist in parallel to each other as they negate each other, but that the conflict/division takes place inside each species. ... We have no choice but to acknowledge this kind of division based on the self-negation of species as a primitive dialectic.

How then should we think about the relation between species' self-negation and the individual? How can the former be the medium of the latter? In order to answer these questions, the structure of species must be further clarified in detail. First, if the species originally includes the element of self-negation in its essence, we would have to put at least a significant limitation on, and add a correction to, our previous idea that species possesses a primitive unity as the continuous whole. That is because, so long as the essence of species is to divide itself through the principle of self-negation—whichever part of the whole that we look at—it would include the conflict of power between the affirmative and the negative, and would then be accompanied by both the division toward the negative opposition through this conflict and the unity of the whole. Species is the constant movement that implies the double opposition, where it tries to diverge through the completely conflicting power of opposition while, at the same time and contrariwise, trying to preserve unity by opposing this division: hence, it cannot be thought simply as a static, fixed unity. No matter how divided it is, the part that is generated from this process still gives the whole and allows the possibility of infinite division; that is because it includes this kind of double power of opposition. As Hegel has clearly demonstrated its essence in the *Phenomenology* (where he discusses the reciprocity of power as the object of understanding), power is the direct unity of opposing negations, where a negation is accompanied by another, thereby constituting a mutual negation, and through that mutual negation, it can be for the first time made real: hence, it is ultimately reciprocal and circular and no matter how far we divide it, we cannot deprive it of its unity as this reciprocal circularity. This serves as the ground for the infinite divisibility of species and provides the reason why we have to think that the unity of continuity does not belong to the geometrical structure of space and time but to the structure dynamics. (See my, "Logic of Species and the World-Scheme.") For instance, reciprocal categories like attraction and repulsion or pressure and tension are mutually established and can coexist while the powers of their contrary movements are mutually negating, so long as they are preserved in the state where these powers can be in effect: if one side exhaustively negates another, the effectiveness of these powers would cease to exist and a simple movement thereby takes place. Moreover, the powers would disappear unless those which coexist in this manner mutually negate and oppose each other. Since it gives the direct unity of this negative opposition and coexistence, no change appears at the surface (so long as there is no generation of movement, or more precisely, the balance of the reciprocity between the powers is not broken); however, despite that, the space where the powers act on each other, or the field of power, constitutes the direct unity of turbulence where the infinitesimal and virtual movement constantly tries to arise without limit while always being suppressed. …

However, if species is the infinite stack of reciprocal activities between these powers in this manner, then does this say something contrary to my previous statement that the relation of multiple species is not the negative contradiction, but only difference and rather end up making it necessary to bring back the old position where multiple species are conceived as that which negates each other? … In the first place, what kind of difference is there between the self-negation of species and the fact that species stands in a negative opposition to [another] species? … We cannot say that … the self-negation of species and the negative opposition between [multiple] species are absolutely the same. Why is this the case? Indeed, the self-negation of species is not different from a species that denies a species. Nevertheless, the negative opposition of species to species does not always indicate the negation of species against its own self. In the case where we interpret the self-negation of species as the negation of species against species, the species that denies and the species that is denied would have to be essentially the same species. Otherwise, we cannot take this to be the self-negation of species. In this manner, when we say that a species negatively opposes a species, we mean that the denying species and the denied species are not the same species [in a negative sense]. Not only that, but we also normally mean that they are [positively] different from each other. This is already shown in the term "opposition" (対立). Of course, we could say that self negatively stands in opposition to the self through self-division. However, the fact that the self opposes its own self in this manner indicates a self-division that is a loss of the self. The self is a self so long as it contains unity: hence, if it divides itself as to lose the unity of the self and stands in opposition to its own self, then it is the same as saying that it does not own the self. The reason why it is called a *self*-division and why the mutually opposing selves as the self that stands against the self are both called "self" is because the unity of self to some degree remains. There is something that should be called "self" so long as the unity of self can compete against the division of the self. In that case, there is a double opposition pertaining to the mutual opposition of contraries that stand against each other in the manner of division and the opposition between this opposition and the unity that can rival it. This double opposition further preserves the immediate and dynamic tension. In this manner, when we say that species negatively opposes species, it formally signifies the same concept, but normally their contents are different. There remains the identity of concept for those of us who refer to them with the same term of "species," but we are not required to become aware of the self-identity regarding the species itself. When there is a conflict between red and blue, the two colors' species stands against another. At this point, we cannot immediately say that both kinds of colors mutually negate or that one of them negates the other. When we say that the relation of multiple species does not give the negative opposition but only signals difference, we mean that when there is mutual opposition between specific kinds of colors, their oppositional relation is only a difference but not a negation; and that since they can coexist, it is not the relation in which one negates and exterminates the other. But if we think about the change in which red is replaced by blue, these colors cannot coexist side by side; hence, in this case, we have to say that one color negatively stands in opposition to the other color. However, of course, we cannot say that this kind of change is the self-negation of species. That one color is changed into the other color indicates their negative opposition in relation to an identical place, but that is because an equipment (like a spinning disk where two colors occupy its halves, thus existing side by side in different places) is possible. What enables the negation in this case is the equipment that exists outside the species .... Generally speaking, when we say that species stands in a negative opposition to species, we mean that two different species that lie extensionally in parallel to each other (like in the example) enter a certain relation in which they cannot be established at the same time and in this relation, they negate each other. I have previously called this kind of thing an "extensional opposition." It is structurally distinguished from the inclusive opposition, where the identical species denies its own self within itself and thereby divides itself. Now, if a species takes self-negation as its essence and gives the infinite layer of the double negative opposition, which consists of an opposition and its suppression, it might look at the outset that different species are negating each other inside a species. However, what is important in this case is that, if those that negate each other are of different species and they coexist with their mutual opposition inside a single species, the species that includes these two would express the characteristics of a genus: hence, it would become something like "color" in relation to red and blue, and thereby it becomes difficult for us to say that the same species constitutes a self-negation. ... Rather, the red itself develops blue, which cannot be established with it at the same time, from inside its own self and, in turn, blue gives birth to red as the negation of self from inside its own self; and thus, for the first time, we can say that [their relation] is self-negative. However, if the other that denies one emerges from inside the one, and it is added to the one, this state of affairs signals a change, where one species only replaces the other; hence, we cannot say in this case that species has the structure of "tensor." It only gives a vectorial motion. In order for species to have the tensorial, mechanical structure, the medium that constitutes its self-negation must be unified to it as the very species without being separated from it. In other words, that which is negative must exist as the species itself in double oppositionality, where its contrary is suppressed in the unity of species. Accordingly, the unity of species constitutes the infinite layers inside itself through its self-negation and stretches the reciprocal tension between itself and that which negates itself, and we can thereby say that it has the structure where it horizontally constitutes the balance between its own self and its negation, vertically the infinite layer inside itself, and overlaps these two. ... However, with regard to the self-negation of species, a change in one side mutually negates as there is a change in the other, and hence, the change itself is simultaneously suppressed from the bottom of the change, thereby constituting the competition between change and unchanged. Since it bears the negative opposition inside the unity of species, the negated species and the negating species are still the same species, and they must compete against each other inside this identical species. Change itself tries to move, but at the same time is it overturned, thereby preserving the dynamic tension between change and unchanged. The waves in the ocean give the layers of contrary movements of ebb and flow and through them the molecules of the sea water do not flow past, but constitute the movement of ups and downs in the same place. In the same manner, the turbulent movement of species' self-negation produces a dynamic tension, where any change brings competition with the unchanged. Accordingly, it is understood as the internal and continuous unity of differences that at the same time does not change as it bears change inside itself. We can think in this manner that, regardless of the fact that difference is incompatible with external negative opposition, it is compatible with the internal unity of self-negation. To say that species does not hold the relation of a negative opposition toward species, but the relation of difference, by thinking the continuous unity that penetrates their difference, they can be mediated through the self-negation of species. The field of power gives continuity as it differs in every place and each of its parts is differentiated from the other. Rather, we should say that difference is an abstraction and the negative moment of continuity. That is because without including difference, we cannot think of any continuity.

3.

When we logically characterize species ..., it gives tensorial, double oppositionality, where the opposition of division and the opposition to it compete against each other for their primal unity. This is the end result of what I was arguing in the previous section. If that is the case, how should we think about the characteristics of the individual in light of species and the relation of the individual to species? ... What directly opposes species in the negative manner is not the individual, but the self-negative moment of the species itself. The individual takes such self-negation of species as its medium. Stated otherwise, we can think of the unity of the opposition between species and its negation as the individual. The tensorial field of power in species, as I mentioned previously, never loses its double structure no matter how small the pieces that it is divided into. This is the characteristic of infinite divisibility, which is particular to species, which also indicates a continuous totality. Thus, it is impossible to reach the individual as that which is indivisible through division [of species]. The individual does not appear through the division of species, but appears as the negative unity of species. What we should call the internal self-return of a specie's self-negation is the individual. Hence, the individual is that which is aware of itself as the unity of the self or of the absolutely negative affirmativeness through the self-negation of species. It always includes the negation of self inside the self .... The dynamic tension of the double opposition of species freely develops the whole of the negative opposition that it includes, and through which, all activities of various powers, which are the moments [of its development] are affirmed, and further this affirmation incurs the mutual negation of the various powers; all immediate powers are ultimately negated and this absolute negation qua affirmation precisely provides that which mediates all these powers through its unity that transcends them. This medium [as the absolute negation qua affirmation] constitutes the content of [self's] being. In this manner, the immediate, continuous whole of species, which constituted the competition of double oppositions as the dynamic tension of self-negation, now appears as the synthetic unity of powers that move in a certain direction as the ordered and balanced movement. ... However, upon further reflection, if species is directly presupposed as the self-negative matter in relation to the establishment of the individual and, if it is nothing more than that, does it not have to be a being that directly exists as the being of non-being? ... The non-being of species does not exist as the being of non-being, but indicates that, as it is being non-being, it is mediated through being, and thereby, being and non-being enter into their communal reciprocity. As I mentioned above, self-negation of species as non-being is turned into absolute negativity and its affirmative content is made to correspond to a specific power as a moment of species and, as they are recognized to have the same volume, [species] becomes possible. In this manner, species is realized in the individual as the foundation of the individual and, at the same time, it does not mean at all that species as that which is already mediated through a moment of power corresponding to the said individual is presupposed before the individual merely as its foundation without any mediation. In this sense, we can say that, as species mediates the individual, the individual also mediates species. We could tentatively say that the former mediation is immediate (or in itself) (*sokuji-teki*, 即時的) and the latter mediated (for itself) (*taiji-teki*, 対自的). The individual as the mediatory moment of species is negated through the self-negative structure of species and further, it is affirmed through the absolute negative-and-positive transformation (*tenkan*, 転換) of species' self-negation. In other words, it enacts negation-qua-affirmation and nothingness-qua-being. However, at the same time, species also enters the absolute contradiction (*hitei-tai*, 否定態) of being-qua-nothingness and affirmation-qua-negation. Species and individual are thus mutually mediatory: they constitute species-qua-individual (*shu-soku-ko*, 種即個) and individual-qua-species (*ko-soku-shu*, 個即種). That is to say, what I just distinguished as the in-itself mediation from the for-itself mediation is, all through the reciprocity of mediation, turned into the in-itself-and-for-itself mediation. This mediatory unity is exactly what I have previously expressed as the absolute genus. That meant the mediatory mode (*baikai-tai*, 媒介態) where, as species realizes its own self through the power of the individuals (which constitute its moment), the individuals as that which have emerged from the foundation of the same species are unified within the whole. It was my interpretation that the state, which can be thought of as the synthetic mode (*sōgō-tai*, 綜合態) that serves as the negative mediation of the specific group of people (*shu-teki minzoku*, 種的民族) and individuals, corresponds to this mediatory unity.

... The individual always takes the negation of self as its medium .... Hence, we have to presuppose the principle of conversion (*tenkan*) where negation is turned into affirmation and nothingness is mediated with being. ... The principle of transformative mediation (*tenkan baikai*) cannot exhaustibly be realized in a single moment, but must be understood as the transcendent, universal unity that exceeds its whole. This so-called universality is not the universality of genus that we ordinary think of as subsuming species that are different from each other, but must mean the inseparable, concrete unity of being and nothingness, or the transformative and mediatory unity of the contradiction between affirmation and negation. The unity of what we call "absolute nothingness" or "emptiness" indicates the meaning of this dialectical universal. Since it provides the unity of contradiction, it cannot simply be thought of as being or existence. And yet, it enables being and existence to be concretely the being of non-being, and existence of non-existence, and also constitutes the principle that enables the individual to possess the structure of nothingness-qua-being and negation-qua-affirmation. Thus, of course, we cannot say that this kind of absolute universal directly emanates the individuals as it determines itself, for this is not the particularization of the universal. It rather includes species as its negative moment, and it is mediated by the species. Since the absolute universal is the principle of the unity of contradiction, of the transformative mediation of negation and affirmation, of the mediatory unity of being and nothingness, it must presuppose the self-negating species as the negative ground where it can be effective, or its non-ontic substrate. Furthermore, to presuppose self-negating non-being means that nothing is presupposed; the absolute universal does not lose its absoluteness. Species as the tension of power that self-negatively fills movement releases the double oppositionality of negation that it includes within itself, freely completes the relation in which infinitesimal powers compete against each other as the layers of such negative oppositions and, at the extremity where it is developed into the absolute negation, its self-negation is transformed into the absolutely negative affirmation. What enables this conversion is precisely the absolute universal. Hence, the absolute negativity that constitutes negation-qua-affirmation of the absolute universal is the principle that turns species at the extremity of its self-negation into affirmation: so, it cannot be that which emanates individuals merely through the particularizing determination of self without the mediation of the species. ... The individual does not directly emerge from the universal at all. Nor does it directly come forth from the particularity of species as its foundation. It is established only through the negative mediation of both [universal and particular]. Not only is it the case that species, insofar as it includes that which corresponds to the realization of individuals, presupposes the individual (as described above), but also, the absolute universal, unless it reaches its affirmation in the individual through the negation of species, cannot realize its work (*hataraki*). When the self-negation of species is turned into affirmation through the mediation of absolute negativity, the order of the transcendent whole is manifested through the emergence of the individual (that it bears), and thereby, the absolute universal is realized as the whole of the development of such individuals. Otherwise, universality of the absolute universal cannot be the for-itself content of self-consciousness. In this manner, since the individual is already included in the whole of the self-negation of species (as the moment that corresponds to it), the transcendent whole of the individual as the realization of the absolute universal is precisely the absolutely negative transcending of the whole of species' self-negation. This is the genus that I previously mentioned that cannot be relativized into species. It should be the absolute genus that is to be distinguished from the specific genus (which is nothing other than genetic species). Species in this [absolute genus] is only the negative moment and is not the classifying species. Accordingly, without being relativized into species, genus falls into species only when it loses its absolute universality through self-alienation. However, at the same time, it is also the individual's process of becoming species as the practice of no-self (自己喪失). ... Yet the genus that takes the self-negativity of species as a medium preserves motion and does not allow it to be fixed. Transcending this motion cannot be achieved by negating any movement, draining the mediation of species, and "encompassing" it. As long as the unity of the absolute universal statically exists as such an encompassing whole, even if it is called "absolute nothingness," it is nothing other than the absolute being. ... However, the nature of motion cannot be transcended by directly negating motion, but rather by pursuing it to the fullest and reaching pure motion, it can be transcended as motion-qua-stasis. We can say that the absolute universal in this sense transcends absolute genus and negates its motion insofar as it takes the self-negating species as its medium. However, this negation is a negation in affirmation: hence, its self-affirmation is mediated through the negation of that which negates it. In other words, transcendence is mediated with immanence, stasis and motion become one with each other (相即する). Apart from this mediation or outside of it, there is nothing that can self-exist as transcendence. Thus, the absolute universal can be called absolute nothingness. ... Even if genus is called absolute genus in the sense that it cannot be relativized into species and is distinguished from a specific genus (genetic species), which is immediate and relative, it is always exposed to the process of turning into species through alienation. It constitutes constant movement in its mode of the absolute negative along with the motion of the individual. ... This pure motion-qua-stasis can be called "absolute nothingness." It is absolute, but at the same time it is inseparable from the relative and corresponds to the absolute nativity side of the relative's self-negation. Even calling this the "negative side" or the "place of nothingness," it has to be at the same time the negation of its side and nothingness of place. In short, it can be thought only as negation-qua-affirmation or nothingness-qua-being. Absolute nothingness cannot exist on its own apart from the absolute negation that takes self-negation as its medium or from the transformative mediation of it. If it could, absolute nothingness would not be nothing but being. ... Given that the individual is the dynamic existence that gives nothingness-qua-being mediation through the self-negation of the species or the negative existence that is constantly in motion, the absolute negation (that accompanies the individual) becomes the mediatory side of the absolute universal as the principle of the negation-qua-affirmation of such negative existence: hence, it does not belong to the individual, but rather to that which negates the individual, and through affirming the individual in this negation, for the first time allows it to exist. This principle of affirmation is the absolute universal. The absolute universal is precisely the static unifying aspect of the absolute negation. Because the absolute includes a mediation, it must have two sides of motion and stasis. The absolute negation is a dynamic side of this, and the absolute universal is the static side. The absolute as the unity of these two dynamic and static sides necessarily corresponds to the negative existence of the individual that is relative and takes the self-negation of species as its negative moment. ...

7.

Species has the structure of space, where time is self-negatively made latent while the individual has the structure of time that negatively mediates space. We should be able to already assume that genus as the synthesis of these two corresponds to the absolutely negative unity of space and time. However, we cannot sufficiently clarify the true meaning of the fact that space and time are negatively unified with each other through the formal dialectic, where we think about space and time separately and then argue that their synthesis must be thought *in concreto* because each of them includes the other in its structure as a moment. It was my viewpoint in the previous section that, just as the theory of relativity empirically reveals the indivisible unity of space and time for the first time by thinking about space as the agent of their mediation, the mutual mediation of space and time that mediates species and individual includes the perpetual occupation of land in the sense of a spacial fixation of time as an agent. ... From this point of view, I further thought of the occupation of land as something corresponding to light as a result of thinking about the mediation of space and time in reference to the agent that, in its essence, has the meaning of substantially connecting both [space and time]. It probably also refers to the spatialization of time. It should normally be acknowledged that the emergence of a society establishes a settlement on a tract of land as its necessary condition. Even nomadic people would have to settle down on land for a short period of time. ... Although, it is unlikely that we could establish a fully intimate community only through this nomadic lifestyle. The clan community based on blood relation in the primitive society would have to be seen as a neighboring community (地緣的 共同体) based on the land. Seen from this viewpoint, can we understand the reason why today's nationalist view of society emphasizes the primordiality of community based on blood and land? At the same time, when a socialist view of society thinks that the primitive community is divided into classes on the basis of private property and that the exclusive occupation of land is the most primitive and important property, we cannot deny that the permanent possession of land has the most fundamental meaning with regard to the structure of society. ... I initially thought about species as blood-related clans that correspond to the direct-unity side of species. In opposition to it, the self-negating and self-dividing side of species is concretized in the land settlement. Perhaps permanent occupation indicates the perpetual occupation of space and accordingly, since we can understand it as the process of turning time into the past, the self-negation of time is exactly made latent in space. The structure where specific space self-negatively conceals time within itself cannot be merely a formal abstraction: hence, through the perpetual occupation of space, the immutability of space is demanded and then realized by negating the motion of time with the identity of the past. In this sense, the land settlement is not only the realization of a specific society, but also a moment of its self-division. It is comparable to an abstraction in classical mechanics, where the finite particularity or contingency of light is forgotten and the status of being the absolute is given to it by demanding its absolute immutability (due to the fact that it produces rapid speed in reality), regardless of the fact that it is the medium agent, which constitutes the temporalization of space. At any rate, we cannot deny that, because species is more than a blood-relation community and accompanied by the perpetual occupation of land, it includes the moment of self-negating division. Perhaps human reproduction does not always maintain the same number of human beings, but produces some degree of increase: hence, some belonging to the new generation are placed where they cannot depend on occupation of the land, but have no choice but to live on their labor. Even if the same number of children to those parents are born, so long as the parents do not die of old age when the children come of age, it is necessary for the two generations to collide with each other. Thus, there is always the period in which the land occupation belongs only to the past and older generation, while the new cannot rely on it. Thus, a society always includes the moment of division. This is the reason why the origin of class conflict is said to lie in the structure of society itself. ...

In this manner, we can think about the determination of species in conjunction with the spacialization of time that is exclusively limited as the medium of specification. Here, we should be able to discuss much more concretely the correspondence (*sōsoku*) between individual and genus that can be thought of as the absolutely negative transformation of such a specie's self-negation. That is because we can no longer think about the individual simply as the temporal negation of space in general or as that which absolutely negates species without any qualifications. Species is not some isotropic or homogenous continuity, but has the peculiarity of discontinuity in a certain direction. Accordingly, the self-negation of the species does not provide the direct power-balance that indiscriminately includes the layer of dynamic movements in infinite directions, but only a layer of contradiction in a certain direction; and all directions take self-negation in this particular direction as its medium. Thus, the species indicates self-negation in each of these directions. At the center of the ocean, waves indicate this transition [in direction]; and we do not see the movement of the molecules in the sea water. This statement only signifies an ideal limit and it is comparable to the fact that, in reality, there is an ocean current that moves in a particular direction in accordance with the shape of the seabed, its position relative to the seashore, the direction of airflow that has something to do with this position, and so on and so forth. ... Stated succinctly, the self-negativity of a specific community includes the societal division (which takes the occupation of land as its medium) as a necessary moment of contradiction within itself; societal contradiction generally takes this moment as its grounding medium. Hence, the statement that the individual comes to be when it converts the self-negation of species into absolute negation does not mean that the contradiction of species is generally negated in the absolute fashion and that the individual is established when the material substrate of the species turns into the subject, but only that possessive contradiction of species is absolutely denied; and when the species is turned into genus as the unity of societal justice (which takes so-called distributive justice as its basic moment), the individual is realized as a member of such genus. As we say that the establishment of the individual right to live is impossible without sublating the class struggle, the emergence of the individual cannot be carried out without social justice. As long as this condition is not met, the individual is in fact not an individual, but simply remains at the level of species. That is because the individual as that which emerges in the standpoint where the self-negation of species is turned into absolute negation would have to be the affirmation of negation and being of nothingness. Through the mediation of such absolute nothingness, individuals become equal to each other, and what makes the individual as an individual lies in the equality of persons who acknowledge the self in the other. Thus, as long as the self-negation of species is maintained through the exclusive permanence of occupation, we cannot expect such equality of persons. ...

As I mentioned earlier, the individual as the affirmation that is mediated by the negation has the structure that is almost like that of irritational numbers: hence, it would have to be an element that represents the whole and in itself creative, just as the irrational number represents the active element in the creative medium of continuity. As Aristotle clearly explained in reference to a moment in time or a point in space in his study of nature, this simple element as a term does not provide a part of the continuity, but a limit. Its simplicity or indivisibility does not derive from being the smallest part that the division will reach at the end of it, but rather, as the limit that constitutes both the end and the beginning of the continuity, it derives from being the union of the opposites, thereby unifying the beginning and the end. The element, as the union of opposites, would have to be actively in motion, essentially as the unifying mediation of negation and affirmation. In other words, through the absolutely negative unity of the sudden moment, it itself represents the whole of continuity, just like the irrational numbers. ...

The individual as such an element would have to be active, creative, and inclusive of the continuity of species within its own self. An individual in a sexual relation creates a new individual through the mediation of its unity with another individual (which belongs to the opposite sex); this can mean that the union of opposites that the individual includes within itself is reflected in the substrate of the species, thereby realizing the continuous productivity of species. Based on this, an individual gives birth to an individual and restores the continuity of the substrate. However, if the procreated individual is still potentially an individual and in its immediacy belongs to species, it becomes aware of itself as the individual when it realizes the significance of being an element of the genetic whole as a member of state while maturing in its body. All individuals that are produced through the creativity of individuals, who restore the continuity of species through their reflection on the species, have the determination of species (deriving from the mediation of the land occupation) in their shared substrate, take the self-negation of species as the absolutely negative conversion, and then each of them can reflect the whole. At the same time, [the individual is] an element or a member of the whole as that which has the creative content peculiar to each of their own positions. I have argued earlier that the individual is temporal in relation to species as spatial and further explained in detail that, in contrast to the species that is comparable to space that self-negatively conceals time in itself, the individual is comparable to time that negatively includes space in a mediatory fashion; however, the individual can be understood as a time that is peculiar to each point of space. In classical mechanics, we think about space and time separately, abstracting each from the other. We rather unify them without any mediation, thereby supposing that an identical time generally corresponds to each point of space. However, in the theory of relativity, the time that is concretely observed is a peculiar time that is relative to each position of space, and when they are mutually mediated through a certain conversion formula, we think that a relative can in turn establish an invariant. An individual as that which constitutes the absolute negative conversion that is peculiar to each position of the species is individualistic, but by taking species as the common substrate, it represents the same genus (with other individuals) from its own standpoint. The reproductive function, where the individual gives birth to the individual, is already seen as the temporalization of space, thereby realizing the active creativity of the species' continuity. Just as the permanent occupation of land is the spacialization of time, reproduction is also the temporalization of space. ... In opposition to the former (the past), the latter includes the meaning of the future, since it is a production of the individual. However, the interrelation between them (as I pointed out earlier) ends up indicating the superiority of the future over the suppressed past. In this case, the individual is not born as the purely free individual, but as a possible member of the genus, as that which is determined by the possession. Generally speaking, the genus is a unity of the possible whole of the individuals. It is not a mere amalgamation of individuals, but the creative whole of the individuals as that which takes species (which serves as the foundation of individual) as its medium. However, as long as it is mediated through the land occupation in a similar fashion to the way in which the determination of the species is mediated by it, it includes the determination of species in itself. Given that the parts of the immediate species as a continuous whole are still species, I previously called the species that directly includes another species as its part the "genetic species" (*ruiteki shu*, 類的種). I also referred to it as the "specific species" in the sense of being a relative genus. Opposed to it, we have to call the genus established at the same time as the individuals as the whole in a mediatory fashion the "absolute genus," but it cannot completely avoid being specific. If the sexual relation in which the individual gives birth to another is the reflection of the individual toward the species, we can say that [this absolute genus] is established in between the individual and species. If we can say this, then genus in its specific determination cannot reach the status of being the truly absolute genus in the sense of humanity. As such, it stands in between this [absolute genus] and the species. The ethnic nation state (*minzoku kokka*, 民族国家) that remains in between genus and species cannot escape such limitation. With regard to its inside, genus is supposed to be that which gives life to the individual as the whole of individuals and, thus, the individual can be said to express its individuality only in this state. However, this relation is not unconditionally established, for only as long as the possessive determination of the species is denied-and-affirmed (*hitei-soku-kōtei suru*, 否定即肯定する) under social justice is it established. The flip side of this is that it is always accompanied by the possibility of a realization that is always mediated by the self-negating and self-dividing possession of species. When this division tends to tear down the social justice and reverse genus into species by denying the individual, the division of the class comes to be. Of course, this is neither equivalent to the species that are continuously connected with each other simply in the relation of difference nor gives the self-division of species itself. The self-negativity that is simply mediated through the perpetual occupation of land only gives the differential competition of the opposite (due to its essential nature as the self-negation) and does not result in the political struggle in reality. Only when the state unity of genus is actually divided, which appears as the struggle of power that denies social justice, does it become the class struggle. We cannot make the determination of the species in its mode of land-occupation cease to exist, since it mediates the structure of the species itself. However, in order for this determination to be absolutely negated, and for the individuals to be established as individuals, they have to be regulated into an organization, inside genus, where the genus does not cause inequality. Thus, in actuality, the determination of the species as land-occupation takes the form of prior-occupation, essentially as the spacialization of time in the past, whereby the prior-occupants naturally come to inherit and divide the species inside of it. Accordingly, it becomes necessary for the part that is removed from the privilege to be in conflict with the privileged and earn the rights to equality. The unity of the genus does not make the union of the self-binding whole—which is constituted by equal individuals as if it were made through a contract—appear in reality, but necessarily preserves social justice through a compulsory bond with the other. The present condition of the state is that it constitutes coercive power relations without having the autonomous organization that spontaneously binds the self with the whole. If there is no mediation of the [land-/property-]possession, the continuity of the species that does not necessarily oppose each other in an exclusive manner must be able to achieve the transformation of individuals into the genus, even when there is the difference of species through the direct unity based on blood-relation. Moreover, in this complete absolute transformation (of individuals) into genus, even when there could be some individual abnormalities, there should essentially be no need for power. Perhaps that is because, in the presence of complete autonomy, coercion is impossible. I thought that such a thing as the essence of the state under the name of the human state (*jinrui kokka*, 人類国家) and logically understood it as the absolutely negative "absolute genus." However, this is different from the real state that cannot eliminate the possessive and exclusive determination of the species and preserve it as the mediatory substrate of its unity: for, [in this situation], there is no room for the power-relation that we think normally belongs to the essence of the state therein. And yet, at the same time, state power is not simply a real force (*jitsuryoku*, 実力). Since the relation that coerces the individual through interruption of her life by resorting to a natural, material force, thereby threatening her life, does not in fact affirm the individual, but denies it, and denies its wholistic unity. This does not render the genus, but remains at the level of species. It is clearly impossible to think that such a thing as the state that has this power. Justice must be the ground for the coercion of power. The mere real force (*jitsuryoku*) stops at the level of material power of nature, which has no ethical significance. State-power must be the real-force compulsion of the ethical. If we think in this way, there is no other way to understand the essence of power other than the compulsory governance that negatively mediates the individual equality of the absolute genus and the determination of the species, and thereby indirectly realizes the equality of the individual through the realization of social justice in the state. Here lies the reason why the state does not simply become an autonomous group, while taking autonomy as a moment of governance. It derives from the necessity of the structure that we cannot easily understand, if we try to think about it simply as a limit of reality vis-à-vis ideality. The mediatory nature of species here maintains the power of determination that we cannot regard as the utterly negative moment that disappears. This is the reason why, regardless of the fact that the state internally takes the idea of social justice explicitly as its principle (as we have discussed above), it externally preserves the immediate determination of species as what it is; hence, it is incapable of extinguishing the conflict that a nationalist state would demonstrate and to thereby present the situation where it looks as though international justice is, after all, only a real-force-qua-justice (*jitsuryoku-soku-seigi*, 実力即正義). In this case, when we look at how an expansion of territories is practiced through a real force, like an invasion and conquest, we can see how land occupation has a basic significance for state organization. However, regardless of that, the exclusivity of land occupation cannot be absolute. We can say that a certain degree of indeterminacy in the ocean, and even more so with the propensity toward indeterminacy in the sky clearly demonstrate this point. Moreover, it is clear that the advancement of mechanical industries as a moment of production adds a certain degree of negation to the determinacy of the land. If nature further opens its resources to us through the advancement of science, and if the limitation of horizontal land is vertically dissolved, more limitation will be added to the determinacy of the land. We can imagine that the development of international law was promoted by oceanic freedom that releases the limitation of land; and today's scientific subordination of nature will further provide a basis to its development. I do not want to give up this hope as a mere fiction. At any rate, even though the specific determination of land occupation cannot be dissolved at the level of an ideal, I believe that the development of human knowledge is beginning to move toward the process of turning it into a merely negative moment. In this manner, the negation of this mediatory substrate naturally leads to the development of the idea of international justice and it will internationally make possible the quality of individual [life], its sublation of the determination of species, and the international expansion of social justice. National conflict would have to be sublated by both substrate and subject. What serves as the most important medium is the advancement of scientific knowledge, toward both nature and history.

Questions for Class Discussions

Q1. Tanabe argues that species is the spatialization of genus (which is to say that a social self could be a historical manifestation of the ideality of humanity) and also that, as such a process of particularization/historicization, species needs to claim its fixed identity with an ownership of some land. If we apply this logic to the example of one's nationality, how do we understand national boundaries? What are the justifications for drawing a line and the basis in which we could dissolve a territorial dispute?

Q2. Tanabe claims that this element of species as the land-ownership leads to a number of economical and socio-political problems (including poverty, wars, class struggles, etc.) and further indicates that an advancement of science could alleviate this deconstructive aspect of species. Do you think that contemporary science and technology have provided us with more resources and helped us overcome these constrains of species? Or do we need to come up with a different kind of solution to these problems originating from the immediacy of species?

Q3. Social justice must be observed: otherwise, species will remain closed and fail to realize its full potential as the open species. What type of individuals constitute these two types of open and closed social selves? Provide examples and explain what kind of social justice is observed or breached therein.

Philosophy as Metanoetics

Notes on Translation

Philosophy as Metanoetics (1946) marks the turning point in the work of Tanabe. After an unusual interval as a prolific writer, Tanabe broke his silence in 1945 with his lectures on metaphysics and philosophy of religion. These marked the end of his illustrious career as a professor of philosophy at the Kyoto Imperial University. It was also a turning point for the country of Japan. The historical and cultural background against which this book was written is itself quite remarkable for contemporary philosophers. Tanabe, as a moral idealist, was sensitive to the fate of his nation (especially when the state authority was mobilizing his students for a war, which made no sense to him). He felt that he was not able to write anything that would satisfy his conscience, as either a citizen of Japan or a teacher of philosophy at a state university. He confessed in this text that he had felt himself as being unworthy of philosophizing since the early 1940s (precisely when he seems to have abandoned the project on "species"). Additionally, his originally weak health was quickly deteriorating during this time. He was practically bed-stricken most days and brought himself to talk about the kind of philosophy he could practice as a powerless and sinful individual, in his university lecture hall. This lecture took place before a large audience, consisting of both students and public intellectuals, most of whom were sensing the end of the Second World War and its aftermath, uncertainty and social chaos. They could not help but listen to a dying philosopher at this time of national crisis.

In this work, Tanabe exhibits intense self-reflection, which recognizes the ultimate finitude and contingency of human existence. He detects a metaphysical and religious hubris in human reason/autonomy that tends to turn itself into various forms of the absolute in the history of philosophy (and here he includes both Anglo-European and Japanese philosophy). As he examines the generous foundation that even allows for this problematic self-(mis-)understanding as the divine absolute in conventional forms of philosophy, Tanabe recognizes the importance of a practical conversion, the turning of self from a self-centered and egoistic self to a selfless and compassionate self, which he describes as a "concrete manifestation of nothingness." In this process of existential transformation, or "metanoesis," he finds the possibility for any future metaphysics, thereby offering a new philosophy that serves as the basis on which we can break down our intellectual and existential impasse, and break through to a liberating philosophy of religion.

In this section, I included the second edition of Heisig's translation of *Philosophy as Metanoetics* (published in 2016 through Chisokudō Publications). This work, as a whole, is approximately 500 pages, but it is important to read the Preface to understand the historical background against which it was written, and the psychological state in which the author of this magnum opus found himself. Moreover, as is typical of the works of dialecticians, the first chapter of this book contains the architecture of the dynamic whole. By carefully reading these two sections, readers should be able to discern the outline of the metanoetic worldview and its historical emergence, and delve more deeply into its rich implications for world philosophies.

A few notes should be made on the inclusion of Heisig's translation. His philosophy of translation has been quite influential in the field of Japanese philosophy since the end of the previous century. In addition to making Japanese philosophical texts accessible to a general audience in such European languages as English, Spanish, and Italian, he has developed a method of translation that has come to be regarded as a benchmark. French and German, among other European translation traditions, are still resistant to this method, and tend to posit an asymmetrical relationship between the source, and the target, language. So, for example, in a French translation, it is possible to sacrifice the grammatical rules of the target language in order to accommodate the sentence construction of the source language. However, when this practice was adopted in Anglophone academia in the 1950s and 1960s, the result was translations, which were unintelligible to those readers who were not familiar with Japanese sentence structure. This was inevitably detrimental to the development of Japanese philosophy in Anglophone academia. To alleviate this problem, Heisig proposed to reverse the relation between the two languages and to emphasize the importance of conveying the meaning in the original by allowing for a more natural flow, so to speak, to the translations developed in the target languages. In other words, the intelligibility of the target language was given priority over the structure of the original or source language.

That being said, in the usual process of translating philosophical texts into English, this "philosophical translation" usually takes place after the appearance of a few editions of the critical translations. That is to say, after a due process of showing one's sensitivity to the structure of the original text, one can begin to provide translations, which more clearly render the philosophical meanings contained therein. This means that philosophy teachers should remain attentive to both the merits and demerits of using these texts for teaching. Indeed, Heisig's methodology has generated some critique among translators of Japanese philosophical texts, who fear its potential violence to the original text.

Having said that, there are several undeniable merits to using the Heisig translation here. In the first place, Heisig's translation of the *PM* is, in fact, rather conservative and does not represent the more controversial style he uses elsewhere. There are many elements of this version that even conservative translators of Japanese philosophy would regard as an original, and even brilliant, way to approach Tanabe's later works. Clearly, more translations are needed if there is ever to be a solid, critical edition in English, but I do not think later editions will deviate greatly from what Heisig has offered us. In the second place, for most undergraduate students with no prior knowledge of Japanese, this version is simply optimal for teaching Tanabean philosophy of religion. Indeed, I am convinced that students will find this translation much more palpable than others.

A few modifications were made to the Heisig translation in this chapter. Tanabe often makes a side remark that only makes sense within a series of arguments. Moreover, as a dialectician, he often repeats the same point to emphasize the interrelation of that point with another. I have eliminated these side remarks and the repetitive modifiers, which are characteristic of dialectical arguments. This allowed me to shorten these two sections. Moreover, the Chisokudō version provides the *romaji* of the technical terms in the body of the text, and their original rendering in sinographs (*kanji*), and syllabaries (*hiragrana* and *katakana*) are provided in the Glossary and Index. For the sake of stylistic consistency and to promote the reader's familiarity with the Japanese language, this edition will insert the original terms at their first appearance.

Philosophy as Metanoetics

Preface

Last summer, when the fortunes of war had turned against Japan and the nation was under the increasing threat of direct raids and attacks, the government found itself at a loss as to how to handle the situation, and in the stalemate that ensued, it showed itself completely incapable of undertaking the reforms necessary to stem the raging tide of history. Instead, government officials tried to keep the actual course of events secret from the people in order to conceal their own responsibility. Criticism of any kind became impossible. All public opinion, except for propaganda in favor of the government's policy, was suppressed. Freedom of thought was severely restricted, and the only ideas given official recognition were those of the extreme rightists. In the midst of economic distress and tensions, and an ever-deepening anxiety, our people were greatly concerned about their nation's future, but did not know where to turn or to whom to appeal.

I myself shared in all these sufferings of my fellow Japanese, but as a philosopher I experienced yet another kind of distress. On the one hand, I was haunted by the thought that, as a student of philosophy I ought to be bringing the best of my thought to the service of my nation, to be addressing the government frankly with regard to its policies toward academic thought and demanding a reexamination, even if this should incur the displeasure of those currently in power. In such a critical situation, where there was no time for delay, would it not be disloyal to my country to keep silent and fail to express whatever ideas I had on reform? On the other hand, there seemed something traitorous about expressing in a time of war ideas that, while perfectly proper in a time of peace, might end up causing divisions and conflicts among our people that would only further expose them to their enemies.

Caught between these alternatives, I was unable to make up my mind and was tormented by my own indecision. In the impasse, I even wondered whether I should go on teaching philosophy or give it up altogether, since I had no adequate solution to a dilemma that philosophically did not appear all that difficult. My own indecision, it seemed to me, disqualified me as a philosopher and university professor. I spent my days wrestling with questions and doubts like this from within and without, until I had been quite driven to the point of exhaustion and in my despair concluded that I was not fit to engage in the sublime task of philosophy.

At that moment, something astonishing happened. In the midst of my distress I let go and surrendered myself humbly to my own inability. I was suddenly brought to new insight! My penitent confession—metanoesis (*zange* 懺悔)—unexpectedly threw me back on my own interiority and away from things external. There was no longer any question of my teaching and correcting others under the circumstances—I who could not deliver myself to do the correct thing. The only thing for me to do in the situation was to resign myself honestly to my weakness, to examine my own inner self with humility, and to explore the depths of my powerlessness and lack of freedom. Would this not mean a new task to take the place of the philosophical task that had previously engaged me? Little matter whether it be called "philosophy" or not: I had already come to realize my own incompetence as a philosopher. What mattered was that I was being confronted at the moment with an intellectual task and ought to do my best to pursue it.

The decision was reached, as I have said, through metanoia, or the way of *zange*, and led to *a philosophy that is not a philosophy*: philosophy seen as the self-realization of *metanoetic consciousness*. It is no longer I who pursue philosophy, but rather *zange* that thinks through me. In my practice of metanoesis, it is metanoesis itself that is seeking its own realization. Such is the nonphilosophical philosophy that is reborn out of the denial of philosophy as I had previously understood it. I call it a philosophy that is not a philosophy because, on the one hand, it has arisen from the vestiges of a philosophy I had cast away in despair, and on the other, it maintains the purpose of functioning as a reflection on what is ultimate and as a radical self-awareness, which are the goals proper to philosophy.

To be sure, this is not a philosophy to be undertaken on my own power (*jiriki*, 自力). That power has already been abandoned in despair. It is rather a philosophy to be practiced by other-power (*tariki*, 他力), which has turned me in a completely new direction through metanoesis, and has induced me to make a fresh start from the realization of my utter helplessness. Metanoesis (*zange*) signifies repentance for the wrongs I had done, with the accompanying torment of knowing that there is no way to expiate my sins. It also signifies shame for the powerlessness and inability that have driven me to despair and self-surrender. Yet insofar as this entails an act of self-denial, it points to a paradox: even though it is my own act, it cannot be my own act. It has been prompted by a power outside of myself. This other-power brings about a conversion in me that heads me in a new direction along a path hitherto unknown to me.

Zange thus represents for me an experience of other-power acting in and through *zange* to urge me to a new advance in philosophy. I entrust my entire being to other-power (*tariki*), and by practicing *zange* and maintaining faith in this power I confirm the truth of my own conversion-and-resurrection experience. In this way, the practice-faith-witness (*gyō-shin-shō*, 行信証) of my *zange* becomes the philosophy of my regenerated existence. This is what I am calling "metanoetics," the philosophy of other-power. I have died to philosophy and been resurrected by *zange*. It is not a question of simply carrying on the same philosophy I had abandoned in my despair, as if resuming a journey after a temporary interruption. It cannot be a mere repetition without negation and change. In the life of the spirit, "repetition" must mean self-transcendence; "resurrection" must mean regeneration to a new life. I no longer live of myself, but live because life has been granted to me from the transcendent realm of the absolute, which is neither life nor death. Since this absolute is the negation and transformation—that is, conversion—of everything relative, it may be defined as absolute nothingness. I experience this absolute nothingness through which I am reborn to new life as nothingness-*qua*-love (*mu-soku-ai*, 無即愛). One might also say that it is an experience of the truth of absolute negation: the confirmation of the Great Nay as the Great Compassion. The truth of my conversion and resurrection in dependence on *tariki* (other-power) is confirmed in the practice and faith (*gyō-shin*) of *zange*.

While I have no doubt that metanoetics is the way to a new philosophy of other-power as the "action-faith-witness" of *zange*, I am but a finite and imperfect being whose *zange* may not be fully pure and true. It may sometimes happen that my *zange* is not accompanied by a resurrection, or that even after a resurrection experience, I may fall away from *zange* into reliance on self-power. I may grow complacent with my accomplishments and in my arrogance imagine myself a wise man. In that case I should inevitably be driven back to my former despair, since anything I achieve apart from true *zange* can only be immediately contradicted by reality itself. Only through continual *zange* can we achieve the faith and witness (*shin-shō*) of continuous resurrection. By acting in and witnessing to the circular process of death-and-resurrection that characterizes *zange* and indeed accords with the unfolding of reality itself, the infinity and eternity of *zange* are revealed to us and the dialectical unity of absolute and relative affirmed. This is in fact the basic principle that shapes history. In terms of its concrete content, metanoetics is a radical historicism in that the continuous repetition of *zange* provides basic principles for the circular development of history.

My experience of conversion—that is, of transformation and resurrection—in metanoesis corresponds to the experience that led Shinran 親鸞 (1173–1262) to establish the doctrine of the Pure Land Shin sect. Quite by accident, I was led along the same path that Shinran followed in Buddhist discipline, although in my case it occurred in the philosophical realm. Reflection on this parallel led me to an interpretation of Shinran's *Kyōgyōshinshō* from a metanoetical point of view. I had, of course, been interested in Shinran before that time. In particular, I found his *Tannishō* and one of the hymns from his *Shōzōmatsu wasan* 正像末和讃 entitled, "Confession and Lamentation," deeply moving for their treatment and tone of metanoesis.

Shinran's doctrine of salvation through the praise and recitation of the name of Amida Buddha, as an expression of faith in Amida Buddha alone, has often been mistaken for a kind of spiritual laxity, especially seen in conjunction with his advocacy of the "easy way" of salvation (*igyōdō* 易行道). This is due to the common error of confusing the realm of the transcendent— where we must speak of people being saved "just as they are," without any merit on their part, as a result of the conversion and transformation brought about by absolute compassion—with the realm of the relative—normal, everyday life. Thus his doctrine of the salvation of people "just as they are" led to the error of disregarding morality, and at times even served the evil purpose of providing excuses for wrongdoings.

In contrast with these abuses of his teaching, Shinran's own faith was based on the bitter experience of metanoesis. This had been my firm conviction from the outset in reading Shinran's works. But I had no idea at the time that his *Kyōgyōshinshō* 教行信証 was in its very essence nothing other than metanoetics. The oversight was a natural one in that metanoesis does not appear as one of the central ideas of the work, even though Shinran mentions and explains the "three kinds of metanoesis" developed by the Chinese priest Shandao 善導 (Jp., *Zendō*, 613–681) in one of his doctrinal discourses, and in his hymns in praise of Amida Buddha we find strong elements of metanoesis at various places. Among contemporary scholar-priests of the Shin sect, Soga Ryōjin 曽我量深 (1875–1971) should be mentioned for his appreciation of and deep insight into the basic notion of metanoesis, as well as for his recognition of its significance for understanding Shinran's faith. I have found his interpretation and doctrinal analysis most enlightening, and owe him a great debt of gratitude in this regard.

Understanding the *Kyōgyōshinshō* as the metanoetical development of Buddhism has not received general approval as a correct interpretation. I myself had long been reluctant to accept such a viewpoint. My innate attraction for the idealistic doctrine of self-power made me more sympathetic to the Zen sect than to sects that taught "salvation by other-power." Although I had never undergone discipline in a Zen monastery, I had long been familiar with the discourses of Chinese and Japanese Zen masters. I was ashamed that I still remained an outsider to Zen and could not enter into the depths of its holy truth, and that I felt closer to Zen than to Shin doctrine. This was why I had taken little notice of the *Kyōgyōshinshō* up until that time.

One of my students, Takeuchi Yoshinori 武内義範 (1913–2002), had published a book under the title *The Philosophy of the Kyōgyōshinshō* (1941). Drawing on the intellectual acumen he had developed through reading Hegel under me, he was able to produce an outstanding interpretation of the work. While I learned much from reading this study, it was impossible for me at the time to develop a philosophy of my own based on the thought of the *Kyōgyōshinshō*. It was only when I set out to develop a new philosophy, a philosophy of metanoetics based on other-power, that I returned to reread the *Kyōgyōshinshō* carefully and was able to find a way to understand it. I regard Shinran with gratitude, love, and respect as a great teacher from the past. As I shall demonstrate in Chapters 6 and 7, his idea of the three stages of religious transformation and his interpretation of the "Three Minds" (*sanshin*, 三心) is unique in the history of the philosophy of religion as an explanation of the structure of salvation. I cannot but feel thankful for the grace of other-power that led me to metanoetics and to reliance on the guidance of Shinran.

I was also surprised to find that once I had arrived at belief in other-power, I found myself feeling still closer to the spirit of Zen, whose emphasis on self-power is generally considered opposed to Pure Land doctrine. Nor was this the last of my surprises. A key to solving a problem in mathematical philosophy, which would at first glance seem to be rather far removed from religious concerns, also emerged at this time. I refer to the puzzle of infinite-set theory, over which I had cudgeled my brains for many years in vain. Moreover, it became clear that a philosophy of history could be based on metanoetics, inasmuch as the content of metanoetics itself consists in a "radical historicism." In this way I grew confident of the range of applicability of metanoetics with its broad and ample perspective, although I must admit that at first I had no idea it was capable of such scope.

Some may contend that metanoesis is so extraordinary a phenomenon in one's spiritual life that it is hardly possible to develop a universal philosophy out of it. But I have been convinced from the start that metanoetics involves social solidarity inasmuch as we are always obliged to practice metanoesis so long as we are aware of our collective responsibility for every event that takes place in our society. In my case, metanoesis was aroused because I had been driven to the limits of my philosophical position as I confronted the desperate straits into which my country had fallen. My distress resulted not only from my own personal inability to execute my responsibilities as a philosopher at the time but also from my feeling the responsibility that each of my fellow Japanese had to assume in his or her particular situation. Naturally, I was indignant at the militarists and the government authorities for having duped the people and suppressed criticism among them, for having had the audacity to pursue the most irrational of policies in violation of international law, causing our nation to be stripped of its honor before the rest of the world. But in the strict sense, we Japanese are all responsible for the failure and disgrace, since we were unable to restrain the reckless ways of the government and the militarists. After those who are directly to be blamed for the disasters that befell Japan, the leaders in the world of social and political thought are most responsible. There is no excusing the standpoint of the innocent bystander so often adopted by members of the intelligentsia.

I am deeply convinced of the fact that, in the last analysis, everyone is responsible, collectively, for social affairs. Once one assumes this standpoint of social responsibility, there can be no doubt that metanoetics is indispensable for each person at each moment. Therefore, metanoetics, like morality, can provide the way to a universal philosophy. Furthermore, when metanoetics is viewed in relation to the *Kyōgyōshinshō* of Shinran, our guide in metanoetical thinking, his profound idea of "returning to this world from the Pure Land" (*gensō-ekō*, 還相回向) suggests a distinctive theory of religious society established on the ideal of "fraternity"—an ideal of equality within the social order, which at the same time recognizes the ranks of elder and younger in the religious sense. This is somewhat different from the equality that emerges from love of neighbor in Christianity. There is no disputing the fact that freedom based on democracy has led to forms of socialism that run counter to the ideal of freedom. The unity of freedom and equality is not a self-evident fact, but a project difficult to achieve. In order to achieve this goal of unity, is it not necessary that the idea of fraternity, restored to its original meaning, mediate in the concrete the conflict between freedom and equality? The idea of "returning to this world" in the Shin sect thus offers a concrete suggestion for a basic principle of social structure, and opens broad vistas in the philosophy of history insofar as it represents the ideal of the compassionate way of the bodhisattva in Mahāyāna Buddhism. We may, therefore, conclude that metanoetics is more than a mere exercise carried out in the realms of abstract thought.

During the fall of last year, I devoted myself assiduously to developing metanoetics into a form of philosophy. From the point of its very inception, metanoetics needs to be developed metanoetically. That is, it should not be a "philosophy of metanoesis" in the sense that it treats an object called metanoesis. Neither should it be a phenomenological or *lebensphilosophisch* interpretation that applies its own established methodology to the investigation of metanoesis. Metanoetics is a philosophy that has to be erected at the very point that all prior philosophical standpoints and methods have been negated in their entirety. It is a philosophical method of "destruction" more radical than even the methodical skepticism of Descartes. It cannot be treated on the same level as philosophy up to the present inasmuch as it is a philosophy achieved through a death-and-resurrection process of transformation. Only one awakened to other-power, who practices metanoetics in "action-witness" (*gyō-shō*), can witness its truth in self-consciousness. In this sense, I gain personal conviction of the truth of metanoetics by means of my own action-witness, and thereby deepen my metanoetic self-consciousness.

In the course of my reflections, I discovered a logic that functions throughout metanoetical thinking, which I call "absolute criticism." Philosophy based on reason can with good cause be described as a philosophy of self-power: the reason it presupposes as its basis is bound to fall into antinomies in the encounter with actual reality. Kant's remedy, as laid out in the *Critique of Pure Reason*, was to narrow the scope of reason to make room for faith. The solution is clearly incomplete. In the radical self-consciousness of being driven to the extreme, reason can only be torn to shreds in absolute disruption, after which such self-affirming reason is no longer of any use to us. Absolute criticism means that reason, faced with the absolute crisis of its dilemma, surrenders itself of its own accord. In the course of this critical task, the subject that is undertaking the critique of pure reason cannot remain a mere bystander at a safe remove from the criticism. The subject of the critique cannot avoid getting tangled in its own web and exposing itself to self-criticism. It cannot avoid dismemberment by the absolute dilemma of its own thought. Yet in the very midst of this absolute disruption and contradiction, the power of contradiction is itself negated: the absolute contradiction contradicts itself. At this point, an absolute conversion takes place and philosophy is restored through the power of the transcendent as a "philosophy that is not a philosophy."

Thus metanoetics includes within itself the logic of absolute criticism. We arrive at metanoetics by way of the critique of reason—reason in both its theoretical and practical aspects—if the critique is pursued radically. This is in fact how the Kantian criticism of the *Critique of Pure Reason* developed into the Hegelian critique of the *Phenomenology of Spirit*. The transcendental dialectic of the former was transformed into the true dialectic of the latter. Still, Hegel maintained that the absolute disruption and contradiction in reason could be overcome by the unity of reason, and that the state of reason prior to the antinomies could be recovered in its simple self-identity, because reason is able to embrace in self-consciousness its own death and resurrection by means of infinite thought in the form of the concept (*Begriff*). This led him to neglect the important fact that the resurrected life of reason is not the same as the former state of reason prior to negation, but comes about only through the activity of absolute transformation—that is, through the activity of absolute nothingness, which is neither life nor death. In the resurrection into new life, self-consciousness is only a temporary axis of transformation posited as a subjective center accessible only through action-faith-witness. But Hegel thought that the identity of absolute contradictories could be grasped in the form of the concept quite apart from any such temporary subjective center, that infinite thinking provided the unity of an infinite circle that could embrace the whole within itself.

Here we see why Hegel's concept of reason was unable to break through the constraints of the Aristotelian logic of identity completely. His failure is itself a negation of the dialectic in that the practical transformation of the self is uprooted at the core under the sway of the objective concept. And since the nonobjectifiable and nonmaterializable subjective self ceases to exist, concept turns into substance and absolute idealism into materialism. We are left with a nonexistentialism that denies the practical transformation of the self any mediating role. Not surprisingly, instead of self-consciousness in absolute nothingness we have only substance as being. As a result, Hegel's thought, which shows an affinity here with the thought of Spinoza, could evolve into Marxism.

In contrast, metanoetics remains grounded entirely on a standpoint of practical transformation and thereby open to the Great Nay-*qua*-Great Compassion (*daihi-soku-daihi*, 大非即大悲). It is a standpoint on which the transformative unity of the death-and-resurrection of the self is practiced and witnessed by means of a radical criticism leading to transformation by other-power, which I would argue is the final culmination of the Kantian critique of reason. The dialectic of absolute mediation that Hegel aimed for but was unable to attain is carried out in practice-faith in a way that was closed to Hegel's contemplation of reason. Here metanoetics is akin to Schelling's theory of freedom which, in opposition to Hegelian reason, probed deeply into Kant's notion of absolute evil. There is also a similarity here to Heidegger's existential philosophy, which, under the influence of Kierkegaard's opposition to Hegel's intellectual philosophy, strove to maintain the authentic self as the center of practical transformation. At the same time, metanoetics is critical of Schelling's speculative philosophy of "construction" insofar as it claims a standpoint of self-consciousness in absolute mediation. It likewise stands opposed to the existentialism of Heidegger, which, by diverging from Kierkegaard's "existentialism of faith" to assert the freedom of the self, has affinities with the atheistic thought of Nietzsche. In contrast with these positions, metanoesis seeks throughout to maintain a standpoint of action-faith through other-power, and thereby to insist on a relationship of reciprocal mediatory transformation between the absolute and the self. Moreover, the redeeming truth that the absolute can function only as the power of absolute mediation can reach self-consciousness by way of reciprocal mediatory activity between relative selves. In this sense, the transformation through vertical mediation between the absolute and the self must also be realized in horizontal social relationships between my self and other selves. Thus, metanoetics is able to overcome the deficiencies of individualism common to both Schelling's doctrine of freedom and Heidegger's existential philosophy, and to make the abstract truth of each more concrete through the realization of responsibility in "social solidarity." Shinran's idea of "returning to the world" (*gensō*) referred to earlier recommends such a doctrine of social solidarity. It gives the idea of a "logic of the specific" (*shu no ronri*, 種の論理), which I have long advocated as a theory of social existence, a new and deeper basis.

In light of the above considerations, I was confident that metanoetics, as a philosophical principle, would provide sufficient grounds for a new philosophy. This is why I was able to return to philosophy with peace of mind. With this idea of a renewed philosophy in mind, I ascended the platform to deliver my final series of lectures at Kyoto Imperial University. Although a new Cabinet had been formed at the time, in accord with the long-suppressed wishes of the Japanese people, it proved no less ineffective in improving the situation. Fears and anxieties grew stronger by the day, as the destitution and disaster continued to spread. While I shared in the deepening pessimism of the people of Japan, I had at least one source of consolation and encouragement. And thus, with a sense of gratitude to other-power, I presented my lectures, which began in October of 1944 and ended in December, under the title "Metanoetics." During this period, I also offered an outline of my lectures in the form of a public lecture with the same title sponsored by the Kyoto Philosophical Society. Such is the history of how my philosophy of metanoetics came to be.

In preparing this last lecture, I developed the logic of "absolute criticism," and through the "destruction" of the Western philosophy in which I had been trained for many years, I attempted a reconstruction from a metanoetical point of view. It was for me a great joy to discover in the course of reconsidering the thought of such figures as Meister Eckhart, Pascal, and Nietzsche that problems I had never been able to penetrate deeply now grew clear to me—at least as far as my limited abilities would allow. Naturally, I concentrated my energies in the main on a metanoetical reading of the *Kyōgyōshinshō*, the results of which filled several notebooks. In order to make a coherent whole of my lectures, I was able to work only on the essentials. A single three-month term was too short; if I had had a year to lecture, it still would have been too short. At any rate, I was approaching the retirement age set for university professors, and on top of that, weak of constitution as I am, I fell ill in

November. But so ardent was my desire to complete the lectures at all costs that I left my sickbed just long enough to deliver them. It was with a great sigh of relief that I completed the final lecture in December, after which I spent the rest of the winter in bed. I have no words to express my gratitude for the kindness shown me by my students and colleagues at that time. Since February of this year I have been legally retired from the university professorship. Looking back over my career of twenty-five years at Kyoto Imperial University, I felt regret for the personal inadequacies that inhibited the performance of my duties, but at the same time I was full of thanks to Heaven and to all those whose help enabled me to see my academic career to its end despite my poor health.

But once I had turned my attention away from my private life to focus on the destiny of our nation, my regret and sadness were without bounds. Even after a second change of Cabinet, there was still no improvement. The mainland of Japan was under attack, and the ravages of war were beyond description. Notwithstanding these calamities and even though the situation was considerably worse than before, I was no longer sunk in despair but endeavored to concentrate on the problems that lay before me. In this I could feel the power of metanoetics. Far from relinquishing myself to despair, I was transformed, converted, by the absolute and elevated to a spirit of detachment. This confirmed my conviction that metanoetics is as strong as we are weak. After a thoroughgoing and humble assessment of my own powerlessness, I experienced the grace of resurrection through the compassion of other-power.

Toward the end of July I decided to move out of Kyoto and into a rural area, the increasing severity of the air raids having made it impossible for me to remain in a large city. It was entirely through the kind assistance of my close friends that I was able to make the transition in safety. Living here in these quiet surroundings refreshed me in mind and body, though I remained quite as weak as before. My spirits rose during the following two months as I began to order my notes into a longer study, the results of which are contained in this book. At first I had no clear idea of how to pursue its publication, though I did consider serializing it in the pages of the *Journal of Philosophical Studies* (*Tetsugaku kenkyū*, 哲学研究) as I had done before with other works.

Then, in mid-August, Japan met with the unhappy fate of unconditional surrender, plunging the entire nation—myself included—into deep sorrow. We the Japanese people have to perform metanoesis when we reflect on how this catastrophe came to be. Looking back, I have come to realize that my own metanoesis of a year earlier was destined to prepare the future for my country. The thought of this coincidence brought me great sorrow and pain. Of course, I despise the shamelessness of the leaders primarily responsible for the defeat who are now urging the entire nation to repentance only in order to conceal their own complicity. Metanoesis is not something to be urged on others before one has performed it for oneself. Still, it is clear that we the nation of Japan, having fallen into these tragic and appalling circumstances, should practice metanoesis (*zange*) together as a people. Since I am one of those who believe in the collective responsibility of a nation, I am convinced that all of us should engage in collective metanoesis (*sō-zange*, 総懺悔) in the literal sense of the term. I feel compelled to conclude that metanoetics is not only my own private philosophy but a philosophical path the entire nation should follow.

Since metanoesis implies remorse and sorrow, it is necessarily accompanied by feelings of shame and disgrace. This is true both in the way that Shinran used the word and in the connotation of the Latin word *paenitentia*, which originally carried a sense of "pang." There can be no *paenitentia*, no *zange,* without pain. But the heart of metanoesis is the experience of conversion or transformation: sorrow and lament are turned into joy, shame and disgrace into gratitude. Hence when I say that our nation has no way to walk but the way of *zange* (metanoetics), I do not mean that we should sink into despair and stop there, but that we can hope to be transformed through resurrection and regeneration. It is true that metanoesis is the activity of conversion and transformation performed by other-power (*tariki*)—I can personally attest to the truth of this through my own "faith-witness" (*shin-shō*)—and I cannot but recommend it to all our people. It is as an act of gratitude that I offer metanoetics (*zangedō*, 懺悔道) as a philosophy that belongs rightly not only to me but to all of you. With this thought in mind, I felt I ought to publish this work as quickly as possible. Of course, in making this recommendation I have no intention of forcing others to accept this philosophy. Nonetheless, it is my sincere desire to offer metanoetics to those of the Japanese people who seek a philosophy at the present time.

In spite of the suffering that goes along with defeat, the suppression of thought that we had to endure for many years has now come to an end through the intervention of foreign powers, and freedom of thought is being extolled as an ideal to which we can all aspire. As is evident to all of us, emancipation from state control has led the people of Japan to rally behind the development of culture as the sole means of rebuilding our nation. I find it a rather curious phenomenon that intellectuals in a country that has just suffered defeat should be stimulated by their freedom of activity to embrace belief in culture. So heavy was the oppression we endured for so many years, at first I am tempted to join them. But can a nation compelled to surrender, with liberalism being forced upon it from without and the development of culture urged from within, be expected to come up with the spiritual resources needed to create a new culture simply because the oppressive controls of the past have been removed? True freedom is not something one receives from another; one has to acquire it for oneself. Even should there be a flowering of new culture in such circumstances as ours, it would be like blossoms on a hothouse plant: beautiful to the eye but too weak and shallow of root to survive in the open air.

Here we see the paradox that true and living culture is not something that can be made by culture worshipers; if anything, their "culturism" is a symptom of the decadence of culture. In general, I have always been critical of abstract ideals like culturism and culture-worship, and I am especially reluctant to approve of the present stress on "culture" since I place no faith in its future. It must be said that the very ones now optimistically espousing the cause of culture are mere onlookers who have no sense of social responsibility to the nation. A moment's glance at some of the current social problems— the hunger and poverty of the vast majority of the people in sharp contrast with the luxury enjoyed by a very few owing to the maldistribution of food and goods, the stagnation and paralysis of industry despite the large number of soldiers returning to the ranks of the unemployed—shows how difficult it will be to rebuild our war-devastated nation. One step in the wrong direction, even one day's delay, may be enough to spell the total ruin of our land. Unless we all undertake the new way of *zange*, free ourselves from the evil institutions of the past, and collaborate in carrying out whatever changes are necessary in the social system, there is no possibility of reconstruction. The only course open to us at present is metanoetics, not culturism. Does not the Old Testament prophet Jeremiah show us the way?

Speaking frankly, I would say that the occupying powers themselves have yet to achieve a harmony between democracy and socialism, and that this will remain a difficult problem for them in the foreseeable future. But so long as that problem is not resolved, it is inevitable that these nations will be beset by a host of difficulties both internal and external. All nations, be they democratic or socialist, have their own need to perform metanoesis. If there is any vocation of significance for world history in the reconstruction of our nation, it lies in the search for a middle path between these two ideologies, a middle path that is neither democracy nor socialism but moves freely between the two systems to make use of the strengths of both. And if this is so, then metanoetics must become the philosophy not only of Japan but of all humanity.

Will not the true meaning of humanity be found when people enter into absolute peace with one another, helping one another in a spirit of reconciliation and cooperation, seeking mutual emancipation and salvation in the conversion of the self-affirming ego into no-self through the mediatory activity of absolute nothingness? For it is the self-affirming ego that is the cause of all conflict among people, while in the life of absolute peace all contribute their best efforts to deepen the joy of fraternal love. For this reason, all people everywhere need to perform *zange* collectively. I do not think I am arguing from a self-centered point of view in making the claim that world history has reached a turning point at the present moment in which all philosophy of any significance should be grounded in metanoetics. Naturally, I have no intention of offering myself as a guide for the world; that would run counter to the very spirit of metanoetics. "Shinran had not a single disciple," wrote Shinran in the *Tannishō*. His idea of a horizontal fellowship, not of a vertical or authoritarian teacher-disciple relationship, laid the foundations for an "equality" in which no one enjoyed any special privilege. What Shinran said of invoking the name of Amida—"It is a matter of your decision whether you accept *nenbutsu* or reject it"—I should also say of metanoetics. And this, too, confirms my belief that metanoetics, carried out in this spirit of freedom and equality, can become a philosophy for all people.

In a spirit of gratitude for having been able to see this work to its completion, I would like, in the first place, to express my sincerest thanks to all those who have assisted me. Their kindness is something I shall never forget. I should also like to mention my gratitude to my wife who, despite her illness, has served me faithfully these many years and enabled me to devote myself entirely to my work. And finally, I would beg the indulgence of my readers for having been made to endure so lengthy a preface as this.

Tanabe Hajime
Kita-Karuizawa
October 1945

1.

The Philosophical Meaning of Metanoetics

The term "metanoetics" (*zangedō*) as I shall be using it here has yet to receive general acceptance as part of philosophical terminology. I for one have never come across the word in the area of philosophy. Someone may object at this point: Are you not merely trying to disguise an obsolescence in your own thought and claim originality for your philosophy by coining a new word? To this question I do not intend to respond with an apology. Since it seems to me an absolutely undeniable fact that philosophy is possible only as metanoetics, it no longer matters to me if my views arouse such suspicions. If there be some selfish motive in my thinking, which distorts the objectivity of my approach, it is I who am responsible for it, and it is I who must reflect on myself and perform *zange* for it.

To my shame I must confess that I am far from being noble-minded and totally free of fault in this regard. The temptation is ever lurking in my heart, and indeed if I examine my motives carefully, the very fact of raising the question myself may turn out to be a symptom of it. Be that as it may, metanoetical reflection urges me to examine myself completely, to recognize this shameful tendency within myself and to perform *zange* for it. Once I have submitted myself to this requirement and devoted myself to the practice of *zange*, I am met by a wondrous Power that relieves the torment of my shameful deeds and fills me with a deep sense of gratitude. *Zange* is, as it were, a balm for the pain of repentance, and at the same time the source of an absolute light that paradoxically makes the darkness shine without expelling it. The experience of accepting this transforming power of *zange* as a grace from *tariki* (other-power) is, as we shall see shortly, the very core of metanoetics.

Hence the claim that metanoetics is the only way to my philosophical revival, and that no other philosophy is conceivable to me than one based on such metanoetical self-consciousness, points to an objective reality beyond all possibility of doubt, despite any arbitrary, subjective, or dishonest motives I may harbor in my breast. So powerful is metanoetics that it sweeps aside all doubt about itself. This may, it seems to me, be taken as evidence of its truth. I can therefore confess frankly and with conviction that metanoetics is, as a matter of necessity, my philosophy. As far as I am concerned, no philosophy is possible without such confession (ὁμολογία) and *zange* (repentance, μετάνοια). It is precisely the self-awakening, which comes to one on the way of *zange* that constitutes metanoetics, or *zangedō*. Intrinsic to the way of *zange* is the self-awakening of those who follow it and the wisdom thus attained. It is for this very reason that metanoetics can be designated a philosophy.

There is another reason for using a word derived from a Western language, "metanoetics," together with the Japanese term "*zangedō.*" "Metanoetics" carries the sense of "meta-noetics," denoting philologically a transcending of noetics, or in other words, a transcending of metaphysical philosophy based on contemplation or intellectual intuition achieved by the use of reason. "Meta-noetics" means transcending the contemplative or speculative philosophy of intellectual intuition as it is usually found in the realms of thought based on reason. Here we have a very important characteristic by which metanoetics is distinguished from ordinary mysticism or philosophies of intellectual intuition: it is not a philosophy founded on the intuitive reason of *jiriki* (self-power), but rather a philosophy founded on action-faith-witness (*gyō-shin-shō*) mediated by the transformative power of *tariki* (other-power). If I may introduce at this point two key concepts characteristic of the teachings of the Pure Land sect of Shin Buddhism—*ōsō* 往相 or "going toward" the Pure Land, and *gensō* 還相 or "returning to" this world from the Pure Land—metanoetics may be described as a philosophy of action following the path of *gensō*, while ordinary mysticism may be described as contemplative speculation following the path of *ōsō*. The doctrine of *gensō* is thus of special significance in enabling metanoetics to bring about a revival of philosophy. The term "metanoetics" helps to express these ideas clearly in that metanoetics implies, on the one hand, a self-awakening through a "way" of repentance, a "thinking-afterward" (μετάνοια), and on the other, suggests a self-conscious transcending of intuition and contemplation (μετανόησις). This is why *zangedō* can be termed a μετανοητική or "metanoetics." The full meaning of metanoetics will be explained in detail later as this work develops, but at least these few comments seemed in order here at the outset.

As mentioned before, the very fact that I advocate metanoetics as a philosophy itself expresses my option for the way of *zange*. Only through metanoetics can I reflect on its philosophical significance. In other words, I discuss "philosophy as metanoetics" metanoetically. Therefore, I am not concerned with how others will take it. All criticism of my standpoint I willingly accept as a further opportunity to perform *zange*. Being evil and untruthful by nature, I feel a deep sense of shame and fear that my confession, or *zange*, must need contain insincerity and impurity. Worse than that, I find myself unable to overcome the ingrained evil of feeling proud over performing *zange*. However severe the criticism against me may be, I cannot possibly excuse my vanity, folly, perversity, and wickedness. I am prepared to accept such criticism with humility; I am determined to reflect upon myself as thoroughly as possible and to perform *zange* for my dishonesty and shamelessness. This, I believe, is the only way left open to me. Indeed my power, by itself alone, is so ineffective, and my folly and wickedness so tenacious, that if left to myself, I could not perform even this *zange*. Nevertheless, the *tariki* (other-power) that acts within me exercises its power in a way so overwhelming that it obliges me to perform *zange*. Thus it is that I perform this action of *zange* solely by following this power. And this is the reason, as I stated before, that metanoetics forces me to treat it metanoetically. In this sense, I may say that the evidence, or witness (*shō*), of the existential truth of metanoetics comes to light. Metanoia is not confined to "meta-noia," that is, a "thinking-afterward" or repentance that implies a painful recollection of one's past sins, or a feeling of remorse accompanied by the profound wish that those sins had not been committed. It is rather the "breaking-through" (*Durchbruch*) of a self that hitherto had moved exclusively within the realms of discursive thinking and reflection. In reality, as long as the self affirms its being directly, true repentance is by no means possible. This is the reason that although repentance is an act of the self, it is at the same time a breaking-through of the self, a forsaking of the self. As Hegel says, when we acknowledge our responsibility for those of our actions that inevitably result in sin, this recognition of our own sin implies the tragic downfall of our own being and a submission to the judgment of fate and destiny. So, too, does *zange*, or metanoesis, imply the downfall and the forsaking of the self. As such, *zange* means simply following a disciplined way toward one's own death.

Moreover, human sin and evil are not accidental phenomena; nor do they signify merely the evil acts of individual persons. They constitute rather a negative determination of our being itself that lies at the foundation of human existence in general, something like what Kant speaks of as "radical sin." As long as *Existenz* is established by determining the existence of the self spontaneously by oneself, one is endowed with a freedom analogous to the freedom of the absolute in order to respond to the transformative power of that absolute. But at the same time, as a consequence of this freedom there is a concealed tendency to forget one's relativity and presume to be the absolute. This clearly is human arrogance and shows how prone we are to extend the "analogous" structure of our being into the extreme assumption of being directly "identical"—namely, to confuse our role of mediatory activity executed in absolute negativity on behalf of the absolute with an immediate affirmation of our freedom, oblivious of the very fact that our existence can be founded only on a principle of transformation, or conversion, that presents itself through self-negation as the result of standing in contradictory confrontation. An "existence" whose principle is freedom cannot by itself eliminate the sort of latent evil we see produced by an innate tendency toward arrogance, the evil most accurately termed "original sin."

Human freedom in its true sense is rooted solely in the grace of the absolute. This grace negates our being in order to convert us to a new being by awakening in us a consciousness of the unfathomable depth of our sin and thereby leading us to recognize that this innate freedom is, in reality, the very cause of our lacking freedom in the true sense, and that only the negation of the former assures us of the latter. It is only when we forsake ourselves and entrust our being to the grace of *tariki* (other-power) that our existence can acquire true freedom. In short, life consists of the continuous practice of "death-and-resurrection." Meta-noesis is practicing, and also being made to practice, this "death-and-resurrection" according to criteria of the value and meaning of our existence, or, more correctly, of the valuelessness and meaninglessness of our existence. It must begin with a casting away of the self that is no longer qualified to exist because it is forced to recognize, through suffering and sorrow, that its being is valueless.

This means that metanoesis (*zange*) is the exact opposite of despair in the ordinary sense, which consists of getting discouraged at ourselves, asserting our negative self, and growing increasingly vexed to the point of forgetting the fact that we have been condemned to original sin. In contrast, *zange* is a true self-surrender that consists not in a recalcitrant despair but in a submissive one, a despair in which we renounce all hope for and claim to justification. Submissive despair thus preserves the permanent wish that our being be as it ought to be. Through such despair we suffer from the serious discrepancy in our being between that which "ought to be" and that which is "as it is." Through *zange* we regard ourselves as truly not deserving to be, and thereby enter fully into a state of genuine despair leading to self-surrender.

Amazingly enough, however, the power urging us to forsake ourselves is at the same time the very power that reaffirms our once negated being. After the submissive acknowledgment and frank confession of our valuelessness and meaninglessness, of our rebelliousness in asserting ourselves despite our valuelessness, we rediscover our being. In this way, our being undergoes at once both negation and affirmation through absolute transformation. In other words, the being that performed metanoesis (*zange*) experiences resurrection by salvation. Moreover, even should this resurrected being sin again, the result would not be to add further negativity to the nature of its new being. For as long as we perform *zange* continuously, there is no change whatever in the process of our being—that is, in the transforming of the negation into affirmation through *tariki*. One who truly performs continuous *zange* is made to surrender self-affirmation, and yet always experiences the wondrous power through which negation is continuously transformed into affirmation. This constancy in one's *zange* is what is called "unshakable or irreversible faith." In this sense the structure of metanoesis is one of infinite spiral process. It is, so to speak, an "eternal recurrence" (Nietzsche's *ewige Wiederkunft*) in the true sense of the term, namely, a genuine "repetition" through the power of the transcendent, and is therefore the fulfillment of the moment by eternity. Accordingly, an increase of finite, particular sins never threatens the fundamental structure of metanoesis in any way. On the contrary, repentance of such sin, the metanoetical awareness of the accumulation of sins, is the true mediating force between our being and the activity of the absolute; it is the infinite element within our finite being. For this reason, we confirm in ourselves the fact that the sins of our being, including even the insincerity of our *zange*, are forgiven, and our being thus is resurrected.

This affirmative aspect of *zange*, as opposed to its negative aspect, is conversion (transformation). Hence the term "metanoia" (μετάνοια) can, as I have stated before, imply both conversion and repentance. *Zange* should be as infinitely continuous as conversion and should, therefore, envelop within itself the infinite repetition of "eternal return." Conversion, however, is transformed negativity, the negativity of metanoesis turned into affirmation through the transforming act of the absolute. This is why we explain them as two aspects of the same thing. The power of salvation through which the self-surrender in our *zange* is transformed into affirmation or conversion inevitably impels us to faith in such power as the absolute power of transformation.

Not only is *zange* accomplished by salvation through *tariki* (other-power), but *tariki* itself is realized in this world through the mediatory operation of *zange*. Thus, the way of mutual transformation and reciprocal interpenetration of *tariki* and *zange* is open to us, and by practicing this religious way of self-consciousness we are able to realize the truth that the activity of *jiriki* is at the same time the realization of *tariki*. In short, religious faith (*shin*) and practice (*gyō*) are one. This means that, although *zange* leads to salvation, it should not be considered the same as "repentance," which is the necessary condition for one's entering into heaven, since *zange* is the "practice-faith" (*gyō-shin*) attained in and through *tariki*. It, therefore, involves both joy and gratitude, which are the very witness (*shō*) of its truth. In a word, *zange* is simply a trinity of action, faith, and witness (*gyō-shin-shō*).

The self-surrender effected as well as performed by one's own free will produces the grace of a resurrected self that brings with it the joy of a regenerated life. Needless to say, the suffering of *zange* is accompanied by the bitterness of repentance and the sorrow of despair. This profound pain, however, is at the same time the medium of joy and the source of bliss. Joy abounds in the midst of pain, not because we are able to participate in the joy of entering into heaven, having reformed ourselves by repentance, but rather because *zange* turns us toward the bliss of *nirvāṇa*, however sinful and perverted we may be. The joy and gratitude that stem from our being included in the compassion of the absolute and thus redeemed from our original sin arise neither apart from the pain of *zange* nor after it. The joy and pain of *zange* interpenetrate each other. Since *zange* itself is not caused by *jiriki* but by the grace of *tariki*, we have only to surrender to the latter, and in our surrender to experience both the pain of negation and the joy of affirmation. Further, the joy thus brought about by *tariki* necessarily leads to gratitude, the expression of which in turn leads to cooperation with *tariki* in assisting others to share in one's joy. Therein lies the proof and witness for the truth of *zange*.

Moreover, since absolute *tariki* (other-power) itself must rely on what, from its vantage point, is "other-power" (namely, human freedom), it functions only when relative beings recognize the mediatory role of their independent self-consciousness. Thus absolute *tariki* manifests itself in horizontal relationships between relative beings, and the witness and evidence (*shō*) for the truth of *zange* is realized as a "return to" the world from the Pure Land (*gensō*). In other words, *zange* is a trinity of action, faith, and witness (*gyō-shin-shō*), so that *zange*, faith, and joy coupled with gratitude for grace become inseparable. This results from the fact that *zange* is a transforming force whose structure may be characterized as *tariki-qua-jiriki*.[1] *Zange* comes about as an absolute transformation by *tariki*; it is not caused by *jiriki* alone. *Tariki* is the power of salvation itself that affirms the relative being of the self that has been negated, regenerating it through "death-and-resurrection." We might say that our salvation is realized through the medium of *zange*. One should not think that the transformation or resurrection we are speaking of here implies a mere return to the routine life of former relativity. It is rather a transcending of the opposition between negation and affirmation, a conversion into a new dimension that is neither life nor death—the realm of absolute nothingness—for the sake of salvation. At the same time, *tariki* performs its salvific function through the mediating activity of relative selves and thus becomes immanent in them. Here we see the true nature of *tariki*. Although *zange* is an act of the self, it does not belong to the self, but is an act of self-surrender and must be an act of absolute nothingness. Thus *zange*, as distinguished from the despair of arrogance, includes the despair of submission in which no self-assertion of the ego performing *zange* remains.

The original vow by Amida Buddha, it is believed by those who profess Pure Land Buddhism, symbolizes this power of absolute transformation or conversion. The compassion of the original vow manifests itself as the Great Nay (*daihi*). It is the quintessence of pure faith in other-power (*tariki*), one may legitimately maintain, that the Great Nay, performed in an act of absolute negation or in the activity of absolute nothingness, becomes the Great Compassion (*daihi*) of salvation through the realization of faith and witness in mature religious consciousness. That "Great Compassion-*qua*-Great Nay," or, in other words, "love-*qua*-absolute nothingness," is realized by one's action-faith-witness (*gyō-shin-shō*) is the very essence of this religious consciousness. It is clear that the Great Compassion should be the Great Nay, or that true love in a religious sense should be grounded in nothingness, since both the Great Compassion and true love must come from the heart of the no-self. But this is only an ontological consideration. Religious consciousness consists in its genuine experience, or precisely in the self-consciousness realized through this experience. ...

To be sure, insofar as the *zange* we have been speaking of does not belong to the performance of *jiriki* (self-power) but is based on *tariki* (other-power), one cannot practice *zange* by oneself alone. It is realized only according to the prompting of other-power. At the same time, because the absolute subject of other-power is absolute nothingness (which is, therefore, the real subject of the activity of the absolute transformation), it must be mediated by the relative self. Instead of having its ground in "the self-identity of absolute contradictories," absolute nothingness must be grounded in the absolute mediatory activity of one's religious existence through "death-and-resurrection." Hence, absolute nothingness can also be called *tariki*, since it is experienced through faith-witness (*shin-shō*) as the principle of the negation and transformation of the self. In this sense, *tariki* inevitably depends *on jiriki* as its mediatory "other." This is why it is written, "Ask, and you shall receive; seek, and you shall find" (Matt. 7: 7).

This reciprocity is also the core of *tariki* faith. Since the Buddha is the one who seeks nothing, one falls into self-contradiction if one *desires* directly to become the Buddha. But if one does not seek at all to become the Buddha, one will never be able to awaken to one's Buddhahood. The way of self-contradiction involved in residing in a spirit of detachment from the desire to become Buddha in spite of a deep aspiration to become Buddha—in other words, of seeking Buddhahood earnestly without seeking it—is the only path open to everyone by virtue of being closed. This is not to say that the contradictions will be solved once and for all. This critical but contradictory way remains forever impassable to any who aspire to traverse it as a being without self-negation; and even if one succeeds in passing through it, one cannot avoid being cut to pieces by the blades of antinomy. This impassable barrier of antinomies, even as it remains closed, will become passable if the contradictions are recognized as penetrable though still unresolved, if one throws oneself into this difficult situation and surrenders oneself in absolute submission to its requirements without any resistance on the part of discursive (discriminatory) thinking, for in so doing one has abandoned oneself thoroughly to the situation and decided to die in the depths of the dilemma of its contradictions. This means that what is impossible with *jiriki* becomes possible with *tariki*, though both *tariki* and *jiriki* remain complementary to one another. The practice of *zange* by *tariki* thus includes within itself at the same time the action of *jiriki*.

On the same grounds that the pivot enabling the transformation of self-*qua*-other or other-*qua*-self becomes self-conscious through the experience of faith-witness (*shin-shō*), we can explain what takes place there as an absolute transformation founded on absolute nothingness. Taken on its own, apart from this experience of faith-witness, absolute nothingness is an unmediated transcendent that in fact remains being even though we call it nothingness. Considered as self-identical, absolute nothingness approaches being insofar as it lacks the mediatory functions necessary for absolute nothingness. Thus it comes to be seen as the content of contemplative intuition, not that of self-consciousness in action. On this view, there is no longer any metanoesis, since there is no need for transformation when one can be confirmed to the absolute identity encompassing the discrepancy between self and others. On the contrary, what characterizes metanoesis is the fact that, although it is my own action, at the same time it is not my own action; or conversely, that the absolute transformation that is not my action nonetheless is my action. There is, therefore, sufficient reason to maintain that we can recommend to anyone the practice of metanoesis. It is in this sense that I recommend following the way of metanoesis as the only way along which we can experience, in our faith-witness, the absolute truth of the Great Nay-*qua*-Great Compassion. ...

Properly speaking, the absolute as a "returning to" this world is the motivating force behind our performance of *zange*. But mystical thinking remains far removed from the true standpoint of faith that Shinran stresses in the *Kyōgyōshinshō*:

> Never discuss whether Amida Buddha accepts you or not: The decisive question is whether you have changed your heart or not.[2]

... It is not possible through the logic of the self-identity of absolute contradictories to determine concretely in what direction the process of absolute transformation is moving or to plot the precise course of its spiral development. That logic remains in the realm of noetics, tied to abstract equations. It has yet to attain the concreteness of absolute mediation, wherein the absolute grants relative selves their freedom, making them the axis around which the absolute itself rotates, serving and assisting in the independent mediatory role of absolute transformation. There each relative self, through its conversion and transformation, becomes in turn the temporary axis of the transformative rotation that we call conversion by the absolute. In this way, the center of the self, which is at the same time the axis of absolute transformation, is located in the decision of each religious existence that constitutes it as a true self. From this standpoint, any point can be viewed as the center of mediation from which coordinates can be drawn to determine the transformative movement of the absolute in time and space. This origin of these coordinates may be likened to the existence of self-consciousness, an existence concretized here and now from among an infinite number of possible points. To claim some other universal *topos* apart from such points would be to diverge from the authentic standpoint of action-faith (*gyō-shin*). ...

We cannot determine the special orientation that the transformative process takes at each point of a mere topological deduction, because a special orientation is produced only as the result of the negative transformation through "death-and-resurrection." This means that a philosophy with such a standpoint lacks the idea of "returning to" (*gensō*) as well as that of a "mediation by the *specific*," which together provide the social determination of our being through ethical action performed in the community. By reciprocity in the specific, the category of species (society in its immediate state) can surpass the state of struggle among forces in competition within it, thus elevating the specific to a concrete universal. Each individual can then represent this concrete universal by bringing together various antagonistic forces within the specific and channeling their opposing orientations in one particular direction. The focus of the dynamic unity of this process is the metanoetical axis around which scattered and opposing forces are organized to work together.

In short, my metanoesis—my conversion—consists in a shift from *jiriki* to *tariki*. Put in positive terms, metanoetics represents the philosophy of other-power. But in deference to the negative way that I have been following so far, I should first like to make clear its negative aspect, that is to say, the transformative power of its negativity.

The methodical skepticism advanced by Descartes represents a formal transformation of reason, even though his true intention with the *dubito* was to gain sufficient evidence for adopting a new starting point for philosophy. The method is not yet free of subjectivity in that its *dubito* is a mere postulate lacking either content or force by itself. In order to supply the formal transformation implied in the *cogito ergo sum* with real content, and thus to establish it as the true ground of his entire philosophy, Descartes had to rely on background motivations—supplied in his case by his own faith in God. ...

True self-consciousness cannot come about through one continuous medium joining God and the relative. The real awakening of self-consciousness in its religious or existential dimension comes only through the "death-and-resurrection" of a negative transformation that takes place between the absolute and the relative. A transforming mediation between self-surrender in metanoesis and resurrection by other-power can, together with the evidence of self-consciousness, provide philosophy with an objective ground. As the sole self-mediating realization of philosophy, it seems to me that metanoesis is, therefore, open to everyone. There is no other way of providing philosophy in the future with a sufficient transcendent ground for its absolute independence than to take the experience of action-faith-witness (*gyō-shin-shō*) as the starting point of our philosophy.

When we consider metanoesis as the path of philosophy, the salvific power of the "Great Nay-*qua*-Great Compassion" mediated by the absolute transformation of nothingness prevails. But is this not what is called *honganbokori* 本願誇 (assurance of one's own salvation and pride in one's trust in the vow of Amida Buddha)? Is there not a clear contradiction involved here in such an expression of self-affirmation? Does this not deny the self-abandonment at the core of metanoesis? If we could have direct assurance of salvation, there would be no need for mediation by metanoesis, and no reason for philosophy to start anew as metanoetics.

When I maintain that the task of philosophy is to bring about the self-realization of salvation through the transforming mediation of *zange*, I do not mean to make either metanoesis or salvation independent and self-sufficient, and the other derivative. On the contrary, I mean that metanoesis, which belongs to one's self-power in the relative sense, is a necessary mediatory element in the work of salvation—that the relative self of metanoesis serves absolute other-power in a mediating capacity, as a result of which the self experiences a wondrous, transcendent resurrection, a conversion from the metanoesis of self-power to the salvation of other-power. Through the self-consciousness of reason that results from the logic of mediation, philosophy therefore attempts to participate in that wondrous transformation, and thus to perform its task of understanding concrete personal religious experience through the abstract and negative mediation of concepts. Seen from the viewpoint of action-faith, and based on its own evidence, philosophy performs its proper task of logical mediation by explaining how metanoesis and salvation neither belong to an original identity nor simply oppose each other, but rather exist in a dialectical relation based on the principle of "neither-one-nor-two," "neither-identity-nor-difference."

If salvation were something that could be secured without any mediation by metanoesis, it could never signify a spiritual relation of one's spirit to the absolute, but could only be an invariable natural objective relation that exists quite apart from the action of the self. It would no longer be a salvation based on action-faith-witness of spiritual conversion. Moreover, if metanoesis were only an experiential or psychological fact with a limited connotation, of mere relative significance like repentance and regret, it could not be regarded as a transcendental, spiritual experience of converting the relative to the absolute through action-witness. If metanoesis were no more than a faculty of the discriminating mind or nothing more than personal psychological experience, it would have no mediating role in the transformation or conversion of the self; it would have no role in salvation.

Spiritual events raise questions requiring philosophy, questions lying beyond the pale of the sciences and the grasp of the principle of identity. Insofar as events are not all mystery and incomprehensibility, some degree of rational mediation can be adopted to make them understandable. Concepts, as determinations of action through the negations and transformations of thought, serve us in assimilating events whose clarification requires the self-consciousness of reason as well as the logical mediation of philosophy. Anything that can simply be reduced to the principle of identity is not a problem for philosophy. For a problem to belong to philosophy there must be something inconceivable in it, and yet by the same token, something altogether inconceivable and mysterious cannot become a problem for philosophy.

To eliminate the mediation of logic and the self-consciousness of reason from our consideration of such spiritual events poses no problem for philosophy. A problem is posed only when there is some clue of a mediation leading to its solution. This is why both repentance—which is not mediated by salvation—and mere salvation—which is simply dependent on the principle of identity and not mediated by metanoesis—cannot furnish philosophy with problems. Philosophical self-consciousness takes its clue for solving problems only from the mutual mediation of metanoesis and salvation that takes place in one's action-faith: the absolute and the relative form a unity through absolute mediation, whereby transcendence and immanence interpenetrate each other in one's action. The soul, mediated by metanoesis, relinquishes its demand to exist and thus abandons all hope of resurrection through salvation. And only such a soul can be transformed and transcendentally reborn by the transformative power of the Great Compassion into a new existence.

This event is something quite incomprehensible, belonging as it does to both the Great Compassion and the Great Nay, which in turn fall outside of any natural necessity grounded on the principle of identity. If I commit the sin of *honganbokori* referred to earlier, I am presuming on the Great Nay-*qua*-Great Compassion contained in the Vow of Amida Buddha, considering it to be a matter of natural necessity—that is, something within my control—and mistakenly supposing, through the vanity of self-assertiveness, that what is beyond my power is actually within my capacity. It is nothing less than a sin of profanity against absolute compassion. It is a betrayal and abuse of holy truth: an act of disobedience against all the Gods and Buddhas. ...

Only through the mediation of metanoesis, where one renounces oneself as unworthy to exist, can one find entry into the realms of salvation. At the same time, metanoesis allows one who performs it to experience the incomprehensible fact that even the sin of blasphemy can become a mediatory moment in service of salvation. In that case, of course, *honganbokori* ceases to be an obstacle; one experiences only awe and gratitude before the inconceivable power of the Great Nay. In my case, it is not only that I possess a tendency to *honganbokori* in virtue of the radical evil I harbor within me. It is a real and inextricable part of me that continues to exist even after metanoesis and salvation. I must perform *zange* and feel ashamed for the fact that, behind my awe and gratitude before the incomprehensible nature of salvation, there lies so much evil and sin that I cannot escape from the tendency to *honganbokori* that survives my conversion and transformation. Through the incomprehensible power of salvation into which the Great Compassion is poured we are redeemed from evil passion and lusts (*bonnō*) without their being extinguished. Since grave sin and the tendency toward it still remain in *zange*, fear, gratitude, and blasphemy flow together and penetrate one another. It is here that a mediatory relationship is set up among metanoesis, salvation, and sin, a circular process wherein the blasphemy and sin of *honganbokori* can be transformed, through metanoetical mediation, into a moment of salvation without the tendency to sin having been extinguished. This infinite structure of metanoesis causes fear and trembling and yet leads one to rely on salvation, since even the betrayal and profound sin of *honganbokori* are transformed into salvation through the mediation of metanoesis. Whatever passions, lust, and sin exist, they are all converted into salvation by metanoesis without being extinguished.

No salvation of any kind can be realized without the mediation of metanoesis. Salvation and metanoesis stand opposed to each other and negate each other. The two never become one, and yet at the same time are inseparable, flowing into each other without duality. They maintain their dynamic unity by virtue of the dialectical tension of nonidentity and nondifference that exists between them. It is in the nature of their relationship to stand in correlation with the constant risk of separation. The very unsteadiness of this bond excludes any unity founded on the principle of identity seen in *honganbokori*.

As mentioned above, it is the same with self-abandonment in metanoesis mediating a conviction of salvation in spite of—or rather, precisely *because* of—the fear and trembling intermingled with awe and gratitude. By completely giving up one's desire to exist and performing *zange* with head bowed, confessing oneself to be a miserable being, a person encounters through faith-witness the wondrous grace of salvation that turns the negation of the self into an affirmation. ... Thus salvation, as the Great Compassion of Amida's Vow, is accomplished through the power of the Great Nay of absolute transformation. This absolute transformation, whose internal dynamic sets up a serious tension in one's mind between affirmation and negation, shows why absolute mediation and the oneness of salvation still require the relative as the affirmative element that coordinates the spontaneity of the metanoetic self with absolute negativity and thus promotes the element of negative mediation.

In short, the mediation between metanoesis and salvation is established by the truly dialectical correlation of the two. In this way it is clear to us that metanoetics opens a way to salvation for ordinary people. It is a way of dialectical logic, in the sense that any affirmation that takes place in the absolute mediation of absolute transformation includes negation and is transformed into negation, whereas negation is converted into affirmation without being simply eliminated. There can be no doubt that through metanoetics philosophy is opened up for ordinary people.

Socrates, the most authentic of all Greek philosophers, pursued the way of metanoetics through the irony of "the knowledge of ignorance." Although in his case faith in a religiously salvific other-power was not present, the most important point of the Socratic irony, that the confession of ignorance mediates the way to a positive wisdom, is similar to metanoesis. The voice of warning of the Socratic *daimon* liberates self-assertiveness and self-attachment from all adherence to immediate affirmation without negation and nonmediation. The mind, thus disciplined, arrives at an absolute negativity totally free from all obstacles. If we take this to mean that complete freedom cannot be attained by self-power, but requires the warning of a *daimon* to convert self-power toward other-power, we can understand Socrates's attitude to the warning of the *daimon* as a consciousness of self-abandonment in metanoesis. This shifts our reading of Socrates from the ethical stage to the religious, as an implicit development from irony to metanoetics. That dialectics originated in the logic of Socrates is only natural, since he was the first to realize philosophy as a self-consciousness of subjective existence. (It is easy to understand here why Kierkegaard entitled his dissertation *The Concept of Irony with Constant Reference to Socrates.*)[3]

Although Socratic ethical intellectualism did not develop as far as the self-reflective (*für sich*) stage of metanoetics mediated by salvation of other-power, metanoesis is already implicit in its ironical dialectics. In contrast, Shinran's teaching in the *Kyōgyōshinshō* establishes a religion almost completely reliant on salvation by other-power (*tariki*). In this doctrine, *zange* does not figure as a special mediating element in salvation but only functions in the background or is used to introduce Shinran's doctrine of salvation. Given that the subject matter is treated from a religious point of view, this is hardly surprising. At the same time, there is no doubt that this has contributed to the degeneration of Pure Land Shin doctrine away from what Shinran taught, and to its failure to preserve the sincerity of the founder's spirit. In this way, so-called believers lack the very ethical, rational element of metanoesis essential to the mediation of religious salvation.

While *shōdōmon* 聖道門, the self-power "Gate of the Sages," retains some elements of discipline and practice, Pure Land believers ... relax in the indolence of worldly life, believing that they will be saved merely by invoking the name of Amida. These have lost Shinran's profound and severe metanoesis, together with his consciousness of how, without the mercy of Amida, humanity is predestined for hell. Their lives are thus empty of all religious significance, and that—one may say without exaggeration—by reason of having lost the way of metanoesis.

I cannot help but to think here of the mediatory role linking ethical reason inseparably to religion, each confronting the other and yet maintaining its independence from the other. Salvation through the Great Compassion of other-power is not bestowed on indolent, shameless persons who, frustrated with the impotence of self-power, turn in admiration to the omnipotence of other-power, forsaking any further ethical effort on their part. Salvation through other-power is achieved only by those who have used every means at their disposal to seek the truth, who have felt the shame of their own impotence, and finally turned to the practice of metanoesis. It is only through the negative transformation wrought by the Great Nay that the Great Compassion comes about. The joy of salvation is bound as closely to the grief of metanoesis as light is to shadow.

Philosophy begins from a consciousness of the self in conformity with the autonomy of reason and from there extends, through the limitations and determinations of the world, to an awareness of the fact that the self exists through the mediation of absolute nothingness, which sets up a relationship of mutual transformation between self and world. Therefore, philosophy must be carried out in the faith-witness that the self is being-*qua*-nothingness, that is, being (*rūpa*) as a manifestation of emptiness (*śūnyatā*) or absolute nothingness. In this way, the self is resurrected to an existence beyond life and death; it receives the gift of a new life. The action mediating this faith-witness is nothing other than metanoesis.

The absolute that philosophy seeks does not exist apart from absolute nothingness. All being thought to be in opposition to nothingness cannot but be relative. Only true nothingness, an absolute nothingness capable of surpassing being and nothingness, can be absolute. Absolute nothingness establishes being as mediatory for nothingness and permits being to exist independently so that it exists as being-*qua*-nothingness beyond being and nothingness.

To practice metanoesis means to be negated and transformed into such being-*qua*-nothingness. The philosophical subject comes into question only after one has been converted in metanoesis. This does not mean, however, that there is some special acting subject that turns us around and effects a conversion in us. When we speak of other-power, the Other is absolute precisely because it is nothingness, that is, nothingness in the sense of absolute transformation. It is because of its genuine passivity and lack of acting selfhood that it is termed absolute other-power. Other-power is *absolute* other-power only because it acts through the mediation of the self-power of the relative that confronts it as other. Only to that extent is genuine, absolute other-power mediated by self-power. In this way, the absolute becomes absolute mediation. The relative cannot be the relative merely because it stands against the absolute. The absolute, as absolute mediation, has not only to mediate with regard to the relative that stands opposed to it, but also to mediate between one relative and another. The relative stands opposed to the absolute only by virtue of the fact that one relative stands opposed to other relatives, and the relative is called relative only insofar as it stands opposed to some other relative. The mutual dependence of relatives brings the absolute into existence to mediate their correlation to one another. For mediation to be absolute it must have this dual character. ...

True absolute other-power has to be made part of one's faith-witness through the mediatory activity of relative self-power. The activity of the absolute with regard to the relative comes about only through the mediation of other relatives which, as relatives, also stand in opposition to the absolute. Thus, the effect of the absolute on the relative only becomes real as the effect of the relative on the relative.

... Precisely because nothingness is mediated by being, and the absolute is mediated by the relative, absolute nothingness is able to be both absolute and nothingness. This nothingness must in turn be realized in the depths of relative mind through action-faith-witness—that is, through metanoesis. Metanoesis, which is the activity of self as well as the activity of other-power, provides the particular content for absolute mediation: the "here and now" of absolute mediation in the self is metanoetics. It is, of course, possible for simple religious faith to be based on a theism of other-power in which grace is experienced directly and without mediation. Indeed, this seems to be a universal form of religious expression. But such simple faith cannot mediate the absolute knowledge of philosophy because the immediate determination of faith in the myths or revelations of theism negates the independence of philosophy and obstructs the freedom of reason. From a philosophical point of view, only in metanoesis can the nature of the mediation of truly absolute other-power be practiced, believed, and made real through philosophical thinking in action-faith-witness. Metanoesis alone preserves the full autonomy and freedom of reason, brings reason to its own limits, and thus prompts reason to self-abandonment.

Contrary to what Kant thought in his critical philosophy, it is impossible for the autonomy of reason to provide its own foundations. Reason endowed with the capacity for self-criticism cannot evade the ultimate predicament of the antinomies of practical reason, since it is caught up in original sin stemming from basic human finitude. The critique of reason needs to be pressed to the point of an absolute critique through "absolute disruption" and absolute crisis, which constitute the self-abandonment of reason. It is precisely this absolute critique through "absolute disruption" and absolute crisis that constitutes the self-abandonment of reason. It is precisely this absolute critique that makes up the rational aspect of metanoesis and provides it with a logic, as I shall explain in the following chapter. I would conclude, therefore, that metanoetics is not merely one possible way among a variety of philosophical ways: it is the *only* way, the ineluctable way. It is the ultimate conclusion to which the critique of reason drives us.

Given the viewpoint set forth above, it is natural to find in Shinran a source of great encouragement and enlightenment. I would argue that the philosophy of religion expounded in the *Kyōgyōshinshō* shows a depth whose counterpart is difficult to find in the Western world. I do not, however, intend to expound a philosophy based on the Shin sect by offering a philosophical interpretation of the dogma of "salvation through invoking the name of Amida Buddha with pure faith in other-power" as it was propounded by Shinran. My real intention is rather to reconstruct philosophy itself through metanoesis in a way corresponding to faith in other-power. In other words, instead of interpreting Shinran's teaching in a philosophical manner, I have it in mind here to remold philosophy as metanoetics, to start afresh along the way of philosophy by following Shinran's religious path. This is precisely how we may learn from Shinran in the true sense of the word, and it is only in this sense that I consider him to be my teacher. ...

For example, in reference to the three kinds of repentance discussed in the section entitled "The Transformed Buddha and Land of Expediency," Shinran quotes from Shandao (Jp., Zendō, 613–668):

> Although there are differences among the three sorts of repentance, those who have practiced *zange* throughout their lives are all accumulating merit. If one has respect for this virtue and respects one's religious master without concern for one's own life, and if one performs *zange*, with compunction in one's entire soul and body, even for the most insignificant of his evil deeds, one will be released quickly from one's sin.[4]

And further, in arguing that *zange* is an appropriate practice, especially in the eschatological time propounded by the Pure Land sect, Shinran quotes from the *An-lo-chi* (Jp., *Anrakushū*):

> Those who practice *zange* and wish to do good deeds and to attain happiness should invoke the name of Amida Buddha. Those who invoke Amida even once can be released from the *karma* performed during eighty kalpas. Even one such invocation has this merit. How much more merit will those receive who invoke his name as long as they live! They are truly ones who have realized *zange*.[5]

These passages make it sufficiently clear that *zange* is universal enough to include the practice of *nenbutsu* 念仏 (invoking the name of Amida), to stand in essential relationship with it, and finally to become one with it, even though *zange* has a negative connotation in contrast with the positive connotation of *nenbutsu*. One may say without exaggeration that *zange* both represents the beginning of the practice of *nenbutsu* and functions as an element in its actual process. ...

Passages like this leave no doubt that the whole of the work is grounded in and sustained by *zange*. Unless one undergoes the same kind of sincere repentance that Shinran had, one will never achieve a profound understanding of the work. At the age of eighty-six—more than thirty years after having established his own faith as expounded in the *Kyōgyōshinshō*—Shinran felt compelled by inner necessity to write another hymn filled with the same spirit of repentance; it begins with these words:

> Even though I have surrendered myself to faith in the True Pure Land,
> there is no truth or sincerity in me. I am false and dishonest, and have
> no pure and undefiled heart.[6]

Only one who could write such a hymn, springing from the depth of his
heart, could be the author of the *Kyōgyōshinshō*.

Without metanoesis, there can be no salvation through *nenbutsu* or faith
in other-power. Metanoetics is indeed a philosophy based upon other-power.
But, as is evident from the preceding, I do not mean to speak of other-power
as operating in me objectively, nor to describe the structure of metanoesis
through self-reflection on how one is transformed by other-power. The
action-faith-witness (*gyō-shin-shō*) in which I myself practice metanoesis is
undertaken for the sake of absolute mediation and pursues the true path of
philosophy, which seeks absolute knowledge.

Philosophy as metanoetics implies taking the path of metanoesis self-
consciously. This is what I understand by philosophy. It is not a philosophy of
metanoesis that seeks to describe metanoesis as an object, but a philosophy
based upon other-power enabling me to practice metanoesis subjectively.
Indeed, the metanoesis of philosophy is itself metanoetics. Metanoesis does
not remain a mere objective presented to philosophy from without as a
problem to be solved or a method to be pursued. As stated above and as
will be explained in the next chapter, a philosophy for which the critique
of reason forms an indispensable moment gives birth to metanoetics when
that critique results in the concept of absolute critique. Metanoetics emerges
from the core of philosophy itself. Philosophy achieves its ultimate end only
when it becomes the metanoesis of philosophy itself.

Being is always relative and cannot be absolute, since the absolute must
be nothingness, as I have stated before. Nothingness means transformation.
Being, as that which mediates nothingness, can therefore be likened to its
axis of transformation. But because being is the mediator of nothingness, it,
too, must be reduced to nothingness. A reciprocity-in-equality exists among
the various pivots of being, each of which serves as an axis of transformation
for the others. As I shall explain later in discussing the three stages of
transformation (*sangantennyū*), the world exists for no other reason than
that of *upāya* ("skillful means"). It is the world of mediation through which
such a reciprocal transformation enables relative beings to move toward
nothingness and to return to the world to serve as a means of enlightenment
and salvation for others. Metanoesis is the mediatory activity of transcending
being in terms of "being as *upāya*."

The relative self, then, as being that serves as the medium—or means
(*upāya*)—of absolute nothingness and yet remains opposed to nothingness,

contains within itself the relative independence of being independent of the absolute. The self, as relative being brought to existence as the medium or expedient of absolute nothingness, contains implanted within itself the possibility of securing its existence in opposition to nothingness and adhering stubbornly to its independence. This is what is termed the "radical evil" of human existence.

Evil does not consist merely of committing evil acts. As Hegel's profound interpretation shows, acts that come to fulfillment in "the true ethical world" (*die wahre Sittlichkeit*) as the synthesis of opposing elements in the form of *both/and* are never brought to our consciousness in the form of an intention or goal. There are always elements hidden in conscious acts that do not reach consciousness, which is why each and every act of ours cannot avoid the stain of sin. Not only are all our acts, therefore, foredoomed to sin, but the independence of our being itself is infected with radical evil. The essence of the relative self consists in the fact that it is a nothingness for mediating absolute nothingness; it is emptiness, void (Jp., *kū*; Skt., *śūnyatā*). This self deceives itself, grows forgetful of its own finitude and relativity, and comes to mistake itself for absolute existence by absolutizing the finitude of its existence. What is more, it shows an innate tendency to cling to this delusion. This is what we are calling radical evil: the self-assertion and rebellion of the relative vis-à-vis the absolute.

Since the absolute, as nothingness, must act as an absolute mediating force, it presupposes relative being as its medium. In contrast with the doctrine of the creation of the world maintained by the theist, or the theory of emanation propounded by the pantheist, historical thinking must begin from present historical reality in order to reconstruct reality in practice, thus producing a circular process of "revolution-*qua*-restoration." For historical thinking, the absolute and the relative, nothingness and being, are interrelated each with the other as the indispensable elements of absolute mediation. Theirs is a simultaneous and reciprocal relationship in which neither can be derived from the other. The relative as the medium of the absolute comes into existence simultaneously with the absolute. The existence of the relative is a *sine qua non* for the absolute as nothingness. And precisely because the absolute *is* nothingness, the relative can exist as being. Conversely, because the existence of the relative is "being as *upāya*" (*hōben*) in the sense that it alone serves a mediatory function with regard to nothingness, and because it is absolutely relative in the sense that it is a being related to other beings in relative reciprocity, it is able to serve as the medium for the absolute mediation of nothingness and thus enable nothingness to realize itself.

That having been said, however, there is no doubt that the relative which serves as the medium for the absolute cannot be derived from the absolute, but must be an independent being in order to function as a self-negating and self-transforming activity within nothingness. The fact that the relative comes into existence as the relative, serving as an element in the mediating work of the absolute, makes it possible for the relative to contain within itself the independence of a finite being, by means of which it can stand in opposition to the absolute. It is here that the roots of evil lie. For the fact that the absolute makes use of the relative for the sake of its mediation also implies that the absolute, as absolute mediation, is a self-negating principle, for which reason the absolute allows the relative—as the negative aspect of the absolute—to possess a relative independence. This is why the relative is disposed toward evil. Since the absolute allows for such a disposition toward evil in relative beings, the latter in turn are able to arrive at the bliss of salvation by confessing the guilt that is theirs as a result of their misuse of the freedom allowed to them and their actualization of this deep-seated penchant for evil. In this sense, the absolute is one with the Great Compassion. This is precisely what I mean by the term "Great Nay-*qua*-Great Compassion."

In this way, the self-awareness of one's guilt, or of one's radical evil and sin, as utterly unavoidable provides metanoesis with a necessary and concrete way to become conscious of the finite self. Suffering arises within a relative being because it is driven into a desperate cul-de-sac by the conflict between the consciousness of past *karma* (unavoidable guilt) and the consciousness of the aspiration for future emancipation from guilt. It is this suffering that characterizes present consciousness as anxiety. Further, the absolute transformation of nothingness leads to equality among relative beings, since the reciprocal conversion and transformation performed by relative beings result in "being as *upāya*" (*hōben sonzai* 方便存在), where each axis of transformation is freely changed into others with nothing to cling to, and becomes "elect" in the sense of being something previously chosen by the absolute. The self-consciousness of relative beings that "being as *upāya*" can exist only insofar as it is one temporary axis of transformation, taking its turn like every other being at being the axis and thus serving as the medium of nothingness, brings to actuality the solidarity of a religious society in the sense of a "returning to the world" (*gensō-ekō*).[7] Here relative beings are all able to exert religious influence on one another, so that they can all be saved through the Great Compassion. In this process relative beings, as pure passivity presupposing no substantial agent other than themselves, surrender themselves obediently to other-power. This surrender is metanoesis. At the same time, such other-power is nothing other than self-power; and conversely, self-power is nothing other than other-power. ...

In contrast with the usual philosophical attitude adopted toward Pure Land Shin doctrine with its notion of faith based on salvation through *nenbutsu* (invoking the name of Amida), I am attempting here to take another approach to the core of that faith. In my view, those who try to interpret the doctrine of Pure Land Shin from a specific philosophical standpoint do not follow the course of salvation by *nenbutsu* to its ultimate conclusions. Theirs is an attitude bearing the unmistakable marks of salvation by the self-power Gate of the Sages (*jiriki-shōdōmon*), and has no connection with that faith in other-power which is the faith of those who perform *zange*. This latter means confessing one's philosophical impotence and, driven to the humble recognition that as an ordinary ignorant and sinful being one has nothing to rely on, letting go of oneself completely. But those who interpret the doctrine according to their own philosophy make their understanding of other-power conform to self-power and never come close to a positive realization of the truth of philosophy through action-witness—that is, according to metanoetics and in a manner befitting salvation by other-power. They remain in the philosophical position of sages trying to save themselves by their own efforts or merits.

There is nothing surprising about this, given the common understanding of philosophy as an activity based on the self-awareness of the autonomy of reason. As for myself, I no longer share this attitude because I can no longer accept its underlying ideal of philosophy. The experience of my past philosophical life has brought me to realize my own inability and the impotence of any philosophy based on self-power. I have now no philosophy whatsoever on which to rely. I now find that the rational philosophy from which I had always been able to extract an understanding of the rational forces permeating history, and through which I could deal rigorously with reality without going astray, has left me.

I feel especially obliged to share in the corporate responsibility for irrationalities like the injustice and prejudice evident in our country. I feel responsible for all of the evils and errors committed by others, and in so doing find that the actual inability of my philosophy to cope with them compels me to a confession of despair over my philosophical incompetence. More than that, I find that this predicament obliges me—the ordinary person, ignorant and sinful, that I am—to admit that such a confession applies not only to me, but to all persons everywhere who are similarly ignorant and sinful.

I hold the view that philosophy consists in the autonomy of reason. In this respect it is similar to science, the difference being that philosophy claims to offer knowledge of the absolute, not of the relative, as is the case with science in general. The claim is an impossible one, however, for the simple reason that as beings who are not absolute but relative, not saints or sages in communion with the divine but ordinary humans wrapped up in ourselves, we remain bound to self-satisfaction and arrogance, try as we may to assume the standpoint of reason. The claim of reason amounts to no more than an ideal that can never be fulfilled completely so long as we maintain the standpoint of self-power. Even if it were somehow possible for this claim to be fulfilled, if we were to acquire knowledge of the absolute and put it into practice, this could not be attributed to an "ascent" of self-power but only to a "descent" of other-power transforming the relative into the absolute and thereby causing the absolute to be mediated through the relative.

In other words, whatever leads the relative self to salvation in religion should also function in the case of philosophy, whose origins are the same as those of science, so that the basic nature of philosophy should undergo a total transformation. And yet philosophy, which, like science, is based on the autonomy of reason, cannot forthwith abandon its basic principle and turn itself into religious belief. The only way for philosophy to achieve this goal of total transformation is for the autonomy of reason, the motivating force of philosophy, to become deadlocked in the self-awareness of its own incompetence. In its despair of self-power—that is, in metanoesis—reason can be led to self-surrender by other-power, until at last it revives as a philosophy of "effortless naturalness" (*musa-hōni*, 無作の作), beyond all opposition between self and other. If it is possible for me to resume the way of philosophy, there is no alternative left but to start anew in metanoesis. ... There was no other way for me to philosophize except the self-awareness of metanoesis in metanoetics. No sooner did I begin this metanoesis, as I said, than my philosophical thinking started anew, yet not as my own doing but as the doing of other-power in me.

The fact that metanoesis is going on within me is not to the credit of self-power. Indeed, I have to admit that even the self-power implied in my practice of *zange* is itself already mediated by other-power, which effects the absolute transformation of my self-surrender and self-negation into self-affirmation. Self-power and other-power converge here and thus penetrate each other. At the same time that I practice metanoesis I am being transformed—converted—into someone who can make a fresh start in philosophy without any intention of doing so. There is no attempt here to continue my old philosophy or to reconstruct it on my own power. The philosophy I am concerned with here is rather a philosophy of the "action of no-action" or "action without an acting subject" (*musa no sa*), because it is mediated by metanoesis and transformed by other-power. I affirm myself only insofar as I, who am a being emptied (*kū-u*) through absolute transformation, can serve as a negative mediator of the absolute. All I can do is submit myself to "naturalness" (*jinen-hōni*) and let the absolute do as it will. My philosophy is simply action-faith-witness in the sense of a self-consciousness of this naturalness. Furthermore, once the standpoint of this metanoetical self-awareness has been acknowledged for what it is, the antinomy mentioned above, which leads to absolute critique because it involves contradiction beyond the capacity of the self-power of reason to resolve, is allowed to remain as it is and to mediate the absolute. From this standpoint the active, subjective moment in historical necessity is made clear, and every attempt of scientific theory to approximate truth is furnished with a necessary meaning relative to its stage in the development of the history of science.

... What happens as a matter of necessity at each stage of history is thus made the result of action-faith-witness. The "way without a way" is opened up by other-power, and philosophy is transported from the standpoint of reason based on the self-power of the Gate of the Sages (*shōdōmonteki jiriki*) to the standpoint of action-faith based on the other-power Gate of the Pure Land (*jōdomonteki tariki*). ... It is only that, when the critique of reason that takes place in philosophy progresses to the point of an absolute critique and thus reaches the end of its tether, a way to the suprarational "death-and-resurrection" of reason is necessarily thrown open, and a corresponding shift takes place from the world of nature to the world of history. This is just what happened when the critical philosophy of Kant opened out into the dialectical thought of Hegel. The difference between the concepts of reason of the two philosophers is the very process we are talking about here. Moreover, the reason that Hegel had to undergo the criticism of Kierkegaard is that Hegel had failed to bring the process to consummation and to emancipate himself completely from the Kantian view of reason. The "death-and-resurrection" of reason necessarily leads to the standpoint of faith in other-power. In other words, metanoetics, as the transrational resurrection of reason, is a reconstruction of philosophy. Viewing matters in this light, one would not be mistaken in the claim that Kierkegaard's existential philosophy also developed a kind of metanoetics.[8]

In short, it has been the destiny of my life philosophy that it necessarily develops into metanoetics. It is not that I mean to graft Pure Land Shin faith in other-power onto philosophy, but rather that the confrontation of philosophy with my personal experience of reality has forced me to develop my thought in this direction. Nevertheless, the fact remains that this my philosophical destiny has given me a new admiration for Shinran and opened the way for me to understand his faith and thought. This is so because, unlike attempts to apply traditional ideas of philosophy to Pure Land Shin doctrine, the development of metanoetics follows closely that of Shinran's Pure Land doctrine. If we assume either philosophy or religious doctrine to be fixed, and then use it to define and interpret the other, we end up in familiar theological dogmatism. In my case, philosophy as metanoetics does not come about exclusively under the guidance and influence of Shinran's thought, but is a necessary logical consequence of the critique of reason pursued to term as absolute critique; but at the same time, my interpretation of the *Kyōgyōshinshō* is not an attempt to interpret Shinran's thought from the viewpoint of an established philosophy. Of course, it is true that my reading of Shinran's religious results is an interpretation peculiar to my philosophy as metanoetics. But the philosophy I am developing here is not intended as a fixed system, since metanoetics grows out of the very destruction of philosophical systems in the traditional sense due to antinomies of reason that usher in the self-surrender of reason's autonomy.

... Philosophy and faith are thus independent of each other and at the same time correspond to each other. They develop spontaneously in reciprocity rather than by one-way determination, with the activity of metanoesis serving as the center of mediation. I find the unification of philosophy and faith here—and indeed, speaking more generally, life itself—to be based on metanoesis through action-faith-witness. Not only in philosophy, but in life itself the self-negation of metanoesis is transformed into self-affirmation: my death in self-surrender restores me to a new life where despair turns to hope. Because my life cannot exist apart from philosophy, nor my philosophy exist apart from my actual life, philosophy as metanoetics becomes the basic principle of my life, the ground on which I can live a life of "death-and-resurrection."

I assure myself through faith that absolute self-negation and pure passivity—in absolute death—is the turning point at which I live in dying and live in being brought to life. ... The process of mediation at work here is metanoesis carried out through "despair in obedience." But when I am moved by other-power to the point of total passivity and obedience, the agent of this absolute transformation is nothingness, which means that nothing confronts me in the way of "being." As agent, being is always relative being and cannot possibly be absolute. Absolute other-power is pure passivity with nothing in the way of "being" as an agent and, therefore, consists entirely of the pure negation of the self, of the mediating character of absolute transformation, that is, of a "naturalness" (*jinen-hōni*) beyond the opposition of self and other. ...

In this way, philosophy—once closed to me—finds a new beginning through self-abandonment. A new philosophical task and its solution are given to self-consciousness through the negation and transformation of the absolute in actuality. For me, philosophical self-consciousness does not mean becoming conscious of the spontaneity of freedom motivated by self-power. On the contrary, it means letting go of myself in obedient despair because of my powerlessness and impotence. ... Since it is through such self-consciousness that I am urged to begin philosophy again in metanoesis, it follows as a matter of course that all pride of supposing I might offer my own philosophical interpretation of the doctrine of Pure Land Shin, as if I were some sort of sage, is swept away. The only thing that happens is that I am allowed to make a fresh start in philosophy, following the path that Shinran once trod to reach the truth of Pure Land Shin. This is why the reconstruction of philosophy in the spirit of Shinran provides a new beginning in philosophy rather than a new philosophical interpretation of Shinran's teachings. It hardly bears repeating that I do not mean thereby to compare myself to Shinran. I mean only that since I am deeply convinced that the metanoetics I am now practicing coincides, as a matter of ineluctable fate, with the spirit of Shinran, I sense the force of his influence and encouragement and revere him as my teacher and guide. At the same time, if I accept him as my teacher and guide, I must have a true understanding of his thought in order to develop my own way of thinking. This is the sense in which I shall be offering interpretations of doctrines like that of the Three Minds and the Three Stages of Faith in the *Kyōgyōshinshō*. It is by discovering my own independent philosophy that I come under Shinran's influence and guidance.

The path of the sage is closed to me. I am but an ordinary person groping my way through dark tunnels and moving in directions diametrically opposite to those of the sage. Metanoetics must only be developed into philosophy *metanoetically*. Metanoetics becomes philosophical self-consciousness when it is mediated by the performance of metanoesis through one's faith-witness. Hence, the posture of *credo ut intelligam* is also applicable here. This posture may be of no use for the absolute standpoint of the sage, which is essentially identical with that of God, but it is indispensable for an ordinary person such as I.

If faith is defined directly in terms of revelation and further determined by dogma, philosophy cannot claim the autonomy or self-determination of reason as grounds for its necessity and universality. This is why the theology of theism leans toward a dogmatism that clashes with the critical spirit of philosophy. Metanoetics, however, is able to avoid this difficulty because it consists in a transformation that can be mediated by faith. ... Though it is hardly necessary to repeat it, the transcendental dialectic set forth in Kant's *Critique of Pure Reason* has made it amply clear that this fundamental predicament is not due merely to some accidental weakness or flaw in the human condition, but derives from a primordial limitation built into the structure of human knowledge and affecting the very nature of human reason itself. For Kant, the way to overcome such doubt is to admit the essential limitations of reason, keep human knowledge strictly within these limits, and thus avoid all pretense of surpassing or transcending these limits ... Thus, faith and knowledge coexist in Kant's transcendental philosophy with a boundary line drawn between them, so that each is assigned its own domain without interference from the other. In other words, theirs is an external relationship, where each is distinguished in terms of its content: the one absolute, the other relative. …

There is no reciprocal mediation to be seen here, no process of transformation intrinsic to the mutual mediation of both terms so that either, having arrived at its limits, is transformed into the other—so that both, in spite of being independent of each other, stimulate and develop each other. Such a reciprocal mediation I regard as characteristic of metanoetics. But I wonder whether the sort of harmonious reconciliation of faith and knowledge that Kant works out on the basis of the self-limitation of each can be brought satisfactorily to fulfillment. In fact, I am convinced that Kant's thought, as developed in the chapter entitled "Metaphysics as a Natural Disposition" in the section of his *Critique of Pure Reason* dealing with the transcendental dialectic, shows beyond doubt that such reconciliation cannot provide a final solution. …

It is therefore impossible for philosophy to stand apart from science in such a way that it presupposes science as a fact for which only a formal basis has to be found. To repeat: the essential feature of contemporary science, the understanding of which was not available to the age of Kant, is that philosophy enters into the content of scientific theories, indeed that science cannot stand on its own ground apart from philosophy and must, therefore, include philosophy within its own theories. Typical examples of this phenomenon are to be found in basic mathematical theory as well as in the new theories of physics referred to above. Seen from this viewpoint, we have no alternative but to conclude that Kant's critique of science has been refuted by science itself. The *Critique of Pure Reason*, the principal section of which is devoted to a critique of science, was unable to resolve the problem of the relationship between science and philosophy. If we also take into consideration the structure of historical reality itself, which poses further obstacles to the critique of reason, we find that it is not only the critique of theoretical reason—taken in the sense of the critique of science—that is doomed to unavoidable antinomies, but the critique of practical reason as well. This confronts the critique of reason with a crisis that threatens to undo it altogether. This is what I have been calling absolute critique, which I take to be the logic of metanoetics. Metanoetics is the logical consequence of conducting philosophy through the critique of reason to its final consequences. Only when science is led to religion, and knowledge transformed into faith, will the standpoint of *credo ut intelligam*—that is, the restoration of philosophy—be open to us. This is what takes place in metanoetics, as I shall discuss at length in the next chapter.

Questions for Class Discussions

Q1. What does Tanabe mean by "absolute critique"? How is his notion of "antinomy" different from the Kantian notion?

Q2. Metanoesis enables one to recognize one's powerlessness and yet, in that state of being ordinary and ignorant (which is exactly what Buddhists mean by the term *bonbu*), the self can realize that it is an infinitely empowered being. How does Tanabe show that this paradoxical self-awareness is possible?

Q3. Metanoia means both repentance and transformation. Why does Tanabe think that these two have to go together? How could repentance help us achieve the transformation of the self from the standpoint of self-power to the selfless embodiment of other-power?

6

Two Aspects of Education in Natural Science

Notes on Translation

The *THZ* volume five consists of eleven essays, which Tanabe published between 1933 and 1939. They were written on a variety of topics, ranging from a general introduction to philosophy, mathematics, religions, humanism, morality, philosophy of science, theoretical physics, education, and even to Dōgen's *Shōbōgenzō* (正法眼蔵). What is really interesting about this collection of diverse essays is the fact that Tanabe was developing the massive "logic of species" at the same time. None of those articles which cover seemingly unrelated topics make any explicit references to the complex theory of social ontology. However, it is undeniable that some of the points Tanabe makes in these shorter works presuppose the comprehensive standpoint that he was trying to establish within a larger and more original framework of thought. In this sense, the essays in the fifth volume of Tanabe's complete works occasionally exhibit clear examples of what the philosopher meant by the "absolute mediation," or an appropriate intermediation, of multiple terms in his rendering of the "logic of species."

"Two Aspects of Education in Natural Science" (*THZ* 5: 141–92) is a great example of this. As mentioned in Chapter 3, Tanabe originally delivered this text as a lecture before a general audience, consisting of natural scientists and government bureaucrats, at the "Workshop on the Study of Japanese Culture Instruction." This event was hosted by the Department of Ideology at the Ministry of Education in November 1936. The timing for this lecture, which was to be delivered to the public at a government building, could not be any more dramatic.

In the previous year, the conventional interpretation of the Meiji Constitution, which regarded Japanese sovereignty as belonging to the state, was overthrown by the military and right-wing politicians. The conventional view was that the Emperor, while constituting the highest official institution, must nevertheless give heed to other political bodies led by the Cabinet. Now it was said that national sovereignty belonged *only* to the Emperor.

On February 26, 1936, there was an attempted coup d'état (now known as the "2.26 Incident"), led by young military officers. The coup resulted in the immediate resignation of the entire Cabinet. The new, so-called, Hirota Cabinet, established the *Thought Criminals Protection and Surveillance Law* on May 29 of the same year. This notorious edict enabled the state to detain, reeducate, and place under surveillance all those who did not affirm the "Japanese spirit."

Not surprisingly, Tanabe, as a leading professor of philosophy at an Imperial University, was invited to justify the significance of "Japonism," and to support the Department of Ideology at the Ministry of Education in its political intervention in the domain of natural science. However, an attentive reader will quickly realize that Tanabe, in this lecture, did not endorse the political propaganda but, instead, systematically spoke against it by emphasizing the importance of never compromising the freedom of those who pursue natural scientific knowledge. This lecture was delivered in terms accessible to the natural scientists (but not to the bureaucrats and government officials) in the audience. If we take into account the political and cultural climate of that time, we can understand why Tanabe was prepared to die for criticizing the government's new policies concerning education in natural science in 1936.

There are three reasons why I decided to include the translation of this article in this volume. First, Tanabe's lecture notes are far more straightforward and accessible to general readers than his representative theoretical works. Many students of the Kyoto School reported that Watsuji Tetsurō and Tanabe Hajime were antipoles as philosophers. Watsuji's lectures, they said, were very difficult to follow since he tended to mumble and stammer during his class, while his writing was absolutely smooth, very clear, and even beautiful to many of them. Tanabe, on the other hand, always delivered logically structured lectures and provided lucid examples by means of which complex issues were logically laid out in a manner accessible to first-year students while his texts were almost impenetrable, even to advanced scholars. This essay clearly shows how Tanabe adopted his style of teaching and explained his complex theory of knowledge in a manner accessible to his colleagues in academic fields beyond philosophy.

Second, this article clearly lays out Tanabe's model of interdisciplinarity, in reference to which readers will be able to discuss what counts as a proper interrelation of multiple modes of knowing. As I stated in Chapter 3, a typical rendering of an interdisciplinary study in contemporary academia follows the manner of "compromise" (or *secchū*) while Tanabe, in reference to theoretical physics, advocates the "mutually exclusive complementarity" (or *sicchū*). In this (scientific and philosophical) manner of thinking, we come to the conclusion that we must pursue a particular mode of knowing to the fullest while recognizing its undeniable relativity to others. What Tanabe envisions here, as a proper form of knowing, is comparable to his notion of "open species." Each academic discipline (as a community of intellectual explorers) must be treated as a particular manifestation of absolute knowing and, as such, it must maintain its openness and relativity to all the others without compromising the other's autonomous development.

Lastly, the political implications of the logic of species are most explicit in this text. While criticizing state politics for compromising the autonomy of natural scientific investigations, Tanabe deploys his social ontology, along with his philosophical understanding of quantum physics, to advocate the open mediation of multiple forms of human knowing. Perhaps his structural critique of the state authority and its policies might have been too subtle for the bureaucrats to clearly understand. Moreover, the fact that the watchdogs of the police state published the text may show that Tanabe's delivery of his message was ultimately poor in terms of its persuasiveness. That being said, in reference to the historical context in which this text was written, we should be able to recognize how Tanabe applied his understanding of self, world, and knowledge to combat the fascist regime. It is clear that he was, intellectually, far removed from compliance with the totalitarian authority, which was determined to eradicate any constructive criticisms that would slow down their imperialist ambitions.

It is my hope that readers of this book will be encouraged to utilize Tanabean philosophical ideas in the same way as Tanabe did. It is only be doing this that that we can move closer to realizing the ideal of "open societies" and achieve a genuine, that is to say, "interdisciplinary," knowledge of ourselves and the world.

Two Aspects of Education in Natural Science

Preface

It may sound impudent for an outsider like me to talk about anything on natural science at the meeting of natural scientists.[1] But I also think that it is possible to "draw a lesson from an outsider" as they say and that is why I came to this meeting. As it is kindly introduced, my presentation is entitled "Two Aspects of Education in Natural Science." First, it is necessary, I think, to talk about what "two aspects" actually means here.

As it is discussed in the opening, this workshop focuses on the education of natural science with the purpose of contributing something to the justification of the emperor as the national sovereign (*kokutai-no meichō*, 国体の明徴). However, what we ordinarily think of as natural science not only has nothing to directly contribute to that kind of problem, but also means that to think natural-scientifically would rather become an obstacle for such a problem of spirit.

Originally, since the way of thinking in natural science holds that all phenomena are bound by the necessary causal relation: hence, if we take this standpoint, we are not allowed to make a value judgment where we argue some should be taken and other should not be taken. We normally think that, according to the natural scientific way of thinking, phenomena that exist in reality should be all equally accepted and studied without any value discriminations. Additionally, if all things have causal necessity from this viewpoint, it would be impossible to add various changes to them in accordance with a certain purpose.

Actually, in that respect, the natural scientific way of thinking is far too powerful such that it brings about a variety of problems in relation to the justification of the emperor as the national sovereign and requires a variety of institutions. It has attracted such circumstances. We cannot say that there is no opinion in our society today that it is rather necessary to place a sufficient limit to the natural scientific way of thinking. If that is the case, then some of you, who have been specializing in the study of natural science or engaged in the teaching of natural science, might think that it would add limitation to the study of natural science itself, that we would not sufficiently exercise our ability to think in the natural scientific manner and instead it would be necessary for us to stop in the middle of it. Also, if you follow through with the natural scientific way of thinking, you might suspect that it would bring about many sorts of inconveniences that are treated today as problems and that there is a risk of arousing philosophy that contradicts with the *Kokutai-*

no hongi. As far as I can see, we cannot say that there is no tendency to make that kind of demand on natural scientists. However, if we are going to fulfill the world historical mission of Japan, the rise of natural science is a much more important matter than many other kinds of institutions. Needless to say, the natural sciences make a great contribution not only for the national defense, but also for the development of industry and, if we overlook natural science, we cannot carry out the development of industry and further the enrichment of armaments necessary for the national defense. We are at the stage where we can positively say today's war is not the war of humans but [much more dependent on the development] of science: hence, we cannot help but to think that, in relation to the future of our nation state, the fact that thought, which hinders the development of natural science and becomes an obstacle to it, is carried out today should be the most troubling for us.

Of course, on the one hand, it is quite necessary for the natural scientific way of thinking to be aware of its own limitation. We must deny though that we can obtain the complete knowledge of all that is, including what is political and further that which relates to a manifold of values, through the way of thinking in natural science. That kind of philosophy must be limited. However, on the other hand, natural science must be developed further in relation to its own unique standpoint. We can think that natural science is today placed in this seemingly contradictory status. What I mean by "two aspects" is not two sides that are standing next to each other, but as it is treated as a problem, two sides that, at first glance, seem to be in a contradictory relation to each other, where, on the one hand, natural science must be absolutely developed and it should be encouraged but, on the other, the way of thinking in natural science itself should be given some restriction. Without establishing these two sides, furthermore, the study of natural science or its education cannot fully demonstrate its significance. I mean these two sides by the term "two aspects" [of the discipline].

Here lies the reason why we have to treat two aspects of natural science as a problem. It does not mean that these two sides are necessary for the development of natural science, but that when the standpoint of natural science is not properly understood in a certain sense, the side that could signify an impediment of natural science and thereby hinder its growth is present today; and however, in relation to which, natural science should be developed to the end when it is seen from the standpoint of nation state. It is placed in such a contradictory position. Here lies the problem. What I mean by the "two aspects" does not signify two sides in relation to the study and the education of natural science that can be carried out in parallel to each other without incurring any contradictions, but as I just mentioned, the two aspects that look to be contradictory at a glance and at the same time without establishing both of them, the education of natural science cannot fully demonstrate its significance. I am talking about the "two sides" in that sense. Since that is one of the important notions that we should pay attention to in relation to the education of natural science, regardless of the fact that I have neither sufficient knowledge of natural science nor the right to talk about it (beyond the fact that I am simply interested in it), I would like to present my personal view with the hope that you will be able to use it as reference.

1. The Positive Side of Education in Natural Science

The summary of my presentation refers to the "positive side of education in natural science." I think it is necessary to further elaborate on what I have just discussed as the "two sides of natural science" and, in doing so, explain what I mean by the "positive side" and what kind of position it occupies [in relation to the former].

Once again, what I mean by the "two aspects" is not the ones that could exist side by side in front of us by saying that "natural science has this aspect and another" without acknowledging any problem, but the two sides that look as though they are contradictory to each other at a first glance. In order to progress the study of natural science and promote the development of natural science, the natural scientific way of thinking must be fully encouraged and promoted to the fullest. However, speaking from the other side, the way of thinking in natural science must be limited; otherwise, when we employ the natural scientific way of thinking on everything, we could arouse a variety of troublesome thoughts: hence, such a way of thinking must be limited. We are facing this kind of situation.

… On further reflection, we can recognize that even inside natural science, such mutually contradictory sides are confronted with the state in which they would have to be unified. I think this is a remarkable fact. Even though my knowledge of natural science is far from being sufficient, I would like to discuss in the following the fact that these two aspects are appearing in the essential content of natural science. Of course, as I have been saying from the beginning, the problem lies in the fact that, without stepping into the content and substance of natural science, the natural scientific way of thinking is placed in the position where it should be encouraged on the one hand, but needs to be restricted on the other. This state is appearing in various dimensions today and as one among them, it is not becoming apparent only in relation to the condition of natural science, but also even in the content of natural science itself. We have to say that this is a very important matter for natural science. Therefore, in order to clarify the two aspects of education in natural science, I would like to borrow concepts included in the theory of natural science and make explicit their state of affairs.

That is the concept of "mutual complementarity," which has been introduced in today's quantum physics. For the specialists in this field, there is nothing that I can add to this concept, but what Niels Bohr has proposed as "complementarity" has become a very important concept in the field of quantum physics. In recent years, some scholars like Pascual Jordan have regarded this concept of complementarity as being extremely important and further argue that it has an important meaning not only in quantum physics, but also even in biology; and I would like to borrow what they talk about as the "concept of complementarity" for expressing the relation of what I have been talking about as "two aspects." This term, "complement," probably meant originally that it simply supplements the lack as it is the case with the term in grammar. When there is a complement to a verb, we cannot know the meaning of the sentence only with the verb or it cannot complete the meaning with the verb even when it is an intransitive one; and in order to supplement it, the complement is used. However, what they say about "complementarity" in today's quantum physics means not only that it supplements because there is simply a lack, but also indicates the relation where one cannot appear in a standpoint where another is manifest, but they are at the same time complementary to each other. In that sense, their characteristic is that they are supplementary to each other while at the same time being mutually exclusive. This is what they mean by "mutually complementary exclusiveness" (*komplementäre Ausschliessung*). Hence, this complementarity means mutually exclusive supplementation. I think that we can flip the words and express it as "exclusive complementarity" (*ausschliessende Komplementarität*). Mutual complementarity and exclusivity are inseparable in today's quantum physics.

If I refer to a concrete example, an electron as the final element in contemporary physics is on the one hand essentially a particle. It means that the electrons can appear discontinuously or at intervals always as a certain integral multiplication of the quantity of electricity. Such particles and their movements can be captured in pictures through Wilson's cloud chamber. In this case, we can clearly think that the particles made movements. However, on the other hand, the electron shows a characteristic of waves just like light. It is accompanied by the phenomena that appear only in the waves of a continuous medium that we say is diffraction or interference. Thus, what we today call "electron" is that which is of particles and also of waves. Two ways of thinking, namely, particle and wave, are by all means necessary for concretely thinking about the electron. On the contrary, instead of thinking about light as wave phenomena (as it has been the case from antiquity), the way of thinking about it as the projectile of particles or as that which jumps out as particles like Newton's understanding of light, which predates Huygen's wave theory, has been proposed as the quantum light hypothesis. We have been thinking about a particle of a material as a kind of grain, but we must think of it as being wave-like at the same time. Simultaneously, the light that we have been thinking as a wave of a continuous medium, in turn, must be thought as the quantum light that has a particle structure. That is how we think about light in today's microscopic physics. If that is the case, then two phenomena of particles and waves cannot appear at the same time; they are exclusive. When we treat light as particles, they are nothing but particles and they cannot be wave-like phenomena at the same time and, in turn, when we treat it as waves, we cannot say that it exists in a certain position as a particle. Here, particles and waves are mutually exclusive. When one appears, the other has to withdraw. However, if they are simply exclusive, can we clarify the true nature of the final element of materials or light? The answer is no. Light is wave-like and at the same time particle-like; an electron is particle-like and simultaneously wave-like. There are those that are exclusive to each other as mutually complementing, namely, there is complementary exclusiveness or exclusive complementarity. That kind of thing is appearing in microscopic phenomena in physics. ...

Now, when we intend the development of natural science in general, it is necessary for us to release natural science for its complete freedom and to complete the natural scientific way of thinking. We cannot randomly add any restrictions to it, which would be a complete contradiction. If we were to do this, natural science could not fully develop itself at all. What troubles me is that there might be a tendency to do this today in our society. Since we can think of a heavy holdover in relation to natural science that does not directly exist in its true nature, we think that we have to put restrictions to natural science, but when seen from the standpoint of natural science, this way of thinking prevents natural science from freely developing itself and tries to suppress it to a certain degree by stopping the development in the middle of it. We have to say that this is not mutually exclusive in the sense just mentioned either. ... However, when the problem of God or the problem of values that does not belong to its standpoint, natural science must withdraw itself [from the discussion]. When we deal with the problem of wave phenomena, the way of thinking [about phenomena] in terms of particles must not appear or cannot appear in physics. This is exactly what it means to be "exclusive." The exclusion does not mean that two things are competing against each other therein, but that when one appears, the other does not. When the other appears, the one does not. Our attitude toward natural science must signify something like this. Two sides of natural science signify the relation in which the standpoint of natural science should be pursued to the fullest for the study and education of natural science, thereby giving a complete and full manifestation of the natural scientific way of thinking, but also be simultaneously withdrawn when the problem of spirit or other problems that the authority and the competence of natural science does not reach. Exactly when the problem of waves appears, the way of thinking that pertains to the particle must leave and simultaneously cannot appear; in that sense, it is exclusive. ... However, two sides that do not compete against each other in this manner have mutual complementarity in that sense that the concrete nature of [what we investigate]—whether it is the light or an electron—cannot be clarified without taking them both into account. That it is say, they are exclusive as they are complementary. I think this is what we should pay attention to as two sides of what we call today "natural science."

Now, if we break down the meaning of this mutually exclusive complementarity by comparing it to things that we would encounter in our general and everyday life, we could say the following. In the case where two things emerge at the same time and where they are competing against each other, these things are continuously connected to each other. What we think as power in an ordinary sense, such as "we are pushing [something] from here" and in opposition to which "the opposing power is pushing [it] from there," means that if it is pushed from here, it is also pushed from there, and they are competing against each other: additionally, they are also present at the same time. In this case, what does it mean for us to take the standpoint of the middle? This is precisely where the concept of "compromise" (*secchū*, 折衷) appears. To make a compromise (*secchū-suru*, 折衷する) means that we are making a demand from here and the opposite side makes another demand; since they are contradictory to each other, if we take one side, the other ends up disappearing. However, in this case, we would be seriously one-sided: so, what do we do when we carry out a *secchū* here? We restrict both sides, thereby making a so-called compromise (*dakyō*, 妥協). The *dakyō* means that we do not completely follow through with one side, but give a limitation to it at a certain point and at the same time, we do not display the power of the opposing side to the full but stop it at a certain point. This is *secchū*. What we mean by this term is that in relation to those that use power against each other, we limit both sides and hold them in the middle. This is not the same as the unity or harmony based on what I am discussing now as the mutually exclusive complementarity.

... When we continue extending "here" gradually, "there" will become smaller and then eventually we have only "here"; whereas, when "there" comes to be extended toward "here," the "here" will gradually become smaller: this is a relation of continuous pushing and being pushed. If we are going to limit our endorsement of the study of natural science with this manner of thinking, this means that we will neither fully pursue our research nor complete our teaching in natural science, but we would have to stop [our engagement with the discipline] at a certain point. We must reject this manner of thinking. Accordingly, I think, we have to eliminate the practice of *secchū*.

Then what kind of relation is established in the exclusive complementarity, which is different from the negative compromise (*secchū*)? As I just mentioned, it converts (*tenkan*, 転換) one to the other. It turns the standpoint. This point of conversion is not "both here and there." The middle in the sense of "breaking in the middle" (*secchū*) or "making a compromise" (*dakyō*) is both here and there. It might be neither completely here nor there, but at the same time, to a certain degree, they are both here and there. That is a compromise. Since we are trying to accommodate both positions at the same time, when we try to establish both of them by giving them limitations, they are indeed established at the same time. That is to say, it is *both* that *and* this. However, when we say "a tuning of a standpoint," it means that when one appears, the other must leave; when the other appears, the one has to go away. The turning point in this case is *neither* there *nor* here. At the border that is neither there nor here, we have no other way but to be either there or here. It is not possible for us to be there and here. That is a negative compromise (*dakyō*) and *secchū*. However, the point of conversion or the moment of conversion in the discontinuous standpoint where one appears when the other disappears is neither here nor there. By setting the boundary at where it is neither there nor here, we have nowhere to stand other than either here or there. If we are going to use simple terms in German and English, the negative compromises like *dakyō* and *secchū* correspond with *sowohl als auch* and "as well as." However, with regard to the exclusive transformation, its point of conversion is neither of them, that is, [the standpoint of] *weder noch* and "neither or." There is no other way for us to stand than being there or here, that is, taking the standpoint of *entweder order* and "either/or." By taking "neither/or" as the boundary, we are either here or there. Or in reference to the neither/nor at the boundary, we turn toward there or turn back toward here. The *as well as* and *sowohl als auch* are continuously attached to both. They can be continuously both. That compromising kind of thing, since it establishes both at the same time, does look like a harmonious standpoint, but it is a standpoint that limits each of them and prevents each standpoint from its free development. If we apply this manner of thinking to natural science, natural scientists would have to stop the study midway while education in this discipline would cease without fully teaching the discipline. We are concerned that this way of thinking is carried out today. I am not a specialist of classical Chinese literature, but there is a word "*shicchū*" (執中) and I wonder that the standpoint that is not of *secchū* corresponds to this one. I do not think that "to take the middle" (*naka-o toru*, 中を執る) is not the same as the ordinary sense of compromise or *secchū*. I do not think that it means stopping at the halfway middle by limiting each side. Rather, "taking the middle" is not being both this and that, but by taking the "neither that nor this" as a boundary, we completely dedicate ourselves to "this" when we focus on it as a problem, and when we problematize "that," we then turn in the opposite direction and fully devote ourselves to it. However, unlike the method of natural science, and perhaps even in the method of natural science, if we talk about not the content of natural science itself, but the natural scientist, that is, the subject of natural science, it turns toward here and then turns toward there. ... Also, to take the middle means that when we take one standpoint, it pertains to a single perspective: hence, it is not everything and we have to completely dedicate ourselves to the one while being aware that there is an opposing side. I think this is what it means to "take the middle." It is not maintaining the incomplete middle, which could be both this and that, by stopping both halfway. That renders the concept of *secchū*. To "take the middle" is to take one side as a problem and when it is necessary, it dedicates itself completely to it. In case the other is necessary, or when the other becomes the problem, it thoroughly investigates the other. However, it is the human being (*ningen*, 人間) that goes here and there. By taking that which is neither there nor here as a boundary, a human being goes here and there. Moreover, when she goes there, she has to be aware that there is there. In this manner, she has no choice but to go either one of these directions and also in the case where she goes to one, the other side is not overlooked or closed off; and in that standpoint, a limit is added self-mindfully to her way of progress. No external limitations are added to this process [of thinking], but one must complete her thinking till the end of this standpoint and yet, she must be self-aware that this standpoint is approved within its boundary and also that there is the opposing way of thinking in the other side of it. I am not sure if these two ways of thinking can be properly understood with two terms of *secchū* and *shicchū*, but I do hope so. And if I am allowed to hypothesize this distinction and use it in this lecture, I am afraid that we are normally thinking [about the bounds of natural science among others] without fully distinguishing these two concepts of *secchū* and *shicchū*; and I think we must tighten our guard against it. Or rather, instead of saying that we are thinking without clearly distinguishing the two, I think that we can say that we are not fully understanding the meaning of *shicchū*, or of taking the middle route. Hence, those who adopt the standpoint of "taking the middle" are often criticized as compromising (*secchū-teki*) and incomplete. Moreover, even though it is necessary to take the middle, we end up committing a *secchū*. However, this happens because we are not making a clear distinction between the significance of *secchū* and *shicchū*. To break in the middle (*secchū*) means that when we take a look at that which is continuously pressing and pressed, that no part of it is an extreme of either side and, moreover, that any part of it includes both sides of being here and there. Instead, when we take a look at it from either side, it is incomplete. Contrariwise, in the case of "taking the middle," once we set our standpoint on one, we have to pursue it till the end. With regard to research and education of natural science, we must fully dedicate ourselves to being natural scientific. The middle space that stays in between the research and education of natural science, or the *secchū* that stops these processes in the middle, brings about no benefit, but only incurs numerous kinds of harm to us. However, when we dedicate ourselves to one side in our study of natural science, it is not the all (there is to study), and rather, it is always accompanied by the opposite way of thinking on the other side. Since, at such a border that is neither that nor this, we are always moving freely by becoming that and then by becoming this, I do think that our study of natural science is necessarily accompanied with the fact that, while thoroughly pursuing the standpoint of natural science, we are to be clearly mindful of a different standpoint, the different way of thinking, on the other side of it. What I mean by "two sides" [of natural science] does not mean that two aspects, which are continuous to each other, are compromised at the midway point; but that they are mutually exclusive and yet at the same time complementary to each other, and that when there is one, the other cannot appear; and, furthermore, it means that they are complementary in the sense that only when there are two sides, the whole can be completed; they are complementary while being exclusive, and exclusive while being complementary, it is necessary for humans as acting subject(s) (*hataraku tokoro-no shutai*, 働くところの主体) to be aware of something like this. If we take this standpoint, we will by no means bring forth a number of inconvenient ideas by going beyond the bounds of natural science. However, at the same time, I argue that natural science should be able to fully demonstrate the capacity of its way of thinking in relation to its standpoint. What I mean by the term *shicchū* is not *the* secchū, but either this or that. Since it is either this or that, the middle space between two sides where they are converted from one to the other, is not "both this and that," but "neither this nor that." We can only describe this [space] with the word "nothingness" (*mu*, 無). An argument that this and that are connected to each other by taking some being as its medium is *secchū*. On the contrary, when we say that there is a conversion at the boundary that is neither this nor that, its betweenness does not exist. The between of either here or there constitutes nothingness. By taking nothingness as a medium, we can freely enter here and freely enter there. I think something like this is necessary for the education of natural science. In this sense, I would like to discuss two sides in the education of natural science, and by focusing on its positive side, I would first like to ask what kind of things are necessary for making the standpoint of natural science as beneficial as possible in education. This is what I mean by the positive side that I mentioned in the beginning [of this section] and even though it has a meaning only in relation to the negative side, I mean something like this by the term "positive side." I would like you to understand that my term, "two sides," correspond to two sides in what we can call today in quantum physics the relation of exclusive complementarity.

2. Knowledge, Method, and Spirit as Its Three Stages

Now, when we step into the content of the positive side of education in natural science, what kind of things should we take into consideration for the purpose of increasing, to a certain degree, the number of benefits? Of course, you should be perhaps more familiar with the actual problems of education, and you may think that I have no right to say anything about them as an outsider. But what an outsider like me has to say about these things might be useful for carrying out your mission; and in that sense, I would like to explain in simple terms what I am usually thinking about these issues.

With regard to the education of natural science, I think we can categorize it into three stages. First, it is obviously necessary for the education of natural science to provide the knowledge of it. Even if we ask the question of "what is the natural scientific way of thinking?" it will be devoid of content when we depart from knowledge: hence, it goes without saying that it is first necessary to provide natural scientific knowledge. You should already know which points we should pay attention to when providing the knowledge and, as an outsider to the field of pedagogy, I have no materials to share regarding the method of teaching. However, if I were to talk about something, to which I personally think I myself should give careful consideration, with regard to the education of natural science, or to the process of providing natural scientific knowledge, what I think we should be really careful about is that particularly when we teach natural science to high school students who are majoring in liberal arts, or more precisely when we present natural science in general or provide common sense of natural science to those who will not be engaged in the discipline of natural science in the future, we need to be as careful as possible about pandering their curiosity in providing them with this knowledge. On the one hand, natural science is necessary today for the prosperity of our nation and because of that, given that Japanese people are poor in scientific thinking, an endorsement of natural science has become almost fashionable. As you can see, newspapers started to include a "science section" and there are some magazines that aim at the popularization of science, which, however, I am not very optimistic about. I secretly doubt that this kind of approach to science would render a great effect. We can teach many unusual things to small children when they are filled with desire for knowledge, asking why this is and why that is. When these things are not unusual or even if they are trivial for our normal common sense, they are rare for children. On that occasion, providing the children with knowledge by appealing to their curiosity and desire for knowledge and enticing them to increase their intellectual appetite (which wants to know this and then also wants to know that) are meaningful and I think they are effective. However, today's popular science magazines or the "science section" in newspapers are not like this, but they are written for adults. The so-called intellectual class in general is their target audience. By the way, when we look at the popularization and dissemination of science in mass media that target the general intellectual class, many of them do not seem to take up the scientific way of thinking as a problem at all. Why a certain thing became a problem and from which principle we are led to a new kind of knowledge and what kind of inventions were made, so on and so forth—these procedures are never questioned. Then it seems that the popularization of natural science tends to talk about things like "how we could not do such and such things before, but now we can do such and such things thanks to an invention of a new machine"; and "thanks to this machine, what we have been finding inconvenient is removed in such and such ways." The popularization of natural science in this sense is probably better than nothing. I am not intending to say that it has no meaning whatsoever. They should have an effect of growing an interest in natural science among general audience. However, regarding the essence of natural science itself, how much contribution does this kind of popularization make? Of course, as far as the things reported in the newspapers and written in magazines would make people think how great the power of natural science, what kind of things it has discovered, and what kind of inventions it has achieved. But that is about it. It does not stimulate and cultivate spontaneity, where each of us obtains this natural scientific way of thinking to any extent nor do we try to think about things and see them in the manner of natural science. I think that this spontaneity of thinking would not be promoted at all by the simple satisfaction of popular curiosity.

I am not sure how you are feeling about this, but I wonder if natural science is far too easily approached and far too popularized, such that we do not perceive the profound truth hidden inside it nor [appreciate] the struggle of scholars to reach the point [where their discoveries are introduced to mass media]; nor even do we comprehend why it was difficult, but we only see the idealistic part of certain accomplishments, which took a long time and were made in the midst of a poor and inconvenient facility; and I wonder if those who are actually engaged in the discipline of natural science would rather feel that this is a desecration of science. In this sense, I cannot help but being pessimistic and skeptical toward the popularization of natural science. Even among scientists, many try to make their science interesting for the general public by explaining it in an accessible manner. In order for that to happen, their writing must be amusing, and so they try to instill scientific knowledge into their audience not in the strictly scientific form, but in the manner of essays; and I wonder if this propensity to a "literarizaiton of science," so to speak, is thriving today even among scientists. Of course, if an excellent scientist has a profound scientific mind and also enjoys a literary talent, this practice could bring forth a valuable result. However, I wonder that those who far too easily handle the popularization of science and turn science into essay material by carelessly making it accessible to the public have an easy-going feeling toward science. I wonder that they might be poor in spirit for engaging in the genuinely scientific study. I wonder that they have a popular and worldly ambition like surprising the masses by submitting something unusual as a scientific result. I cannot hold back this kind of doubt. Also, for teaching at schools, I do think that when providing scientific knowledge, those who are involved with education should avoid at all cost appealing to students' curiosity and leading them to have an easygoing feeling toward science.

In fact, I am sensing from the sideline that the courses on natural science for students in the faculty of letters are incredibly difficult to teach. We have assigned less hours for these courses and, since students from the outset dislike natural scientific subjects, they entered the liberal arts programs. They also think from the beginning that, when they major in law or economics, natural science will hardly have any use for them. I am sure that providing them with the knowledge of natural science and giving courses on the subject under that circumstance would require much effort and many different methods of teaching. However, even then, I do think that we should be careful about the ways of teaching in education, the ways that look like simply appealing to students' curiosity, cultivating in them an easy-going feeling toward natural science, where they could think that natural science is an easy subject, the ways where, we are afraid, natural scientists themselves could look as though they are making fun of science. Hence, it is necessary to provide the knowledge for the students and surely to raise their interest in terms of education: however, it is necessary to keep teaching them, without pandering to their curiosity, in such a way that the students would learn the difficulty of natural science and the struggles of natural scientists. I believe that this is the main point of creating different methods for those who are engaged in teaching this subject. If we are going to teach what students find unusual by appealing to their curiosity, we do not really need to devise different methods. This could be done by anyone and this way of teaching would not be effective for cultivating a scientific way of thinking among Japanese or the development of scientific thinking (*kakagu shisō*, 科学思想) in Japan. In some cases, I secretly suspect they could even be harmful. Well, I am not intending to propose any active methods for providing the knowledge of natural science to students, but I feel I would like to request a little bit more of the passive caution that I just mentioned.

However, needless to say, teaching natural science is not irreducible to the process of transmitting the already made knowledge of natural science to students. Probably this does not bear repeating for you. For instance, when teaching natural science to the students of letters, we are teaching that all things are governed by principles, individual things do not exist independently of each other in isolation, but are interrelated with various phenomena, and they are governed by a universal principle. In other words, it probably goes without saying that it is necessary to gradually keep inspiring the method of science in students. This applies to any academic discipline, and also for natural science what is important is not only the result. The process of reaching the result is important. Even if a person cannot render the result due to various obstacles, she could obtain a new way of thinking or a new method; and even if her circumstance does not grant her with a complete result, we can anticipate that her successor could achieve the new result based on her method and leave the new research result. In that sense, the process is important. The result is just that. However great the invention, if students are taught about it only as the result in terms of knowledge, then they learn only that. But clarifying the method, or which procedures and what ideas led us to the invention and discovery can be an effective reference not only for the solution of this specific problem, but also for other cases; this has an effect where we do not stop with the solution to the problem, but with the same method we can go beyond it.

Thus, even though it is first necessary to grant the knowledge obtained through natural scientific research, if we are going to talk about the degree of importance, we can safely say that it is the lowest. What is more important is the method. I think it is necessary to teach the method of natural scientific study and the natural scientific way of thinking to our students. This way of teaching is especially important when we instruct students who will major in natural science in the future or more precisely students who would study the hard sciences in the broadest sense of the term. But also, in the case of teaching natural science to the students of letters, it would be necessary to adopt this method as much as possible. Well, I say "method" and "method," but I am not saying at all that it is necessary to teach a so-called methodology from a standpoint outside of natural science, as something like philosophy. I think the kind of abstract theory of natural science that stinks of philosophy would be rather harmful and devoid of any good effects. What I mean is that I would like natural scientists to focus on transmitting the method of solving many concrete and real problems from inside the standpoint of natural science to students and pay attention to it such that the students will achieve this method.

In that case, when teaching natural science to the students of letters, there is something that I would like to suggest as an outsider. To begin with, we only have a very short period of time for courses on natural science at the faculty of letters. Also, since students are not going to study any of the hard sciences in the future, they are hardly interested in them. Many of them enter the humanities programs because they did not like the sciences: so, I believe, it is a great struggle to catch students and make them eager to attend the lectures. But what I think might be helpful for alleviating these struggles is that perhaps you should discuss a bit more about the history of natural science to the students in the humanities. At any rate, given the small duration allotted for these courses, even if you are going to give them the knowledge of natural science, we do not really have time to do anything more than just very simply discuss what is really important in the field. And since students are not initially interested in this topic, unless you are going to talk about something really unusual, they would not studiously listen to your talks. However, these students would have a great interest in the history of natural science; and since we are indicating the development of science from the historical side of lived humans, they would be really interested in the subject. What do you think? Of course, I easily say "history," and since you have limited time for these courses, you wonder what kind of things we should do: so, if I were to say a word about this, I would like to point out that the ways of thinking in natural science are not limited to natural science, but the ways of thinking that are particular to each age and each group of individuals (*minzoku*, 民族) are reflected in the natural scientific ways of thinking. At the same time, moreover, the natural scientific ways of thinking have an influence on the general ways of thinking in each age and each group of individuals. Might not taking these things into consideration be useful for the natural science courses at the faculty of letters? What we call the method and the way of thinking in natural science is by no means irreducible to natural science, but it is playing a greater role in a large area in relation to the development of general humanity and the development of history. Hence, I think that students in letters would be interested in courses on natural science if you talk about these things to some extent or touch on them to any degree.

For example, generally speaking, there are, of course, precursors to the later atomistic theory in ancient Greek philosophy. Roughly speaking, [ancient Greek thinkers] statically see the world and regard it as the result of a certain teleological arrangement of things that take on a harmonious and beautiful pattern. Such unity of matter and form gives the characteristics of the Greek view of nature. Now, since things take on the harmonious and beautiful patterns in this manner, they themselves become a teleological view of nature. The original nature of natural things is to take on such harmonious shape; no matter how chaotic they look nor how filled with contradictions at a glance, if we pay closer attention to them, they exhibit a very beautiful harmony. It is just like snow: even though it does not appear to have any shape at a glance, once we pay closer attention to it, it consists of beautiful, crystalized shapes. What we call nature, moreover, is moving toward its beautiful shape from chaos. The whole of nature is arranged in an order that extends from the kind of things that have beautiful shapes to those which possess incomplete shapes. When there is a change of movement, it precisely means that the incomplete things are trying to move toward a complete and beautiful shape. In this sense, the essence of nature lies in what we call the harmonious form. That which realizes this form is eternally unchangeable; it would neither move nor change. That is because, as I just mentioned, [ancient Greek philosophers] thought that change or motion is proof of incompleteness. Stated succinctly, in Ancient Greece, as we know, natural philosophy and natural science were originally one. In Great Britain, even when I was a student, I think there were more books that were entitled "natural philosophy" than "physics." Even in the British tradition, natural philosophy and physics were one, as they were, of course, also one and the same in the Greek tradition. In a word, that sort of view of nature was static, not dynamic. We could perhaps describe it with a term "staticism." However, the modern view of nature is completely different from this one. The purpose of natural cognition does not lie in this kind of unmoving form, but primarily in clarifying the motions and changes. When we build a machine by utilizing nature, we have to grasp the laws of motion in nature. Thus, natural science in modernity is essentially dynamic. Contrary to staticism, we have "mechanism." It primarily focuses on the motion of things. Hence, as you already know, it is a matter of course that the physics of Galileo and Newton play the central role [in modern natural science]. That is largely different from the Greek view of nature or Greek natural science.

However, after the nineteenth century, we cannot say that the view of nature still pertains to mechanism. As you know, since there has been the development of Faraday's and Maxwell's notion of the "dynamic field," the view of nature by no means constitutes mechanism. Its characteristics are something like this: instead of saying things are simply in motion, the motion of things is always thought through the medium, which is the field of force. It is not mechanism, but dynamism. Instead of posing that things separately move and thereby seek the law in the progress of their motions, it focuses on the medium that is supporting them. ... They also thought about human beings as a machine, as there is a book like "Man, a Machine" that tries to explain human beings simply as the motion of various elements. That pertains to mechanism. However, recent biology does not take this way of thinking. Its outstanding character is that it always thinks about living beings *in* the environment. Thinking about living beings and environment as constituting their inseparable, interrelating unity, instead of thinking about the mechanistic relation of them, precisely indicates an instance of dynamism.

This might be a very simple fact, but each way of thinking in ancient, modern, and contemporary natural science has its unique character and they are different from each other. Moreover, they are not only different in the domain of natural science, but as I just mentioned, the differences of staticism, mechanism, and dynamism can also be said about things outside natural science. ... In this manner, if you actually talk about scientific knowledge by taking into account that natural science or the natural scientific way of thinking has historically changed when it is seen in a relatively broader perspective, students in letters would be interested in your discussion, and also for students that are majoring in hard sciences, it could have the effect of giving them a more general and broad outlook on their discipline. In this sense, I would like to express my wish that, if time allows, you would think about discussing the history of natural science in your courses.

Nevertheless, the method is, after all, a means for a human being to accomplish its mission. The method is just a path. What moves in that path is the spirit of natural scientists. After all, I cannot help but think that the highest mission in terms of value for the professors of natural science is inspire the spirit of natural scientists or the natural scientific mind into students as much as possible. It is, of course, necessary to pass the knowledge of science or have students acquired the method. However, I think it is most important to stimulate the spirit of natural scientists or natural scientific spirit, in other words, the mind that believes in reason's governance of things and tries to unfold this reason (*dōri*, 道理). Indeed, reason is not at all an idea or rational quibbling that we think only in our heads. It should not signify the rational arguments that we abstractly lay out on a desk. Those kind of rational arguments cannot actually function inside things as the reason. The reason that acts inside things would have to be that which can be drawn from empirical facts, the facts that we can actually verify. Put simply, the spirit of natural science must take that kind of empirical mind as its first content. However, the empirical spirit only teaches us about the reality of the particular but unifying reality and giving a certain lawful order [to it] would rely on the rational demand of humans, or more precisely, the demand to think about the reason of things. Hence, natural scientific spirit is first the empirical spirit and second, the rational spirit. It is important to think about this empirical and rational character in terms of the relation based on the exclusive complementarity that I discussed in the beginning. Insofar as it is empirical, when we know things, we must accurately receive the facts that we actually observe and experiment. Today's new physics, as it was already the case for Einstein, and it is still so with young quantum physicists such as Heisenberg and Jordan, claims to inherit the spirit of the positivist Mach. I think the spirit of contemporary physics is to go beyond Mach's positivism while succeeding it. In fact, both for the theory of relativity and for today's quantum physics, they start by accepting the empirical facts as what they are no matter how incompatible they are with our conventional way of thinking in physics or with our common sense. For instance, it is indeed very strange that light is made of particles. It is very difficult to accept that the final element of materials that we call "electron" is at the same time wave-like. If we are speaking from the conventional standpoint, it is quite difficult to conceive of these things. Also, regarding the theory of relativity, we are thinking that we can measure time without having any relation to space, and at the same time, we are not thinking that time is related to our measurement of space, and wherever we stand, one hour is an hour and one meter is one meter. However, the fact is otherwise. The time that we measure in physics is relative to the motion that belongs to it. Accordingly, time includes a spatial element within it. The length of the spatial cannot be thought apart from the motion of what is being observed. In other words, a determination of time is included in the determination of space. In this manner, what we normally conceive as two separate things, like space and time, that we think we can measure independently from each other is now shown to be connected to each other. However contradictory to our common sense, if the empirical fact shows that this is the case, we have to construct the theory that ultimately supports the facts. We must not manufacture the theory in advance and bend the facts toward it. That is precisely the spirit of positivism.

However, the positivist spirit cannot continue acting on its own at all. When we carry out an experiment, we are implementing some kind of theory. When we set up equipment for an experiment, we cannot leave it to accident to make it work. A theory must be used for the experiment even if it might be later revised or completely denied due to its result. Here, the positivist spirit must primarily focus on the experiment in relation to experience, but we must say, when it takes the standpoint of experience, the positivist spirit rather presupposes, on the other side of experience, the theory that is not appearing at the same time; that is to say, it maintains the complementary opposite. It is at least exclusive. There is no theory when we interpret experience by resorting to the senses. However, since there is a theory on the other side of observations, we can devise equipment for them. If that is the case, then it is clear that theory and experiment hold the mutually exclusive and complementary relation to each other.

In that sense, this is why a true study [of natural science] cannot be carried out unless the positivist spirit, while preserving the empirical facts, is after all tied to the rational spirit, which theoretically constitutes the facts into a system devoid of any logical contradictions, in the relation of exclusive complementarity. On the one hand, a true researcher [of science] must be positivistic through and through. Today's science requires positivists. However, on the other, their study must be rationally organized. I think that the positivist and the rational spirit, which are seemingly contradictory to each other, establish the relation where we can deem them to be the two sides, which are necessary for constituting the spirit of science. I think that, to inspire the scientific spirit that has two sides in this sense is an indispensable requirement in teaching natural science to students at high schools.

Then, what does it mean to inspire that kind of spirit to students? How can we do this? Once again, I hesitate to say anything about it from the standpoint of those who are not engaged with the actual study of natural science. And once again, if I am allowed to say that it is possible to "draw a lesson from an outsider," I would like to say the following. To inspire the spirit cannot be done by words. To breathe in the spirit is the relation between people. When students can sense that their teacher is actually on fire with the spirit of natural science, that she carries out her research and teaches classes by making good use of the spirit, only when that happens, the spirit is inspired in the students. Also, this belongs to the other side of spirit that cannot appear as the object of natural science. Even if we tell them to have the spirit by explaining theories in a naturally scientific way, conducting experiments, and analyzing equations, the spirit cannot be imbued in the students. The inspiration of spirit can be done only through the relation of people, the relation of spirits, and the living community (*ikita kōkan*, 生きた交感).

This might be stepping into the topic too far, but I would like to hope that those of you who are teaching natural science to students at high schools and vocational colleges to continue to pursue your own research no matter how incomplete your facilities are, no matter how poor your budgets are, and no matter how destitute your circumstances might be. (Of course, I am aware that some of you are already doing this.) As you all know, it goes without saying that, unless we have a large-scale facility that requires a massive budget; it is extremely difficult to help science make one step forward. However, the number of people who can carry out their research at such a complete facility is very small. Of course, we can expect that this small number of scientists are very excellent in their capability. But there are those who are in circumstances where they cannot do research in that kind of facility regardless of the fact that they are also very talented in science. We cannot argue that one is superior to the other in capability and talent because one is a scientist that has access to the great facility, while the other only has access to poor equipment. It might be misleading to say this, but if we are to say that those who belong to the research institute with a great facility and pursue the mission of advancing science are the scientists that stand in the front line, we could say that those who have access only to relatively poor facilities on the one hand and are engaged in teachings at schools on the other are the scientists standing in the second line. This does not mean at all, however, that the first scientists are necessarily superior to the second in every respect. It is a matter of human affairs that those who have abilities should be in the front line while others have no choice but to stand in the second for many reasons. Also, those who are standing in the first line end up being there due to circumstances regardless of the fact that they do not have sufficient capabilities to work there. Of course, those in the second could be transferred to the first due to some circumstances as well. Therefore, if the scientists in the second line take themselves lightly and belittle themselves by saying that, since we are the scientists in the second rank who have access only to incomplete facilities, we should leave the advancement of science to those in the front line; even if we try, we would not achieve anything; it is useless to try; and then, if they only focus on teaching classes [by thinking about these things], I do not think that they can be the source for inspiring the spirit of natural science to students.

It goes without saying, Faraday and the biologist, Mendel, for instance, made great accomplishments at terribly mal-equipped facilities. Of course, this is a different age today. However, I cannot help but think that, if you are scientists who are alive with enthusiasm for scientific studies, you can necessarily sympathize with, and be moved by, the spirit that drove these great scientists to accomplish their discoveries and inventions that advanced science toward the new age in the present, despite the fact that they were placed in positions where they were too poor to devise any equipment at their terribly deficient facilities. Under whatever circumstances they are placed, and no matter how poor their facilities are, these kind of people cannot help but think out some way of studying. I do not know the details, but I am really happy when I come cross with journal articles that introduce the works of school teachers whom we could expect to be working at incomplete facilities. I think that these are gratifying phenomena for the improvement of science in Japan. When teachers provide the knowledge that they gained from books, the knowledge that is not connected to their living experiences, even if they look like they know science very well, sensitive and naïve students could immediately feel their differences from teachers that are working on some project of their own. It was actually the case when I think about my experience during my middle school years. The students felt that the teachers who were working on their own projects, even if they were terrible at teaching, had something deeper than what they were saying in classrooms. We could say that he is simply teaching what is written in the textbook, but somewhere deeper inside, there is a living spirit of scientists and the teaching is carried out through communication or a resonance of living spirits between human beings; and I think this is an undeniable fact. The teachers that are engaged in that kind of study necessarily move students. I would like to say that this is exactly the most efficient means to breathe in the spirit of natural science. These teachers' projects might be trivial to the researchers in the front line. However, we cannot know for sure if the trivial research will forever end up being trivial. We cannot be absolutely certain that a project, which looks like a trifle in terms of the study of natural science, would not turn out to be something that revolutionizes the theory itself. We cannot determine the significance of ongoing particular studies immediately from within today's standpoint. ... Zen monks would say that, even if they cannot achieve true enlightenment (*satori*), if they have the courageous heart-and-mind to achieve self-awareness (*kenshō*, 見性), that alone is enough for them to be saved when they die. I think this has a profound meaning. You all are quite busy and even if we keep saying "research and research," it would be fairly difficult to achieve any results at incomplete facilities. But still I think you can always maintain the spirit that continues thinking about the problem emerged in your project and intends to solve it by any means. This will eventually be the force that moves students. In that respect, the fact that the scientists in the second line continue holding their hearts and minds for working on their own projects without belittling themselves would almost be the only way to inspire the spirit of natural science. But I am sure, depending on the situations and also on your interests, you cannot easily realize this in practice. In these cases, what I would like you to take into consideration is that you would study the biography of scientists and the history of science. As long as you have access to books, you hardly need anything else including a facility. Even if you are so busy and do not have a considerable amount of time to do an experiment, you can read for one hour every night and you can familiarize yourself with the history of science and come to know the lives of great scientists. Especially if the biographies of great scientists naturally have an influence on your hearts, and even if you cannot work on your own project, but satisfy your heart and mind for doing the study by sympathizing with the study of these great scientists, I think students would be able to feel and receive your spirit. Perhaps because natural science in Japan is young, we do not pay close attention to the biographies of scientists or to the history of science. Among the universities abroad, there are some that provide courses on the history of science.

Regarding the history of science, and especially what we are now talking about as its spirit, if you read into the paths of scientific investigations in the biographies of great scientists, and even though you yourself may not be able to carry out any experiments, by satisfying your desire as a scholar, you could induce some emotional response from your students. I think that the highest stage of the positive side [in the education of natural science] is for you to inspire the scientific spirit in your students in this sense.

3. The Awareness of the Limit of Natural Science as the Negative Aspect of the Education in Natural Science

I discussed the positive side in the two sides of education in natural science yesterday. I would like to talk about what we should call the negative side today.

As I mentioned yesterday, this relation of the two sides, the positive and the negative, is slightly different from what we ordinarily think as "two sides" of things. When talking about the negative side today, I might repeat myself here, but I would like to add a few more explanations to the concept.

The relation of the two sides that I discussed yesterday cannot be a compromise in the sense of *secchū*. I am not entirely confident if this expression is appropriate for describing this relation, but still, as previously mentioned, we can pose the notion of *shicchū* in opposition to that of *secchū*.

When we talk about this *secchū*, two things that are broken in the middle are in the relation, where each of them tries to claim and affirm its own standpoint as much as possible; hence, when one is stretched, the other would have to shrink. We sometimes say the "relation of rising and falling" (*shōchō-no kankei*, 消長の関係) or that there is a conflicting relation of competing power. There is this kind of relation between them. In order to break somewhere in the middle of them and establish a compromise, we have to shave the excess and combine them (by breaking them) at the point where they will not clash against each other. This is what we mean by the term, *secchū*. We also say in this sense that a compromise (*dakyō*) is established. .... So, I described yesterday that this kind of "rise and fall" of continuous powers indicates the relation in which they push against each other through the medium of being (*u*, 有). I have been saying from yesterday that my conception of "two sides" do noes not stand in this kind of relation.

What then is the difference between this relation and my rendering of the "two sides"? The "two sides" that I am thinking about does not mean that they are in competition through the relation of power nor that they limit each other nor even remain mutually restrictive. ... Rather, each of these sides will complete their standpoints respectively. However, since each of these sides does not constitute the whole on its own—despite the fact that it can complete its account by itself—it always remains (self-)aware that it is accompanied by the opposite and always thinks about contributing to the whole that contains both sides. In this manner, when one standpoint appears, the other cannot appear therein. This is the meaning of exclusiveness that I mentioned yesterday. Of course, the term "exclusiveness" might be used to describe the competing "rise and fall" relation in an ordinary sense. We do not need to be fixated on this term. But because the concept that those who play a central role in contemporary physics are equivalent to what I mentioned as "exclusivity," I borrowed it to talk about this. What I mean is the concept of exclusiveness in what they call "exclusive complementary." The English translation of Bohr's book uses the expression "natural exclusion." This must also refer to exclusion (*haita*, 排他). At any rate, when I say "exclusion" it does not mean that two things are pushing against each other and one eliminates the other, but the relation in which when one appears, the other cannot appear. Perhaps, we could use the word "contradiction" instead of "exclusion" in order to avoid some confusions. In short, it means that they are not established at the same time. The relation in which contradictories complement each other is what I mean by the relation of two sides. Accordingly, when we say this, it does not mean that which limits one exists outside of one's own self, but that it lies in oneself. The whole can never be established unless there are both of these; hence, in order to contribute to the whole and establish it, the self limits itself. It does not mean at all that, that which limits one is the other that exists outside the one, but rather for the whole that establishes them in a complementary relation, the self must limit itself. Originally, the self is not the whole, but it is accompanied by the other side, and only when they complement each other is the self established inside the whole; and since the self is aware of this fact in itself, even though the other does not appear when it takes its own standpoint, it limits itself in order to establish the whole in a mutually complementary relation with the other. This is what I mean by the relation of two sides. *Shicchū* precisely means to take the standpoint of this whole that is nothingness.

As I mentioned yesterday, when we think about the light as waves, the particle-like nature of it does not appear. When we think about the particleness, the wave-like characteristics do not appear. However, the true nature of light would be incomplete if we only think about either side of them and only when we wait for both can we, for the first time, establish the whole of what we call "light." Now, the scientists themselves can freely enter both sides of these contradictory positions (which cannot be established at the same time) and by unifying them into the whole through the medium of nothingness, they can clarify the true nature of light. When they take one standpoint, they would never mix the other standpoint for the other while holding the one and limit this standpoint that they are taking in the middle of it by mixing the other into the one. They would never face the case where, when they look at any part of their study, it gives a composite or a compromise of these two. When they take each of them, they focus on it till the end. However, real physicists think about both. Or we could call this subjectivity or if we speak not from the side of objectivity but the subject, by freely entering and exiting each side of the two through the medium of nothing, they manifest the whole therein. Such a relation gives the relation of "two sides" that I am now describing as the relation of the terms as the "positive" and the "negative."

Thus, when we are standing on the positive side when teaching natural science, we do not have to think that this standpoint is limited from the outside or that, since there is that kind of power out there, we would have to be making a compromise here. When we hold the standpoint of natural science, dedicate ourselves to the study, and teach the subject, it is right to do the best we can in order to demonstrate the full effect of this standpoint. However, at the same time, this is one side of the whole. To think in a natural scientific manner is not the whole of human thinking. It is one side of it. There is another side. Yet we can freely enter in and exist from both sides. No, we dedicate ourselves to the study of natural science by taking the natural scientific standpoint. We are not forced to do this, but do it in freedom. So long as we take this standpoint, we must focus on completing both research and teaching so that we can prove the natural scientific spirit. But that is one side of the whole. There is the other side. ... The limitation in self-awareness is the limit that the self puts on itself: hence, it is not externally forced to it, but belongs to its freedom. Freely limiting itself is the meaning of such limitation.

If I am to bring up an example for clarifying a bit more about this [concept of limitation], I wonder that the problem of the relation between state rule and individual freedom, which is our actual problem today, might need this way of thinking. Normally, since the one rules and the other claims its freedom, we tend to think of them in terms of the conflict between two incompatible forces. However, I think that there is a huge difference between interpreting this relation in this standpoint or in terms of the [contradictory] relation that we are thinking of right now. If the rule means the relation of coercion by force, it refers to the relation of power conflicts. It only means that the stronger subjugates the weaker by force. When they are going to make a compromise with each other, they will do it reluctantly. The limitation of freedom in this case is not the limitation that the self gives to itself, but is implemented from the outside. If we are going to see this from the side of the ruling party, it wishes for that which stands against it in any sense would not exist at all; and this indicates the standpoint of power conflicts. What is ideal in this case (we have to say) would be that there is absolutely no demand for the freedom of individuals and that the relation in which everything mechanically and blindly follows the will of the ruler would be established. However, that kind of relation is by no means mutually complementary. If we stand in this relation, dedicate ourselves to one side, and remain oblivious of the other, then we would act as though we [as the self] are constituting the whole, even though we are not the whole; and consequently, we will fall victim to a contradiction somewhere down the road and fail to avoid the situation where the [neglected] other shows its face to us. Naturally, when we talk about the rule, there is something that moves out of its initiative, freely and spontaneously moving against this rule; and only then, what we call "rule" has some meaning. It does not mean anything to say "rule" to that which, from the beginning, moves exactly in line with the will of the ruler. And if we exclude that kind of thing from its scope, this kind of rule would be utterly powerless. There is no way [for the ruler] to fully demonstrate its concrete power when it controls that which blindly follows it in a mechanical fashion. The state of being concretely ruled has to mean not that the limitation is externally imposed on something that freely and spontaneously moves, but that the self enters into the rule in the sense of freely limiting itself. Put simply, only when the self fully agrees and cooperates with the ruler, we can fully prove the significance of the term, "rule." The self recognizes the rule not as that which is forced upon it from the outside, but as that which it has put on itself and collaborates with the rule by spontaneously adding itself to it; this is the truly concrete rule. But at the same time, freedom avoids the fate of stepping into a contradiction, where its arbitrary whimsicality will be dragged around by its selfish desires, thus reaching true freedom where the self spontaneously rules itself. This is precisely rule-qua-freedom (*tōsei-soku-jiyū*, 統制即自由) and freedom-qua-rule (*jiyū-soku-tōsei*, 自由即統制).

We generally use the word *soku* (即) like "A-*soku*-B" and, in this case, we are saying "rule-*soku*-freedom." The meaning of this term does not mean that A and B are exactly the same. If they are identical, there is no reason why we should describe them through the relation of *soku*. They are different from each other: hence, rule is rule and freedom is freedom. Each of them at least has its own standpoint and is independent. However, as I just mentioned, for establishing one of them, only when there is the opposing other can it demonstrate its meaning as one side of the whole. *Soku* means that the two sides, in this manner, wait for each other to be unified into the whole while being different from each other. Thus, *soku* does not signify the same (*dō*, 同), but rather, as I have been saying since yesterday, a sort of a relation in which two things, which are in their exclusive and contradictory opposition, intermediate each other. That kind of relation is described by the concept of *soku*. When we say *kleshas-soku-buddhi*, it does not mean that giving free rein to (negative) desires immediately reaches enlightenment. But rather they are contradictory. To some extent, they cannot be established at the same time. However, the concrete truth is where these things that cannot be established at the same time are mediated. The true nature of human action, I think, is to mediate these things that look to be incompatible with each other. To act is not to realize the self's demand, that is, to have one's own way, but to kill the self and to let the other live. By killing the self and letting the other live, it can in turn let the true self live. This space between the self and the other (*jita-no aida*, 自他の間), as I discussed yesterday, is not continuously connected from one side to another through the medium of some being. No, since it is completely discontinuous and moves like a transformation from one to the other through the medium of nothingness, the "I" that moves in this manner must also be nothingness. If there is something that we can call "I" and that "I" acts, then I am afraid it cannot make most of the whole, which is nothingness, by establishing the mutually contradictory and yet complementary relation that I just mentioned. That the "I" acts in fact means that the "I" comes to nothing. This means that, when the "I" disappears, the reality lives. When the "I" governs the reality as it is, it enables the conflicts of power that we previously distinguished and it is absolutely unattainable. When the "I" comes to nothing and reality lives, it becomes for the first time the act of the "I." However, when the I disappears and reality lives, this reality is not the one that was standing in position of the "I," but at the same time the true "I" itself. That reality begins to act when there is no "I" means that the true "I" has emerged therein. The reality becomes the "I." This reality is not that which stands in opposition to the "I," but "I"-*soku*-reality. In this case, the disappearance of the "I" is to become the true "I"; hence to kill the "I" is to let the "I" live in the true sense. This does not mean at all that the "I" dies out and is gone because the power that puts a certain limit on it from the outside wins over, but that the "I" freely disappears. The fact that the "I" freely goes to nothing comes to mean that the freedom of the "I" is truly realized.

Of course, what we call "reality" does not perfectly manifest its reason as it is all the time. If it were the case, there would be no reason for humans to make any effort or to keep improving upon all things. Reality is always living and moving and human beings act in this moving medium. Hence, it is the fact that there is always a mixture of standpoints in reality. It could happen in reality that one forces the other [to do what one wants], or that each of them wants to exercise its freedom as it wishes, through the conflict of power. However, the true relation of the rule and the freedom would have to be the relation in which the self takes the other as the medium of denying itself and in turn the self is affirmed.

If we think about this kind of relation in reference to today's natural science, we have to say that it is necessary for scientists to be aware of the negative side of natural science in opposition to the positive side in themselves and to remain attentive to the fact that natural science is not all-encompassing, but contains the other side that is standing over against it in a completely contradictory relation. However, this kind of self-awareness is that which is held by living human beings themselves, the natural scientists that have this self-awareness mediates both sides that are contradictory to each other. The small "I" disappears and brings itself to nothing, both sides are mediated [with each other through the self-negation], and thereby the concrete whole of nothingness is manifested. However, when we hold the position of a natural scientist, the standpoint of natural science is indeed more positive. Hence, after all, we have to use the term "negative" and since, when you study and teach natural science, you have to stand on the side of forming the natural science, the negative standpoint in relation to it is not that which externally gives a limit to the positive side, but points in the direction of self-awareness, where the self internally limits itself. I would like you to think about the negative side in that sense.

It is of a great significance, I think, that the two sides, which constitute the relation between the positive and the negative in this sense, have clearly appeared in today's natural science. Even some physiologists, including Haldane, think that the essence of life is to maintain the orderly unity between living beings and their environment and regard a wholistic rule of two sides as an axiom of biology.[2] The fact that this kind of philosophy has started to appear in biology where the mechanical interpretation had been dominant certainly has the significance that marks a new era in this discipline. This is the so-called physiological orientation of physics. The aforementioned physicists, including Jordan, call the two sides that are in this kind of relation a "duality," but what they mean by it is that two contradictories are complementary to each other. In this sense, we can say that reality is entirely dualistic. Moreover, such duality constitutes the unity of the whole through each other in the manner of their complementarity, but since this whole is a contradictory unity, it would have to be not being, but nothingness. The dual is brought into one in the whole of nothingness.

These doubleness (*nimensei*, 二面性) and wholeness are acknowledged not only in physics, but also much earlier in biology. The discipline of biology requires the standpoint of element analysis on the one hand, as Jordan writes in his books, it acknowledges various discontinuity on the other and accordingly requires the complementarity. I do not know about this topic in detail, but I would like to briefly introduce in the following what Jordan argues in his books for those of you specializing in biology. So, for instance, we can think that Mendel's laws of heredity, like the quantum in physics, clearly demonstrates an instance of discontinuity in nature. As you already know, when we think about heredity, things that have different traits, for instance, in Mendel's experiment of peas, when we think about the new species generated from breeding two parents that have different colors, if we think of them as being continuous, the result of crossbreeding A and B, which have two different traits, as we can expect commonsensically, a crossbreed emerges as a combination of both A and B. This is precisely a "mixed" type seen from the standpoint of continuity. At first glance, it seems that this kind of mixture is natural. However, in the actual study of genetics, this is not the case. The next generation shows the traits of one of the parents. That is exactly a discontinuity: if one parent has the trait A and the other has B, and if the child is born out of them, it seems that it is going to be a crossbreed in the middle between them, but that is not the case; according to Mendel's experiment, the child shows only the characteristics of either parent, the so-called dominant traits. However, this does not mean that the other traits that do not immediately appear in the next generation are completely gone somewhere, but rather they can appear in a later generation like their children's children. These recessive traits are not completely gone .... This is the discontinuous and dynamic inheritance and it is transmitted [to the next generation] with a certain unit. There is a unit in inheritance and it is indivisible beyond it. It must discontinuously appear or not appear, and this has to be either/or. As I mentioned yesterday, the discontinuous way of thinking would have to be a compound, which could be both this and that. It is both/and. However, the inheritance that appears in a discontinuous fashion is an either/or. Mendel's law of heredity is established as a law of discontinuous phenomena. These kind of things are gradually discovered in other fields as well. The conventional framework of physics tended to carry out its observation in a mechanical fashion. That is because it was thinking that it could explain all natural phenomena as a continuous interaction of things. However, discontinuity was made explicit in quantum phenomena and the field of physics had to clearly acknowledge complementarity and duality. Some have referred to this confrontation with the facts of microscopic experiments with an exaggerating phrase, "The Renaissance of Physics" (as in Darrow's book published in 1936). However, this is something that the field of biology had already acknowledged, and further, I think this is not anything unusual if we think about this in reference to human beings. In fact, I think we have been thinking like this since ancient times. For instance, a human spirit is on the one hand always conscious. Today's psychology starts with the consciousness as the object of its study. However, can we exhaustively understand the phenomena of the human mind? The answer is no. As an extreme example, the Freudian theory argues that unconsciousness (*muishiki*, 無意識) is always playing a great role in the life of the human mind; and that, even though the result of its work appears in consciousness, what supports the appearance of consciousness is the unconsciousness. However, even though unconsciousness occupies a very broad area in the life of the mind in this manner, it is not possible to see it directly. There is no way but to estimate unconsciousness in the background of consciousness by taking what appears therein as a medium. Then, we can say that consciousness and unconsciousness in psychology are in the relation of mutually exclusive complementarity. Or, if we take a look at what appears in the conscious side, consciousness consists of simple elements like "sensations" and in opposition to this element theory, there is a wholistic unity—in psychology, it is described with the important concept we call "*Gestalt*"—these two ways of seeing [consciousness] with elements and the wholistic Gestalt are once again in the relation of the exclusive complementarity, where neither one can be reduced to the other. It is necessary to always think about the whole and the elements with regard to the cognition of the mind. Also, when we think about consciousness, we must not forget that unconsciousness grounds it. Thus, we can perhaps say that this represents the duality in psychology.

Moreover, if we are going to think about society, formal sociology conventionally thought that a society consists of interactions of individuals or their interrelations. However, this way of thinking is rather peculiar to the formal sociology that emerged from the individualistic and liberal standpoint and it cannot comprehend things like a specific group of individuals (*minzoku*, 民族) or the state. If we think about the state from that kind of standpoint, we have no choice but to think of it as a group that is established through the contract of individuals. However, we cannot understand the primitive unity of an ethnic group or the essence of the state through this standpoint at all. Therefore, today's sociology discusses "society as a whole" as a very important concept in relation to these topics. However, if the society as a whole, as I mentioned earlier, gives the whole that absorbs individuals inside it and both dissolves them therein, it will at the same time lose the meaning of being a whole. The whole can be what it is only when the individuals were let live inside it. Then, we would have to acknowledge the whole and the independence of individuals that constitutes it as members at the same time in relation to a society. An individual becomes the true individual in such a whole and, by letting the individual live, collaboratively participate in the whole, and spontaneously contribute to its unity, we have the "whole" for the first time as the "living whole."

Contrary to our expectation, things that give a complementary unity of duality started to appear in material nature, and thereby nature is no longer seen as a continuous motion of material elements in a mechanical fashion, but is acknowledged as the unity of discontinuity and continuity; and furthermore, with regard to life, spirit, and society, this kind of duality is clearly acknowledged [in corresponding disciplines]. This is the present state of contemporary academia. As I mentioned yesterday, I think this is something that we should fully take into account when we teach natural science to students.

4. The Limit of Causality in Uncertainty and *Zenkisei* (全機性)

These things are clearly demonstrated especially in reference to the problem of causality today. Perhaps it is not necessary for me to say this to those of you specializing in hard sciences. But just for those of you who are not, or if I am to say something within the bounds of what is comprehensible to nonprofessionals, causality in short means that, in a single system of nature that we observe, when a certain kind of phenomenon takes place at a certain point of time, it is always accompanied by another certain kind of phenomenon that takes places at an antecedent point of time. In this manner, causality is the temporally sequential relation of phenomena, where their occurrences are necessarily accompanied by each other. When a certain kind of phenomenon appears in a certain system, the other certain kind of phenomenon always appears after it; then, in order of us to observe this as a causal relation, what is presupposed as the necessary condition is that our observation of it neither introduces any disturbance nor brings about any changes to the system. It presupposes that, whether or not we observe it, the causal relation would always take place in the same way.

However, when it comes down to the motion of a very small particle like an electron, even though the motion in general is described by the quantity of the material object's movements or the speed, or, for example, when determining the position of an electron at a certain point of time, we cannot measure it without shedding light on the particle. Needless to say, the light possesses an energy; hence, if we direct a considerable amount of light on the electron to clearly show us its position, the quantity of the electron's movement changes due to the energy of the light and its speed also changes. In this case, it means that we cannot precisely measure the position and the speed of the electron as well as the quantity of its motion at the same time. If we provide a substantial amount of light, the quantity of the electron's motion ends up changing due to the light. If we reduce the light to not disturb it and refrain from providing any light, then we cannot determine its position in an exact manner. But then, when we causally understand the motion by describing it, we cannot clearly observe the position and the speed (or the quantity of the motion) at the same time in reference to the particles that are indispensable [for the very process of the observation]. If we precisely determine the one, the other becomes uncertain. This is what we call the "principle of uncertainty" or the "uncertainty principle." Because there is such a principle, the procedures of our observation add disturbance to the system that is to be observed. Accordingly, the causal description becomes impossible. Hence, we can say that the conventional framework of the causal relation or the mechanical worldview are applicable to the ordinary phenomena that we can physically witness, but when we cannot see through our eyes except by making the microscopic electrons the object in our observation of phenomena, we cannot determine the causal relation. The observation gives disturbance to the phenomena and it prevents us from determining an intrinsic causality. This is also something that we could acknowledge as a very mysterious event only when we limited our thinking of the natural phenomena within the phenomena in physics through some equipment for a very large-scale experiment; but if we think about this, this is something very simple that we already know. When we become angry and then decide to reflect on our "self," and try to observe it, our anger disappears before we know it or at least it is softened. In other words, the same self observes itself in its state of being angry. Then the "I" is divided into two sides: the angry "I" under observation, and the "I" that observes the fact that it is angry. Thus, since they are the same human being, when this intellectual act of observing the self-observation enters in its attempt at observing the angry "I," the anger under observation is disturbed and thereby no longer possible for the "I" to observe itself in the original state. This is a very common thing in terms of psychology.

However, this has greater significance for the human spirit. The veteran in today's physics, Planck, often talks about human free will, but his theory of free will is, I think, attempting to argue for the similar idea to what we have been talking about; namely, given that the cause-and-effect can be disturbed by our observation, there is room enough even from the standpoint of physics to be able to think about human freedom. Put more succinctly, when we deal with the problem of free will, we have to distinguish and think separately about the two sides in relation to the "I," that is, the willful "I" and the intellectual "I" that observes it. We then decide that, either the human will is free or necessarily/causally determined. However, as I just said, when we observe a cause-and-effect, even in physics, we have to acknowledge that the observation itself, when it comes to the microscopic event, is turned into the phenomenon that is to be observed and that it brings a disturbance to the object under observation. That is to say, with regard to the human spirit, we observe whether or not the "I" is causally determined; and that which observes is also the "I." Since the "I" that is observing regards the willful "I" under observation as the same ego, when it acts as the observer on the one hand and the ego already undergoes a transformation on the other, thanks to this act. If we can put the ego somewhere beyond ourselves and validate whether or not this ego as a willful ego is causally determined, and just by the fact that we can do this, we can determine that, either human beings are causally necessary in their entirety or that they have freedom. In the same way as we observe in physics the macroscopic phenomena that we would encounter in our everyday life, we could determine the causal nature of the human will, but even in physics we now know that we cannot do the same for the microscopic phenomena. It is more so in human psychology: since both the "I" that observes and the "I" that is observed are the same "I," we cannot admit any causal determinations here. We could think that freedom is grounded in this causal indetermination. Planck tries to argue that human free will is possible in this manner. However, of course, freedom is experienced as such when the self begins to act: hence, so long as we put the self over there for an observation and debate whether or not it is free, freedom does not actually become real. An act of a human being as an object would have to be understood as that which is causally determined. However, the acting self would have to be free. That which is not free is not the "I." This "I" is free as the act of what I previously called "nothingness." Therefore, if we are thinking in the same way as Planck, we can only say that freedom is after all not impossible, but we cannot say that we are actively free. As long as we are saying that causation is both denying and limiting the "I" and clarifying that there is something beyond its reach, we are only showing that there is room for the other side to act. Only when we actually put the other side into practice will we be able to actively say that there is indeed the other side. But, of course, unless sufficient room is given, we cannot positively fill the other side; and only in that sense could we say that Planck's theory of free will has a significance that we cannot ignore at all. At any rate, I am thinking that this has a great significance for making us recognize the limit of natural science.

Materialism overlooks the human spirit, thinking as though material motions alone constitute existence, and treats the human spirit that observes these very motions as an incidental phenomenon that emerged in conjunction with the materials. Our knowledge, in this case, only mirrors the movements of such materials. It does not have any positive principle of its own, but merely reflects the material movements. It holds the idea that so-called knowledge is copying. However, the limit of causality just mentioned, or more precisely, uncertainty, does not allow this way of thinking at all. So long as it can be disturbed and transformed by observation, knowledge cannot be copying. It is established as a result of the collaborative intermediation between subject and object. If we take the materials alone as reality and recognize the spirit as an incidental phenomenon therein, we cannot understand knowledge. The theory of knowledge as copying in materialism would have to be denied by today's new theory of physics. In that sense, we can become aware of the limitations in the mechanistic view of things/nature or the limitations of the materialistic worldview in reference to various results of contemporary natural science. The other side that shows up as these limits is not the matter, but the spirit. Once again, these matter and spirit are in the contradictory and complementary relation with each other. When both sides are negatively mediated, the whole of nothingness begins to act. Moreover, we cannot be (self-)aware of the act of nothingness from the side of matter, but only become such from the side of spirit: hence, we must say, not the matter, but rather the side of spirit is the realization of the whole. Nevertheless, so long as spirit is the concrete manifestation of the whole, it is not the spirit that stands over against nature or matter, but nature-*soku*-spirit and matter-*soku*-mind. Natural science is also spirit when it is seen not from the side of the object, but from the side of its act. This is where the work of nothingness as the whole or what we call "dynamic whole" (*zenki*, 全機) is manifested. It is, in turn, reflected on the side of object and thereby becomes the uncertainty principle; and furthermore, in biology, the principle of "dynamic wholeness" (*zenkisei*, 全機性).[3]

As the cause-and-effect changes do the laws then disappear in natural science? Of course, the answer is no. The statistical law appears instead of it or the law that we think is causal in relation to these phenomena is actually statistical. The statistical law is the certainty of uncertainty. The certainty that includes uncertainty, we could say, is precisely the statistical law. The individuals that constitute the whole where the statistic is established show completely irregular movements when they are seen apart from the unity of the whole. They do not make an orderly movement as the whole, but carry out irregular movements. Yet this does not mean a simple irregularity or disorder because they spontaneously reach an average and constitute a kind of regularity on their own. That is the statistical law. Accordingly, we can say that the statistical law is the uncertainty of certainty and the order of disorder. The flipside of this is that the individuals demonstrate their freedom in the whole and thereby establish the order of the whole. As a whole, they are moving in a certain direction, but in it, each of them can carry out its own particular movement. We can understand the statistical law, in this manner, as allowing the freedom of the individuals while being the order of the whole. However, with regard to the statistical law in a simple sense only means that the whole allows the freedom of individuals; and it does not mean that these two sides are mediated with each other, and thereby the act of the whole becomes the content of individual's freedom. It does not mean that the act of freedom, which belongs to the individuals, denies the [individual] self and thereby the whole fills its content. We cannot acknowledge here the intermediation of the contraries like the whole and the individual, where one lets the other live by limiting one's own self and by doing so, in turn, one is allowed to make the most of its own self. Statistics does not have that kind of profound meaning. It is after all the object of observation. However, the fact that the statistical law is there as a law proves that the individual and the whole are dualistic and mutually complementary in the sense that one cannot be reduced to the other. This dualistic complementarity is made aware in ourselves, it no longer gives a simple statistical law, but the order of the state and the society. The state must let the individuals live inside itself and realize the unity of the whole through their spontaneity and, at the same time, the individuals can become free for the first time in the state; this kind of concrete relationship is the positive fact that fills the space pointed out by the statistical law. We cannot speak clearly and positively about these things in natural science. However, it is important that the study of natural science leaves open the space that it should fulfill through this kind of concrete self-awareness. Through that, we should become aware of the other side in reference to natural science. It is necessary to fully make this kind of self-awareness explicit in our teaching of natural science; and, I think, the way for recognizing the limit of science by using the materials available therein is open to us all in today's academia.

There might be things that I have not fully explained. Since I talked in a hurry, some of my points are confusing as well. But since the time is up, I would like to stop here.

Questions for Class Discussions

Q1. Explain two types of compromise: (1) *secchū* and (2) *shicchū*. Think about a concrete case in which we are confronted with two contradictory perspectives, e.g., A and B; show if it will be understood in reference to these two types.

Q2. Think about an example of interdisciplinary studies including multiple disciplines that you are thinking about pursuing as your major and/or minor. How does the interdisciplinary study look in relation to these two notions of compromise (namely, *secchū* and *shicchū*)?

Q3. What are the great examples of positive outcomes that we can draw from Tanabe's rendering of interdisciplinary studies? Discuss some examples of them from the intellectual history of your country or from your personal experience of studying multiple academic disciplines.

Teaching Notes and Further Reading

Chapter 1

The threefold sense of "self" in the *LS* argues that one sense cannot be fully articulated or properly understood without taking the others into account. This chapter takes nationality as an example of species and discusses other senses in relation to it. However, there could be many other examples of the specific that could be qualified as a social self or as a group of individuals that play an essential role in determining one's self-identity. Make sure to enumerate as many examples as possible during the class discussion.

Some of these examples could pose a challenge to Tanabe's *LS*. For example, a group of individuals who form their community through the internet does not necessarily require "land-occupation" as Tanabe states in his exposition of the logic of species (cf. Chapter 4). A religious community that celebrates the solidarity between the living and the dead also seems to deviate from his notion of species and, moreover, seems to require a different sense of "shared space." Additionally, a Kierkegaardian understanding of the "individual" (as the "knight of faith") or Bergson's portrayal of the "ethical hero" indicates a sense of the individual who seemingly goes against the notion of species. Some of these problems could show why Tanabe had to rearticulate the sense of the social self through metanoetics (where the community of individuals are no longer limited to the living beings, but also include the dead while maintaining attentiveness to the irreducibility of the singular). It is important to revisit these limitations of the *LS* after consulting Chapters 2 and 5.

Tanabe draws the distinction of "open-" and "closed-species" from Bergson's concepts of "open-" and "closed-society." Show the similarities between these two sets of concepts to students and then introduce the fact that Tanabe devoted a great number of pages to explain how Bergson's distinction is abstract and problematic. The "open society," in other words, looks more like an abstract genus rather than a concrete species. Tanabe further points out that the open–closed distinction should neither be binary nor sublationary. Explain how this is the case by consulting Bergson's argument and by demonstrating how Tanabe's rendering of species modifies this distinction.

- Henri Bergson, *The Two Sources of Morality and Religion*, trans. R. A. Audra and C. Brereton, with W. H. Carter. Notre Dame: Macmillan Press, 1977, 18–27, 45–65, 229–34.

- Matteo Cestari, "The Individual and Individualism in Nishida and Tanabe," *Re- Politicising the Kyoto School as Philosophy*, edited by Christopher Goto-Jones, 49–74. London; New York: Routledge, 2008.

Chapter 2

One of the major difficulties in teaching the Kyoto School philosophy to students at universities in Europe and North America is the fact that philosophers assume readers' familiarity with East Asian (and especially Japanese) history, culture, and language. This is precisely the reason why they do not always cite or explain in detail the terms deriving from the intellectual history of Japan. When Tanabe is read by students that are not familiar with East Asian histories and cultures, they will focus on the parts that they can understand, which will be written predominantly in European philosophical terms. As I mentioned in this chapter, Tanabe looks as though he is just revisiting the dogmatic past and/or reconstructing a theology by substituting God with the East Asian term "nothingness."

To alleviate this problem, teachers are recommended to talk about the concept of nothingness in *The Heart Sutra* with an emphasis on the historical fact that European intellectual resources were not available to Japanese scholars until the middle of the nineteenth century. Jettisoning assumptions that derive from the Abrahamic tradition and/or the Hellenistic metaphysical framework students will be able to see that the notion of nothingness neither indicates a naïve divine transcendence that stands in a simple opposition to the standpoint of philosophy nor remains reducible to the sense of the religious. But nothingness in the Kyoto School philosophy (and especially in the works of Tanabe) insinuates both nihilism and its overcoming. The seemingly simple equation of form and nothingness paradoxically results in a liberation from their binary opposition in *The Heart Sutra*. Through this intellectual exercise of reading two pages of the Buddhist text, students will better appreciate the paradoxical death-and-resurrection of philosophy that maintains its openness to the sense of the religious that is inclusive of both the Abrahamic and Mahayana Buddhist traditions.

The concepts of self-power and other-power from the Pure Land sect of Buddhism play a central role in explaining the significance of metanoetics. Tanabe refers to a variety of European thinkers (in addition to a plethora of insights drawn from the Japanese intellectual tradition). Instructors are highly recommended to read through the full translation of the *Philosophy as Metanoetics* (2016) or refer to its index to pick out the European thinkers that with whom they are familiar. So, for instance, the excerpt from the

PM made available in Chapter 4 of this book only refers to Kant and his antinomies. However, the rest of the *PM* refers to a number of other thinkers in the history of European philosophy and Tanabe argues that they are more or less falling victim to the problems of self-power philosophy, namely, the existential antinomies of self. These sections will help instructors bring Tanabean insights closer to their areas of competence and help students show how they can approach Tanabe's distinction of self-power and other-power not only in reference to the intellectual history of Japan, but also to that of Europe and beyond.

- *The Heart Sutra*, trans. Red Pine. Washington, DC: Shoemaker & Hoard, 2004.
- *The Heart Sutra*: A Comprehensive Guide to the Classic of Mahayana Buddhism, trans. Kazuaki Tanahashi. Boston & London: Shambhala, 2014.
- Tanabe Hajime, *Philosophy as Metanoetics*, trans. James W. Heisig et al. Nagoya: Chisokudō Publications, 2016.
- John C. Maraldo, "Tanabe Hajime's Philosophy of Metanoetics," *Japanese Philosophy in the Making 2: Borderline Interrogations*, 145–208. Nagoya; Brussels: Chisokudō Publications, 2019.
- James Heisig, *Of Gods and Minds: In Search of a Theological Commons*. Nagoya & Brussels: Chisokudō Publications, 2019.

Chapter 3

Tanabe provides two examples of Niels Bohr's "exclusive complementarity." He refers to the original sense of the notion in physics; and this chapter and Chapter 6 prove this point. In many other places (especially in his later philosophy of religion), he also refers to the discipline of math when mentioning the "Dedekind's cut" as an example of this complementarity. He seems to suggest that the structure of absolute mediation in the *LS* or the absolute dialectic in metanoetics is synonymous with the ways in which physicists explain the dual nature of light/electrons or mathematicians tried to create a theoretical framework in which they can ground the continuum or the theory of real numbers in arithmetic.

I highly recommend the instructors to familiarize themselves with the basic notion of the "Wave–particle duality" and how Bohr's notion of "complementarity" plays a role in this context. There are decent Wikipedia articles that can help us understand the gist of these concepts in addition to a number of scholarly publications, which discuss their applicability to the fields beyond physics. As for the Dedekind cut, I highly recommend to watch a short clip explaining how the Dedekind's cut aims at grounding the continuum of real numbers by defining the irrational number in its relativity to the rest of the continuum. As indicated below, this can be found at the *Insights into Mathematic*s channel at the YouTube.

Tanabe consistently argues that a definition of X always requires its openness to what is not X and the dialectical relation of these two opposing terms cannot be reduced to the sublationary synthesis of Hegel's self-determining infinite. But the finite remains irreducible to the infinite and vice versa while they are always already in a mediatory relation to each other. This intermediation of self and other, Tanabe claims, is possible when there is an open space between them, thereby preserving irreducible duality (or "doubleness" as he describes in Chapter 6) without falling victim to dualism.

Tanabe's references to physics and mathematics are great examples of how he is thinking about the mediatory relation of X and non-X, including self-power and other-power, finite and infinite, reason and faith, among other relevant metaphysical terms, in reference to his understanding of the world. Instructors are advised to understand the scientific and mathematical examples of the dialectical model and further to evaluate whether or not this insight is applicable to fields beyond theoretical mathematics and natural sciences as Tanabe seems to claim in his *LS* and *PM*.

- "Difficulties with Dedekind cuts | Real numbers and limits Math Foundations 116 | N J Wildberger," https://youtu.be/jlnBo3APRlU.
- Arun Bala, *Complementarity beyond Physics: Niels Bohr's Parallels*. London: Palgrave McMillan, 2016.
- Dean Brink, *Philosophy of Science and the Kyoto School: An Introduction to Nishida Kitaro, Tanabe Hajime and Tosaka Jun*. London: Bloomsbury, 2021.

Chapter 4

This is a translation of an article from Tanabe's *Logic of Species*. The compilation of twelve essays, written between 1932 and 1941, officially constitutes the *LS*. They are compiled into vols. 6 and 7 of the *THZ* with a small book published in 1947, entitled *The Practical Structure of the Logic of Species* (種の論理の実践的構造) at the end of the vol. 7. David Dilworth translated a small portion of this book in 1969. However, this translation is too short to provide any substantial picture of this book as a whole, let alone the rest of the *LS*. As mentioned in Chapter 1, Tanabe left a note saying that the *LS* should be read in its entirety before criticizing any part of it, while the whole work amounts to more than 900 pages in heavily bound two volumes of *THZ*. It is important for an instructor to emphasize that what is made available in English here for the first time in the history of philosophy is a fraction of the massive work that the author had put forth during his prime as a professor of philosophy at the leading university in the midst of the most controversial moment of modern Japanese history.

Tanabe's language could occasionally come across as being militaristic or nationalistic in a negative sense (especially when he talks about "land occupation" or "national unity based on blood" through the concept of species). However, it is important to note that the concept of species does not promote military expansionism or colonialism as many criticisms of the Kyoto school at the end of the last century have argued. This point must be emphasized by talking about the importance of "open species" and the necessity for "social justice" to realize the full potentiality of "species."

- Tanabe Hajime, "The Logic of the Species as Dialectics, *Monumenta Nipponica*," vol. 24, no. 3 (1969): 273–88.
- Christopher Goto-Jones, *Re-Politicising the Kyoto School as Philosophy*. London: Routledge, 2007.
- Sugimoto, Kōichi. "Tanabe Hajime's Logic of Species and the Philosophy of Nishida Kitarō: A Critical Dialogue within the Kyoto School," *Japanese and Continental Philosophy: Conversations with the Kyoto School*, edited by Bret W. Davis, Brian Schroeder and Jason M. Wirth, 52–70. Bloomington, IN: Indiana University Press, 2011.

Chapter 5

The *Philosophy as Metanoetics* (1946), *Existence, Love, and Practice* (1947), and *Dialectic of Christianity* (1948) constitute the trilogy of Tanabe's later philosophy of religion. A comprehensive treatment of these three works and a summary of each with an extensive reference to secondary sources are available in *Faith and Reason in Continental and Japanese Philosophy: Reading Tanabe Hajime and William Desmond* (2019). Part of the sections on Tanabe in this monograph is revised in Chapter 2 of this book. An extensive bibliography of the secondary sources on Tanabe, most of which are written in Japanese, is available in this book.

This chapter is an excerpt from James Heisig's acclaimed translation of *Philosophy as Metanoetics* (Chisokudō Publications, 2016). Please make sure to consult the TOC of this book as a whole and explain to students what Tanabe is doing with the Preface and the first chapter. The position of these excerpts in relation to the later parts of the book is similar to Hegel's Preface in his *Phenomenology of Spirit*. They are an architectonic of the rest of the book and thus the end toward which the whole text guides its readers. As mentioned in the notes to Chapter 3, Tanabe extensively talks about the history of European philosophy to ground the significance of metanoetics in the rest of the book. If instructors are not familiar with the works of Kant or Hegel (which Tanabe talks about in the selected writing for this chapter) or are more comfortable with other philosophers that Tanabe refers to in other parts of the book, I highly recommend to survey the whole work and select sections of interest. It would be useful to read European philosophers and Tanabe side by side in order to discuss why Tanabe argues that European philosophers have fallen short of metanoetics and, moreover, why they have more or less subscribed to the idea of "self-power philosophy."

Last, the Appendix to the translation of *PM* provides an intellectual biography of Tanabe. It is not only a comprehensive summary of the historical aspects of Tanabe's life, but also shows the ways in which we can apply the metanoetic insight to our understanding of the life of an individual. If the selected reading is too abstract for some of the students in class, this section can help make the main concepts more concrete.

- Takeshi Morisato, *Faith and Reason in Continental and Japanese Philosophy: Reading Tanabe Hajime and William Desmond*. London: Bloomsbury, 2019.
- Hase Shōtō, "The Structure of Faith: Nothinngess-qua-Love," *The Religious Philosophy of Tanabe Hajime*, edited by Taitetsu Unno and James W. Heisig, 89–116. Berkeley: Asian Humanities Press, 1990; Nagoya & Brussels: Chisokudō Publications, 2020.
- Heisig, James W., *Philosophers of Nothingness: An Essay on the Kyoto School*. Honolulu: University of Hawai'i Press, 2001.

Chapter 6

Instructors must keep in mind the historical context in which this article was written, presented, and published. As stated in Chapter 3, it was initially delivered as a lecture at the "Workshop on the Study of Japanese Culture Instruction" hosted by the department of ideology at the ministry of Education in November 1936. It was compiled into the volume *Japanese Culture Series* published by the same department in 1937. Modern readers should be able to feel the serious breach of academic freedom just by looking at these titles. But it is important to keep in the mind the following historical and cultural backgrounds.

There was an attempted coup d'état, organized by a group of young Japanese army officers, on February 1936, which is known as the "2-26 incident" (*ni ni-roku jiken*, 二・二六事件). As a result of this political and military turmoil, the prime minister and the admiral at that time, Okada Keisuke, and all of his cabinet members resigned from their posts. Under the following Hirota cabinet, the "Thought Crime Probation Law" (*shisō-han hogo kansatsu hō*, 思想犯保護観察法) was established on May 29 in the same year. Coupled with the notorious "Peace Preservation Law" (*chian iji hō*, 治安維持法), the Japanese government was quickly paving its way to the total control of citizens' physical and intellectual life. A couple of the Kyoto School thinkers fell victim to this law and died in prison toward the end of the Second World War.

This movement toward totalitarianism and military dictatorship was already in place when the Okada cabinet declared "*kokutai meichō seimei*" (国体明徴声明) or what is commonly known as "*Kokutai-no meichō*" (国体の明徴) in October 1935. The right-wing military officers and politicians argued that the conventional interpretation of the Japanese emperor (and the imperial house) in the Meiji Constitution is subservient to the nation: that is to say, the emperor must wait for instructions from the ministry (which ultimately holds the rights of sovereignty and can function against the emperor as the ruler of the state). Note also that the Meiji Constitution was based on a German model. Hence, the rise of national socialism in Germany and their increasing affinity with Japanese officials in the early 1930s were great incentives for the Japanese government to publicly turn the emperor into the sole ruler of the state.

For modern readers, Tanabe's article does not clearly speak against right-wing nationalism. Nor does he explicitly critique military dictatorship. As we can easily imagine, he was invited to pay lip service to the political interference of natural science at the workshop organized by the department of ideology. However, when we read that he says natural science and academic autonomy must be kept intact for each discipline, it is not surprising to learn that Tanabe was "prepared for imprisonment and subsequent death"[1] when he delivered and prepared this paper for publication.

Instructors are also recommended to list the interdisciplinary courses available at their universities. Use the distinction between the positive and the negative compromise (namely, *shicchū* and *secchū*), categorize what is being studied at the interdisciplinary courses, and examine if Tanabe's model of interdisciplinarity (*shicchū*) is beneficial for the development of each field and if his critique of *secchū* applies to some of these examples.

- Himi Kiyoshi, "Tanabe's Theory of the State," *The Religious Philosophy of Tanabe Hajime*, edited by Taitetsu Unno and James W. Heisig, 303–15. Berkley, CA: Asian Humanities Press, 1990; Nagoya & Brussels: Chisokudō Publications, 2020.
- John C. Maraldo, "National Identity, Modernity, and War," *Japanese Philosophy in the Making 2: Borderline Interrogations*, 145–208. Nagoya; Brussels: Chisokudō Publications, 2019.

Notes

Acknowledgments

1   I would like to thank the great Italian translator of Japanese philosophy and literature, Lorenzo Marinucci, for checking the proverb.

Preamble

1   Cf. *PM*, 64. Tanabe supports this metanoetic reading of the logic of species. The pagination of the *Philosophy as Metanoetics* refers to the English translation: Tanabe Hajime, *Philosophy as Metanoetics*, trans., Takeuchi Yoshinori, Valdo Viglielmo, and James W. Heisig (Nagoya and Brussels: Chisokudō Publications, 2016).

Chapter 1

1   *THZ*, 6: 176.
2   *THZ*, 6: 176.
3   *THZ*, 6: 127, 131–2, 141. To differentiate it from the relative notion of nothingness as a mere negation of being, he often calls it "absolute nothingness" (*zettai mu*, 絶対無).
4   In some cases, it is much more complicated to identify the nationality of an individual. Additionally, citizenship of a nation-state undergoing a violent socio-political-economic turmoil is almost always detrimental to its holder. However, this does not deny the fact that her belonging to the specific nation-state is foundational to the fate of her life as an individual. Regardless of the positive or negative outcome of the belonging, the socio-political substratum itself is undeniably significant for the life of an individual.
5   *THZ*, 7: 267.
6   *THZ*, 6: 313.
7   *THZ*, 6: 315. For the "self-negating structure of species," see *THZ*, 6:321; and for the "absolute-negative transformation of species," see *THZ*, 6: 484–5.
8   Notice how the language of "positive" and "negative" in Tanabe's account is quite paradoxical. The great negation, especially self-negation, is a very positive point in his philosophy.
9   These two types roughly correspond to Heisig's interpretation of "open" and "closed species" (even though Tanabe's formulation of open society will end

up having a religious dimension that extends to the realm of the dead in his later philosophy of religion, thus stretching the scope of the open–closed distinction). See his rendering of it in relation to the political discourse "Tanabe's Logic of the Specific and the Spirit of Nationalism," *Much Ado about Nothingness: Essays on Nishida and Tanabe* (Nagoya and Brussels: Chisokudō Publications, 2016), 329–31.

10 *THZ*, 6: 306. Cf. *THZ*, 6: 302–3. Tanabe means here that, in the process of establishing itself a continuous whole, the species requires a number of individuals to dedicate themselves cross-generationally to its preservation. In this case, many individuals must die to maintain the whole as it provides a foundation for sustaining the life of individuals. The preservation of species, in this sense, paradoxically provides a ground for the life of individuals and takes them for maintaining its determinate identity.

11 *THZ*, 6: 196.

12 *THZ*, 6: 306.

13 *THZ*, 6: 109. See also *THZ*, 6: 119.

14 *THZ*, 7: 80.

15 *THZ*, 6: 124.

16 *THZ*, 6: 112.

17 This point concurs with Heisig's analysis of the "absolutizing of the specific." See Heisig "Tanabe's Logic of the Specific the Critique of the Global Village," *Much Ado about Nothingness: Essays on Nishida and Tanabe*, 280.

18 *THZ*, 6: 59.

19 *THZ*, 6: 218.

20 *THZ*, 6: 218.

21 *THZ*, 6: 402; *THZ*, 6: 506.

22 *THZ*, 6: 404.

23 Tanabe remains inconclusive in the *Logic of Species* regarding the source of the self-negating self-transcendence of individuals as the concrete manifestation of genus in open species. In *Philosophy as Metanoetics*, however, he will clearly state that it should originate from the nature of nothingness.

24 In this sense, genus remains as a mere ideality when it is understood in itself or mistakenly conflated with the closed species, but when it is properly placed in a mediating relation to other terms, it is manifested as the principle of self-negation through the self-negating act of the social and the individual self.

25 *THZ*, 6: 402; 7: 168, 289.

Chapter 2

1 *THZ*, 6: 364, 400.

2 *THZ*, 6: 241, 246.

3   *THZ*, 6: 264.

4   *THZ*, 6: 289.

5   *PM*, 117.

6   *PM*, 118.

7   *PM*, 125.

8   *PM*, 118.

9   *PM*, 118.

10 *PM*, 124–5.

11 *PM*, 55.

12 *PM*, 55.

13 *PM*, 125.

14 *PM*, 102.

15 *PM*, 103.

16 Kant, *Religion and Rational Theology*, edited by Allen W. Wood, George di Giovanni, and translated by Allen W. Wood (Cambridge: Cambridge University Press, 1996), 77 (6:29).

17 *PM*, 124–5.

18 *ELP*, 344.

19 *PM*, 81.

20 *PM*, 190.

21 *PM*, 394.

22 Nishitani Keiji, "Reflections on Two Addresses by Martin Heidegger," *Heidegger and Asian Thought*, ed. Graham Parkes (Honolulu: University of Hawai'i Press, 1987), 151.

23 *PM*, 394–5.

24 *DC*, 25. See also *PM*, 221: Tanabe talks about this resurrection as naturalness or the state of being "be restored to life as one who has died to the world and to self."

25 *PM*, 276.

26 *PM*, 276.

27 *ELP*, 284. Cf. *ELP*, 318; *DC*, 305; *PM*, 273 and especially 175.

28 *PM*, 415–16.

29 *PM*, 337. The Shin/Pure Land tradition tends to talk about this in terms of "vicarious suffering," but as you can see, Tanabe purposefully introduces the notions of love (i.e., eros and agape) in reference to the Judeo-Christian tradition.

30 *DC*, 126, 237–8.

31 *PM*, 63. Cf. PM, 340–1.

32 *PM*, 3.

33 *PM*, 338. Cf. *ELP*, 374–5.

34 *ELP*, 365.

35 *ELP*, 365. Cf. *PM*, 436–7.

36 *ELP*, 365.

37 *PM*, 290. Cf. *DC*, 141, 210.

38 *PM*, 235, 273–4, 279.

Chapter 3

1 Not surprisingly, since they ask about the intermediation of a particular form or the whole of human knowing to what is other to it, we should be able to find great consistency in Tanabean answers to these questions, but roughly speaking, we can find the answer to the first question in metanoetics and to the second question in the logic of species.

2 *PM*, 55.

3 *PM*, 54.

4 *PM*, 110–11.

5 Augustine's *credo ut intelligam* certainly does not mean that we accept everything written in the scripture before starting to philosophize (especially if we pay attention to the whole of his *Confessions*). However, I am afraid that most contemporary (secular) readers would read this phrase to mean the primacy of faith at the cost of free thinking.

6 With this in the background of reading Tanabe's texts, it is very difficult to refrain from characterizing his critique of the Kantian philosophy of religion as an existential defense of religious absurdism:

> In speaking of a "restoration," I do not mean that reason is restored to its former state, but rather that reason is brought to the self-consciousness of an action-faith-witness that transcends reason. Kant proposed a "religion within the limits of reason alone," but in truth there can be no such religion. The principle of absolute goodness which furnishes a basis for religion and is able to overcome the radical evil in humanity belongs only to God. Religion consists in the faith of those who participate in the work of establishing the Kingdom of God on earth and who, as members of the Kingdom of God, submit to the supremacy of divine providence. The faith in God to which Kant was pointing was rational and universal, as distinct from faith based on God's revelation as a historical event. Genuine faith, however, is an absolute negation of reason, worthy of being termed religion only when it transcends mere rational thinking.

This assessment of Kantian philosophy of religion seems to lead Tanabe to a conclusion that we need neither autonomy of reason to ground the authenticity of human existence nor philosophy to defend our faith in religious transcendence.

7 *PM*, 418.

8 *PM*, 269, 270.

9 *PM*, 172: Nothingness is by no means immediate.

10 *PM*, 223: Nothingness cannot function apart from the cooperation of being, which is why self-consciousness of nothingness consists in nothingness-qua-being and arises wherever the center of the relative self is established

through death-and-resurrection. The Zen saying, "Light and darkness, side by side" (*meian sōsō*), seems to point to just such a reciprocal penetration and correspondence between nothingness and being.

11 *PM*, 414–15.

12 *PM*, 415.

13 *PM*, 259.

14 *PM*, 124.

15 *PM*, 125.

16 *PM*, 125.

17 Cf. *PM*, 179: "This change of standpoint takes place when the relative self, lacking the power within itself to break through the antinomies, is forced by absolute critique into the ultimate predicament of finding contradiction itself driven to the point of absolute nothingness (in a negative sense). At this outer limit of 'absolute contradiction,' contradiction brings itself to unity, as it were, through a contradiction of contradiction; the absolute disruption is made whole again in nothingness; and the powerlessness of the self—the metanoetic practice of self-abandonment—restores the self as a mediator of nothingness."

18 When we live in prosperous and democratic countries like contemporary Japan, in Europe or North America, it is hard to imagine how an intellectual like Tanabe could not speak up against the military government and publicly engage in social activism to undermine the military government. It is much easier for us to praise those who were persecuted (e.g., Tosaka, Miki, among others) and also to question those whose reputations did not suffer much from censorship during the war (e.g., Nishida, Tanabe, among others). I do believe that philosophers must speak up against evil regardless of the fact that it might incur serious inconveniences (including death). However, it is not reasonable to deem Tanabe as a right-wing fascist or defender of the Japanese imperialist policy in the 1930s. This article clearly shows that he was critical of the government's nationalist educational policy. In fact, some students report that he was fully aware of the possibly that he might be arrested and possibly die in prison after delivering his criticism at the government office.

19 *PM*, 287.

20 James W. Heisig, et al., eds., *Japanese Philosophy: A Sourcebook* (Honolulu: University of Hawai'i Press, 2011), 670 . See also Heisig, "Tanabe's Logic of the Specific the Critique of the Global Village," *Much Ado about Nothingness: Essays on Nishida and Tanabe* (Nagoya: Chisokudō Publications, 2016), 261. Heisig explicitly explains the reason for substituting "species" with the "specific" to remove any ambiguity from the term. However, my contention is that the very ambiguity is key for elucidating what is missing at the surface of the logic of species. For my critique of Heisig's translations of Tanabean terms, see *PM*, 469–73.

21 *THZ*, 6:141. Cf. *THZ*, 6: 303: "The continuous whole of species should precisely give the continuous whole of life. The individual living being

takes species as the ground of its life and yet as a product of the will to love that does not reflect on the sacrifices of numerous individuals for its preservation, it remains irreducible to species." See also, *THZ*, 6: 358: "An individual living being is an individualized species."

22 *THZ*, 6: 212.

23 *THZ*, 6: 272–3.

24 *THZ*, 6: 296–7: "Hegel's philosophy ignores nature's independent, negative opposition to mind and that is why it tends to be interpreted as painting nature as a result of mind's self-alienation within itself. In this case, when claiming nature as existing externally to mind, this transcendence cannot indicate that which is negative to immanence as a moment of the absolute mediation. But it can only signify ideal transcendence within mind. Here, the peculiar meaning of the transcendence of space, discussed in overture to philosophy of nature is lost, whereby nature is reduced to ideality. However, nature that ultimately remains in immanence as that which is emanated from absolute spirit cannot be the mediatory moment as the substrate of existence."

25 *THZ*, 7: 179.

26 Cf. *THZ*, 7: 156: "In action, self does not remain to be self alone, but while entering nature beyond itself and working on it, nature goes through formative change through the mediation of self and takes the self into itself. The act is established through the transformative mediation where self's work becomes nature's and vice versa. In short, in act, self as the acting subject and nature as the object that is worked on are transformed through absolute nothingness and thereby self becomes nature and nature becomes self. That is to say, through the transformation of absolute nothingness, both self and nature negatively become one. This serves as the ground of comparative studies between nature and human action."

27 Tanabe identifies this renewed sense of nature as "historical nature" (in opposition to an ordinary sense of it as "material nature"). Cf. *THZ*, 7: 164: "The concepts of nature, causation, and technology can have a broad meaning of the negative moment of historical and ethical act in general. … Historical nature is more concrete than physical nature. The concept of material itself comes to be historicized and comes to have historical meaning."

28 *THZ*, 7: 233.

29 *THZ*, 7: 156.

30 Tanabe classifies biology as one of the disciplines in science that becomes a component of history. See *THZ*, 7: 341.

31 *THZ*, 6: 364.

32 *THZ*, 6: 364.

33 *THZ*, 5:143.

34 The best example of this would be Rousseau's *Social Contract*.

35 *THZ*, 5: 151.

36 *THZ*, 5: 153–4.

37 *THZ*, 5: 154.

38 When one appears, the other does not and, since both need to be established, these terms, which stand in the mutually exclusive and complementary relation, are not continuously connected with each other: hence, we cannot make them compromise by stopping each of them at a certain point. Just as when we move from the standpoint of particle to that of waves, the transition is discontinuous.

39 The middle position of *secchū* … is both A and B. It might not be entirely A or B, but at the same time to a certain degree simultaneously both A and B. That is a compromise. … This transformative point of conversion is neither A nor B. The compromise gives the position of both/and while in the exclusive conversion it point of transformation gives neither/nor.

40 *THZ*, 5: 156.

41 *THZ*, 5: 156.

42 Of course, one person can pursue multiple disciplines at the same time and move from one domain of knowledge to another. However, Tanabe's point is that she cannot look at the text *both* as a historian *and* philosopher at the same time, but must hold the position of neither/nor where she can alternate her perspective from one to another.

Chapter 4

1 Tanabe Hajime, *The Logic of Species* (種の論理), edited by Fujita Masakatsu (Tokyo: Iwanami Shoten, 2010).

Chapter 5

1 [The "*qua*" here refers to the Sino-Japanese copulative "*soku*," which functions as a sort of pivot around which two terms revolve and interchange with each other as mutually defining elements in a single dynamic.]

2 [Wherever possible, references to the *Kyōgyōshinshō* will be taken from the abridged English version, *The Teaching, Practice, Faith, and Enlightenment*, vol. 5 of the Ryukoku Translation Series, published in 1966 in Kyoto (RTS). Suzuki Daisetsu's translation, *The Kyōgyōshinshō* (SD), was published in 1973 by the Eastern Buddhist Society in Kyoto. Passages unavailable in either of these translations will be taken from the more complete, but dated translation of Yamamoto Kōshō, published in 1958 by Karinbunko in Tokyo (YK).]In the passage cited here, Shinran is quoting Zendō; see *YK*, 133.

3 English translation by Lee M. Capel (New York: Harper & Row, 1965). [Tanabe read Kierkegaard in the German.]

4 *Kyōgyōshinshō* 6: 10; see *YK*, 251.
5 The passage is cited in Shinran's *Yuishinshō mon'i* (*Exposition of the Words of Seikaku*). See Kaneko Daiei, ed., 親鸞著作全集 (Collected writings of Shinran) (Kyoto: Hōzōkan, 1979), 563–4. Hereafter references to this collection will be abbreviated as *SZ*.
6 *SZ*, 457.
7 [*Ekō* refers to the transference of merits by Amida Buddha to sentient beings. In its *gensō* phase, it enables those who have been saved to return to the world to save others; in its *ōsō* phase, it is composed of action, faith, and witness.]
8 See especially the *Philosophical Fragments* and *Concluding Unscientific Postscript*.

Chapter 6

1 For the original of this translation, see *THZ*, 5: 149–92.
2 [J. S. Haldane, *The Philosophical Basis of Biology* (Doubleday: Doran, 1931).]
3 [Hashida Kunihiko (橋田邦彦) extensively talk about his interpretation of Dōgen's *zenki* in the field of biology and Tanabe must be referring to his work here.]

Teaching Notes and Further Reading

1 *THZ*, 5: 510.

Bibliography

Haldane, J. S., *The Philosophical Basis of Biology*. Doubleday: Doran, 1931.

Hashida Kunihiko, *The Dynamic Whole of Organisms: The Collected Works of Hashida Kunihiko*. Tokyo: Kyōdō Isho shuppansha, 1977.

Heisig, James W., John C. Maraldo, and Thomas P. Kasulis, eds., *Japanese Philosophy: A Sourcebook*. Honolulu: University of Hawai'i Press, 2011.

Heisig, James W., *Much Ado about Nothingness: Essays on Nishida and Tanabe*. Nagoya and Brussels: Chisokudō Publications, 2016.

Kant, *Religion and Rational Theology*. Edited by Allen W. Wood, George di Giovanni, and translated by Allen W. Wood. Cambridge: Cambridge University Press, 1996.

Kierkegaard, Søren, *The Concept of Irony: With Constant Reference to Socrates*. Translated by Lee M. Capel. Bloomington: Indiana University Press, 1968.

Nishitani Keiji, "Reflections on Two Addresses by Martin Heidegger." In *Heidegger and Asian Thought*. Edited by Graham Parkes, 145–55. Honolulu: University of Hawai'i Press, 1987.

Ryukoku Translation Centre, trans., *The Kyōgyō Shin Shō, (Ken Jōdo Shinjitsu Kyōgyōshō Monrui): The Teaching, Practice, Faith, and Enlightenment* (abridged). Ryukoku Translation Series, vol. 5. Kyoto: Ryūkoku University Press, 1966.

Shinran, *Shinran Chosaku Zenshū* 親鸞著作全集 (Collected works of Shinran). Kyoto: Hōzōkan, 1979.

Shinran, *Shinran's Kyōgyōshinshō: The Collection of Passages Expounding the True Teaching, Living, Faith, and Realizing of the Pure Land*. Translated by D. T. Suzuki. Oxford: Oxford University Press, 2012.

Tanabe Hajime, *Philosophy as Metanoetics*. Translated by Takeuchi Yoshinori, Valdo Viglielmo, and James W. Heisig. Nagoya and Brussels: Chisokudō Publications, 2016.

Tanabe Hajime *Tanabe Hajime Zenshū* 田辺元全集. Tokyo: Chikuma Shobō, 1963–1964.

Yamamoto Kosho, trans., *The Kyōgyōshinshō, or the "Teaching, Practice, Faith, and Attainment."* Tokyo: Karinbunko, 1958.

Index